THE USE OF

HAND
WOODWORKING
TOOLS

THE USE OF
HAND WOODWORKING TOOLS

Leo P. McDonnell

•

Alson Kaumeheiwa

COPYRIGHT © 1978
BY DELMAR PUBLISHERS INC.

10 9 8 7 6 5

LIBRARY OF CONGRESS CATALOG CARD NUMBER: 76-48504
ISBN: 0-8273-1098-6

Printed in the United States of America
Published simultaneously in Canada
by Nelson Canada,
A Division of International Thomson Limited

DELMAR PUBLISHERS INC. • **ALBANY, NEW YORK**

PREFACE

Technological developments in building materials have brought about improvements and advances in the tools and equipment of the building construction trades. The invention of new tools and the improvement of existing tools require a constant updating in the instruction of the use of tools. The purpose of this text is to provide an up-to-date and complete coverage of the use of hand woodworking tools.

The Use of Hand Woodworking Tools deals with nonautomatic hand tools. There are fourteen units of instruction: Safety, Measuring Tools, The Rafter and Framing Square, Layout Tools, Testing Tools, Sawing Tools, Refitting Handsaws, Bench Planes and Special Planes, Edge Cutting Tools, Boring Tools, Fasteners – Nails, Fasteners – Screws and Others, Smoothing Tools, and Coated Abrasives.

Basic principles and related information concerning carpentry practices, computations, and descriptions of tools are included in each unit where appropriate. The instructional units contain only basic operations common to the use of hand tools. Since each operation involves the teaching of basic trade theory and fundamental processes, both are included in the instructional units. To facilitate correct application, the principles governing the use of tools are established before procedural instructions. Safety is highlighted at the points in the procedure where it must be observed and is also the subject of the first unit in the text.

Each unit ends with review questions designed to check the student's mastery of the information contained in the unit. Key operational points are emphasized in these reviews. A variety of testing techniques (such as short answer, discussion, identification) are employed to make the reviews more motivating and interesting to the students.

Several changes have been incorporated in this revision of *The Use of Hand Woodworking Tools* to ensure a thorough presentation of the subject. An important unit on safety practices has been added at the beginning which covers unsafe acts, unsafe conditions, and safety rules for the use of tools. An Appendix has been added at the end of the text which includes useful tables such as decimal equivalents of number and letter size drills, and decimal and millimeter equivalents of fractional inches. New photographs replace many line drawings to better illustrate the tools and their uses. Each unit has been reviewed for readability and logical presentation.

This revision was prepared by Dr. Alson I. Kaumeheiwa, who is the Chairman of the Department of Industry and Technology at Northern Michigan University. He has over a decade of experience teaching industrial arts courses at the postsecondary level. Dr. Kaumeheiwa is a member of several organizations including the American Industrial Arts Association and the American Council of Industrial Arts Teacher Educators.

This textbook, with its companion text, should provide the foundation upon which advanced carpentry skills can be developed. Texts in related series include:

Portable Power Tools
Concrete Form Construction
Framing, Sheathing and Insulation
Interior and Exterior Trim
Simplified Stair Layout
Introduction to Construction
Blueprint Reading for Carpenters
Basic Mathematics Simplified

CONTENTS

        The author and editorial staff at Delmar Publishers Inc. are interested in continually improving the quality of this instructional material. The reader is invited to submit constructive criticism and questions. Responses will be reviewed jointly by the author and source editor. Send comments to:

                    Delmar publishers Inc.
                    Editorial Department
                    2 Computer Drive West Box 15-015
                    Albany, New York 12212

Unit 1 SAFETY

Safety is a skill. It is something that must be learned and then practiced. As one learns to skillfully use a tool, it is also important to learn to work safely. Practice must be added to skillful use of a tool. Thus safety must also be practiced.

Learning and practice are important parts of safety. Both of these help people develop a sense for safety. The ability to sense unsafe conditions is gained from all past experiences in safety practice. Sensing dangerous conditions depends on each person's feeling toward safety. This feeling is an awareness or "sixth sense" about hazardous conditions. It is generally explained as common sense. Common sense is noticing the similarity of hazardous conditions from one situation to another. For example, a hammer with a loose handle creates an unsafe condition. Similar tools with loose handles will also create an unsafe condition.

What is an accident? An accident is an unplanned, uncontrolled, and unwanted event that interrupts an activity. The key points in an accident are (1) it is unplanned, (2) it results from the lack of control, and (3) it results in an unwanted outcome.

What causes accidents? Safety educators feel that accidents are the result of unsafe acts and/or unsafe conditions.

UNSAFE ACTS

Unsafe acts are acts that differ from accepted practice. Not every unsafe act results in an accident. However, unsafe acts increase exposure to hazardous conditions, increasing the chance that an accident will occur.

UNSAFE CONDITIONS

Physical conditions include work areas as well as the condition of tools. Either might lead to an accident if left in an unsafe condition. Again, an accident does not always occur because of an unsafe condition. However, the risk that an accident will occur is increased.

HAND TOOLS

Hand tool safety begins before one uses the tool. When a tool is being purchased, the following features should be considered: (1) built-in safety features, (2) type of wood (ash, hickory, maple) and grain pattern of tool handles (straight grain), (3) grade of steel and proper tempering of punches, chisels, and hammers, and (4) the overall design and construction of the tool.

Hand tools should also be checked before and after each use. In industry, tools are checked regularly. They are inspected for any conditions that would affect safe operation with that tool. Figure 1-1 is a hand-tool appraisal checklist.

In addition to the checklist for safely using hand tools, the following are some general safety rules when using all tools.

- *Keep the work area clean.* Cluttered areas and benches invite accidents.
- *Avoid dangerous environments.* Do not expose tools to rain. Do not use tools in damp or wet locations. Keep the work area well lit.

- *Keep children away.* All visitors should be kept a safe distance from the work area.

- *Store idle tools.* When not in use, tools should be stored in a dry, high or locked place – out of the reach of children.

- *Do not force a tool.* Use a tool in the way it was designed. It will do a better, safer job.

- *Use the right tool.* Do not force a small tool or an attachment to do the job of a heavy-duty tool.

- *Wear the proper clothing.* Do not wear loose clothing or jewelry that can catch in moving parts. Rubber gloves and footwear should be worn when working outdoors.

- *Wear safety glasses.* Wear safety glasses while operating tools. Also, face or dust masks should be worn if the operation is dusty.

- *Secure the work.* Use clamps or a vise to hold the work. It is safer than using one's hands. It also frees both hands to operate the tool.

Tool	Unsafe Conditions	Unsafe Acts
Screwdrivers	A badly worn, splintered, or broken handle A bent blade or shank A dull or poorly shaped blade	Using a screwdriver as a chisel, pry, or punch Holding a screwdriver in one hand and the work in the other Using the wrong size of screwdriver
Knives	A dull blade A worn handle	Cutting toward the body Placing the knife in an unprotected position Not using the protective sheath
Chisels and Punches	The head mushroomed The head and point too hard (look for chipping at the cutting point) The body of the tool is too short to allow a safe grip	Not wearing safety glasses Not holding the tool in a safe manner
Mallets and Hammers	A loose, split, or rough handle (tape should not be used on the handle because it covers defects) The head poorly or loosely fitted to the handle	Using the wrong type of hammer (carpenter's hammer for machine work) Exposing the free hand to the hammer blows
Files	A missing handle The file teeth covered with foreign material or dull	Using a file as a pry or punch Hitting a file with a hammer
Wrenches	The jaws worn or sprung Mechanical defects	Using the wrong type or size of wrench Using a pipe on the handle to get more leverage Using a wrench as a hammer
Saws	An improper set A loose or splintered handle	Starting a saw with a downstroke instead of an upstroke
(A partial list from **Modern Safety Practices** by Russell DeReamer.)		

Fig. 1-1 Hand-tool Appraisal Checklist

- *Do not overreach.* Keep the proper footing and balance at all times.
- *Maintain the tools with care.* Keep tools sharp and clean for the best and safest performance.

(Partial list of Safety Instructions from Power Tool Division, Rockwell International.)

REVIEW QUESTIONS

A. Short Answer or Discussion

1. What is safety?

2. Name two important parts of safety.

3. What does it mean to have common sense about safe practices?

4. Why is it important to learn and practice safety?

5. What is an accident?

6. What causes accidents?

7. What is the term for behavior which differs from accepted practice?

8. An axe with a loose head is considered an unsafe act or an unsafe condition?

9. When does hand tool safety begin?

10. When should a hand tool be inspected for its condition?

B. Identification and Interpretation

1. Indicate if the following are unsafe acts or unsafe conditions.

   a. A dull blade

   b. Not wearing safety glasses

   c. Nontempered glasses

   d. A very short-bodied punch

e. A split hammer handle

f. Horseplay

g. A loose mallet head

h. Prying open a paint can cover

i. Using a pipe on a wrench for more leverage

j. A wet floor

k. Working off-balance

l. Using a wrench to drive nails

m. A cluttered work surface

n. Loose clothing

o. Being overtired

Unit 2 MEASURING TOOLS

There are several things to consider in laying out work accurately. The first is choosing the correct tool for the job. The second consideration is using the tool correctly. It is also necessary to know how to read the graduations on different measuring tools.

Measurements made by carpenters vary with the type of work. The 50- or 100-foot steel tape is used for taking long measurements such as foundation lines. Shorter measurements are taken with pocket tape rules, spring-joint rules, and other types of folding rules. The framing or steel square is used for taking measurements such as spacing joists, studding, and rafters. The framing square is an important tool (see unit 3).

Each of these measuring tools is used for a specific purpose. They all incorporate the same systems of linear measure.

SYSTEMS OF MEASUREMENT

There are two systems of measurement. The traditional system used in the United States is the *customary system.* It is based on the English system of measure. The second is called the *SI* system (metric system). SI stands for Système Internationale d'Unités or International System of Units. The metric system, based on the meter, is now becoming widely used in the United States.

The customary system of linear measure uses the yard as the basic unit of length. The yard is divided into three equal parts called feet. The foot is divided into twelve equal parts called inches. Fractional divisions of an inch are found by dividing the inch into equal parts. The more common parts of an inch are halves, quarters, eighths, and sixteenths, figure 2-1. Where greater accuracy is needed, the inch is divided into thirty-seconds. The fractional parts into which a rule is graduated depends on the type and use of the rule.

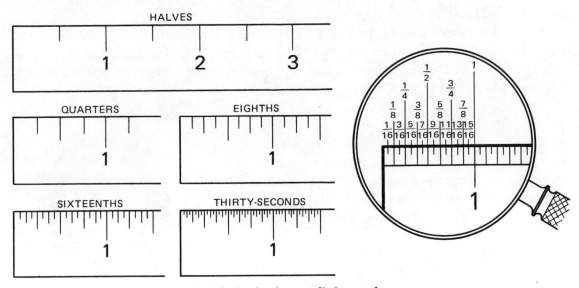

Fig. 2-1 Graduations applied to a rule

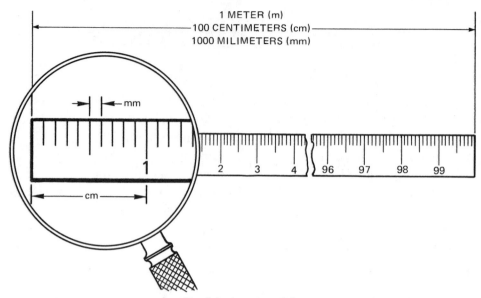

Fig. 2-2 A meter stick

Measurements longer than twelve inches are expressed in terms of feet, inches, and fractions of an inch. For example, the length of a board 7 feet, 10 and 11/16ths of an inch is written as 7'-10 11/16". A dimension such as 6 feet and 3/4 of an inch is written as 6'-0 3/4".

Fractional parts of an inch are always reduced to the lowest denominator. For example, 6/32" is reduced to 3/16"; 10/16" to 5/8"; and 5/4" to 1 1/4".

The SI system of linear measure uses the meter as the basic unit of length. The meter (m) is divided into 100 parts. Each part is called a centimeter (cm). Each centimeter is divided into ten parts. Each part is called a millimeter (mm). There are 100 cm in a meter and 1,000 mm in a meter, as shown on the meter stick in figure 2-2.

In architectural drawings the basic unit is the meter. In machine drawings the basic unit is the millimeter.

Fractions are not used in the SI system. Figures that are part of a meter or millimeter are written as decimals. The measurement of 5.05 meters is read as 5 and 5 hundredths of a meter or 5 and 50 thousandths of a meter. Therefore, 5.05 meters can be written in the following ways: 5.05 m, or 505 cm, or 5050 mm.

STEEL TAPES

Steel tapes, figure 2-3, are used to measure lengths up to 200 feet. There are many types made to suit special needs. The tape is made of flexible spring steel. It is stamped in graduations of feet, inches, half inches, quarters, eighths, and, in some instances, sixteenths of an inch.

Metric steel tapes, figure 2-4, are made in lengths up to 50 meters. They are stamped in graduations of meters, centimeters, and millimeters.

Fig. 2-3 Steel tape

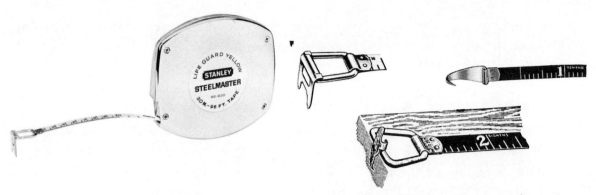

Fig. 2-4 Metric tape

Fig. 2-5 Types of hooks used on measuring tapes

The tapes shown in figures 2-3 and 2-4 indicate that each tape has a ring. This ring can be used to anchor the tape over a nail. Some steel tapes have a hook on the ring for anchoring the tape at the ends of boards. Several types of hooks are illustrated in figure 2-5.

The steel ribbon is uncoiled from the case by pulling outward on the ring. This should be done in the direction the measurement is to be taken (A, figure 2-6). Pulling the steel ribbon, as at B, damages the tape. The winding handle is opened by pressing on the center of the opposite side of the case.

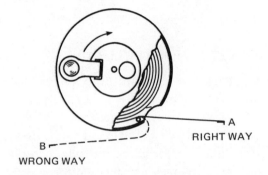

Fig. 2-6 Right and wrong methods of withdrawing the tape from the case.

At times the tape can stick. Tapping the side of the case against a flat surface helps to free the tape. Do not step on or twist a steel tape that is unwound. The tape can kink and crack. Treat the tape with oil. This should be done often, particularly after using the tape in damp weather. This is done by uncoiling the tape, then wiping it with an oily rag.

Measuring Distance with a 50- or 100-Foot Steel Tape

1. Attach the ring end of the tape to the point from which the measurement is to be taken. This can be done by driving a nail at that point. Then, adjust it so that the ring

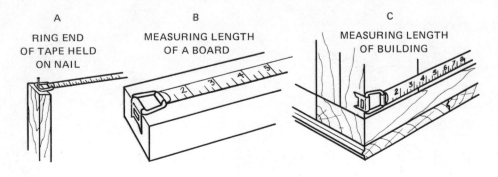

A
RING END OF TAPE HELD ON NAIL

B
MEASURING LENGTH OF A BOARD

C
MEASURING LENGTH OF BUILDING

Fig. 2-7 Applications of the steel tape

of the tape slips over the nail with the outside edge of the ring directly over the point from which the measurement is to be taken (A, figure 2-7). If the tape has a hook, it can be used as shown in B or C.

2. Uncoil the tape from the case. Pull in the direction of the point to which the measurement is to be made. Be sure that the tape lies flat and is free of kinks.

3. Pull the tape taut to the point of measurement. Mark the desired point directly opposite the graduation on the tape. Be sure that the uncoiled tape lies flat on the surface.

4. For measuring the distance between two points, read the graduations on the tape. Note which line on the tape meets with the point of measurement.

5. Recoil the tape into the case after the measurements are taken. This is done by opening the winding handle and turning it clockwise.

POCKET OR PUSH-PULL RULES

Pocket steel tapes (also called push-pull rules, figure 2-8) are shorter types of steel tapes. They are generally made in lengths of 6 to 20 feet. They are more useful for taking short inside or outside measurements. Also, they can be used for measuring the circumference of cylindrical objects.

Fig. 2-8 Push-pull rule

The end of the tape is fitted with a hook. The graduations are printed on only one face of the tape. Both edges are graduated in sixteenths. In some cases, one or both edges of the first several inches are graduated in thirty-seconds.

Taking an Inside Measurement

1. Put the end of the tape against one side of the opening. Uncoil the tape across the opening toward the opposite side.

Fig. 2-9 Taking an inside measurement

2. Hold the tape at the starting position. Continue extending it until the outer edge of the case butts against the opposite side of the opening. See figure 2-9.

3. Add the width of the tape case (usually two inches) to the indicated reading. Another type of pocket rule allows direct reading of the inside measurement by a small red pointer, A, figure 2-10.

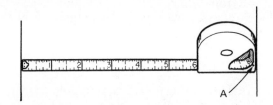

Fig. 2-10 Push-pull rule with pointer (A) for direct reading of inside measurement.

Taking an Outside Measurement

1. Pull the tape out from the case until there is enough tape to allow measuring the required distance.

2. Hook the end of the tape over the end of the object to be measured. See figure 2-11.

3. Read the dimension on the tape. Observe which graduation lines up with the point being measured.

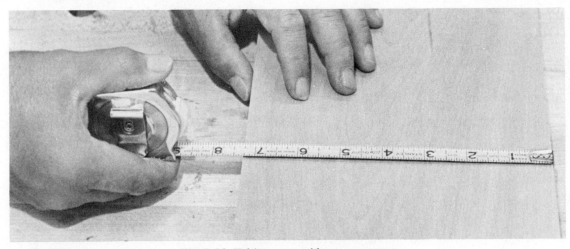

Fig. 2-11 Taking an outside measurement

Measuring the Circumference of a Cylinder

1. Pull the tape out a short distance. Hold the end close to the cylinder as shown in figure 2-12.

2. Pull the tape around the cylinder as though to wrap it. The end is held in a fixed position as the tape is uncoiled from the case. Completely encircle the cylinder with the tape. It should go beyond the point where it first made contact with the surface of the cylinder.

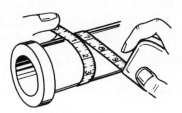

Fig. 2-12 Measuring a circumference with a push-pull rule.

3. Note which graduations are in line where the tape crosses at the starting point. If the 1-inch and 7-inch graduations are in line (figure 2-12), the circumference is found by subtracting the 1-inch reading from the 7-inch reading. This leaves 6 inches as the circumference measurement.

THE SPRING-JOINT FOLDING RULE

The spring-joint folding rule (zigzag type) is shown in figure 2-13. It is the rule most often used by carpenters. The rules fold to about 6 inches and fit easily into a pocket.

Wooden folding rules (A, figure 2-13), are usually graduated in sixteenths on both edges of each face. Metal rules are made with either one or both edges graduated on each face (B, figure 2-13).

Spring-joint rules have some weak points. When unfolding them, it is best to unfold one section at a time. Be sure that the pressure of the hand is directed in line with the unfolded sections. In this way, the thrust on the joint is as it should be. A sideways pressure has a bad effect on the joints and can cause the joints to break.

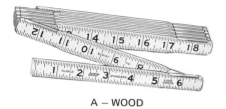

A – WOOD

B – METAL

Fig. 2-13 Six-foot spring-joint folding rules

Using the Spring-Joint Folding Rule

1. Hold the rule in one hand. With the other hand, unfold the sections one at a time, in order, as shown in figure 2-14. Unfold the sections until the rule is long enough for the required measurement.

2. Hold the rule flat on the surface to be measured. Place one end at the starting point. Decide the correct dimension by noting the measurement on the rule. When measuring large openings, the rule may bend or sag. The measurement should then be made by using a rod and taking the correct dimension from it. The extension measuring stick can also be used.

THE EXTENSION RULE

The extension rule is a zigzag type folding rule. It has a brass slide which can be extended or removed from the rule. Inside measurements can be made with the extension slide. Hole depths are also measured with the extension slide. Graduations on the slide must be added to the measurement on the rule, figure 2-15. Hole depth measurements are read directly off of the slide, figure 2-16.

Measuring the Thickness of a Board

1. To measure the thickness of a board, hold the rule in the right hand. Place the rule on its edge across the surface to be measured. Guide the rule with the thumbnail until the end of the rule is even with the left edge of the work. See figure 2-17.

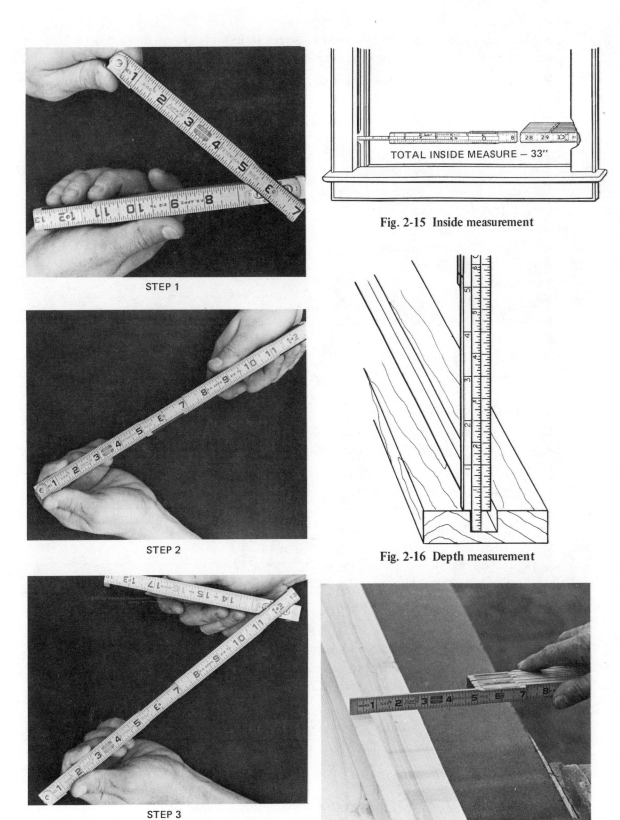

STEP 1

Fig. 2-15 Inside measurement

TOTAL INSIDE MEASURE — 33"

STEP 2

Fig. 2-16 Depth measurement

STEP 3

Fig. 2-14 Unfolding the spring-joint folding rule

Fig. 2-17 Measuring with the folding rule

NOTE: Lengths or widths less than two feet should always be measured by placing the rule on edge. In this way, error in reading the rule is lessened.

2. Read the graduations on the rule from left to right. Note which graduation on the rule lines up closest with the right-hand edge of the work.

THE CALIPER RULE

The caliper rule is made as a separate rule or it is incorporated in a folding rule like the extension on an extension rule (A, figure 2-18). The sliding brass rule is graduated in sixteenths and thirty-seconds. This rule is particularly useful for taking small, accurate measuren.

The two types of caliper rules are shown in figure 2-18. Note that type A can be used only for taking outside measurements, whereas type B can be used for taking either inside or outside measurements.

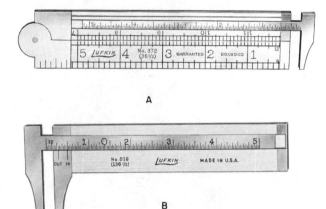

Fig. 2-18 Types of caliper rules

Taking an Inside Measurement

1. Close the sliding rule so that both rounds easily fit into the opening to be measured.

2. Insert the round into the opening. Move the sliding rule outwards until both rounds lightly touch the sides of the openings as shown in figure 2-19.

   NOTE: To get accurate results, the caliper should be held square to the opening.

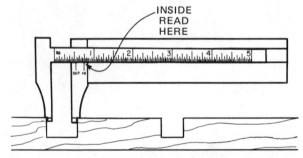

Fig. 2-19 Application of caliper rule for taking an inside dimension

3. Read the dimension by noting which graduation is in line with the indicating arrow for inside measurements. Reading of the caliper can also be done when it is removed from the opening. However, the removal should be done carefully so the sliding rule is not moved.

   NOTE: When taking inside measurements, do not use too much pressure on the rounds of the caliper rule. Too much pressure can spring the caliper which results in inaccurate measurements.

Taking an Outside Measurement

1. Move the sliding rule outward so that the caliper opening is greater than the size to be measured.

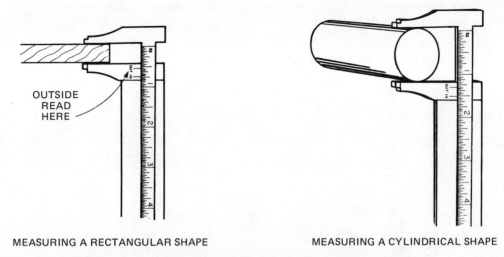

MEASURING A RECTANGULAR SHAPE   MEASURING A CYLINDRICAL SHAPE

Fig. 2-20 Applications of caliper rule for taking outside dimensions.

2. Place the calipers so that they enclose the object to be measured.

3. Move the sliding rule inward so both faces of the calipers slightly touch the surfaces of the object as shown in figure 2-20.

4. The reading is then taken by referring to the indicating arrow on the caliper for outside measurements.

The caliper rule should not be used to measure the outside diameter of a cylinder having a radius greater than the depth of the caliper opening. This is shown in figure 2-21.

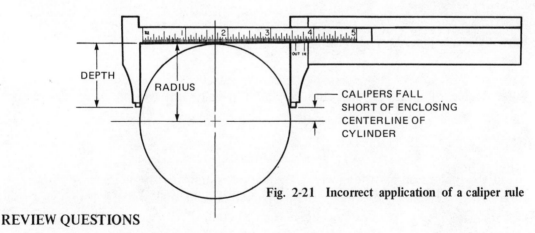

Fig. 2-21 Incorrect application of a caliper rule

REVIEW QUESTIONS

A. Short Answer or Discussion

 1. Express the following in feet, inches, and fractional inches as required.

    a. 49 12/16″   c. 52′-15 9/16″   e. 11′-22″

    b. 4 2/3 yds.   d. 61 6/32″   f. 4′-11 8/32″

 2. What is the purpose of the hook on the ring of a steel tape?

 3. In what direction should a steel tape be withdrawn form its case? Why?

4. How does the pocket steel tape combine the features of both a tape and a rule?

5. Describe three uses of the pocket rule.

6. What rule does the carpenter use most often? Why?

7. In using any type of rule, why is it best to use a type which is longer than the distance to be measured?

8. Describe three uses of a caliper rule.

9. What is the limitation in using the caliper rule for measuring outside diameters of cylinders?

10. What precautions should be taken in using the caliper rule for inside measurements?

11. Which of the measuring tools used by the carpenter are designed for the most accuracy?

12. Why is the rule placed on edge for measuring short distances?

13. What degree of accuracy does the carpenter usually not exceed in routine work?

B. Multiple Choice
1. A dimension such as eight feet, ten and three-quarters inches is written as
   a. 8'-10"-3/4"   c. 8'-10 3/4"
   b. 8-10-3/4"   d. 8'-10 3/4

2. Eighty-one and twelve-sixteenths inches should be stated as
   a. 81-12/16"   c. 81 12/16"
   b. 81 3/4"   d. 6'-9 3/4"

3. Unless the direct-reading type is used, use of the pocket rule for inside measurements requires adding which of the following to the indicated reading.
   a. 2"   c. width of the tape case
   b. height of the tape case   d. 2 1/2"

4. A pocket rule used to measure the circumference of a pipe shows the graduations 2″ and 10″ in line. The circumference is

a. 12″   c. 6″

b. 9″   d. 8″

5. Show by arrows where the measurement is read on the two illustrations of caliper uses, figure 2-22.

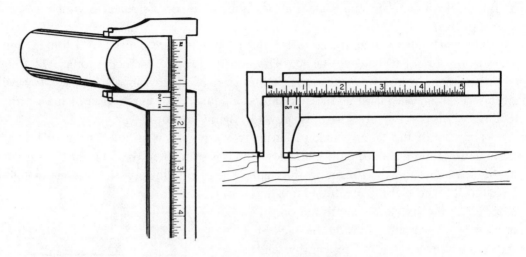

Fig. 2-22 Caliper rule applications

C. Match each item in Column I with the use in Column II for which it is best suited.

Column I	Column II
1. Caliper Rule	a. The length of a building about 30′ long.
2. Extension Rule	b. The circumference of a pillar.
3. Six-foot Zigzag Rule	c. The inside measurement of a wall register opening about 12″ wide.
4. Six-foot Pocket Rule	d. An outside measurement about 4″ long.
5. Fifty-foot Steel Tape	e. The layout of a building line about 75′ long.
6. Hundred-foot Steel Tape	f. An accurate measurement of the width of a small dado cut.

Unit 3 THE RAFTER AND FRAMING SQUARE

A carpenter's rafter and framing square is often called a steel square. It is used to measure spacing for studs, joists, rafters, and general layout work. This instrument can be termed the carpenter's rapid calculator. The beginner should become familiar with the uses of this tool. There are many graduations and tables on its surfaces which save hours in layout problems.

The parts of a standard size rafter and framing square consist of a tongue and body. These form a right (90-degree) angle. The body is usually 24 inches long. The tongue can be either 16 inches or 18 inches long. Other sizes of squares are also made. However, they are not as commonly used as the standard size square. An illustration of the square, giving its dimensions and the terms used, is shown in figure 3-1.

The face of the square is identified in two ways. It is either (1) the side which bears the manufacturer's stamp, or (2) the side which is seen when the body of the square is held in the left hand and the tongue in the right. The graduations on the face are in eighths and sixteenths. The eighths are found on the inner edge; the sixteenths are found on the outer edge. The graduations on the back of the square are in tenths, sixteenths, and twelfths. The outside edges are graduated in twelfths. The inside edge of the body is graduated in sixteenths and the inside edge of the tongue is graduated in tenths. (See figure 3-2.)

A hundredths scale is also found on the back of the tongue, located in the corner of the square. The scale is limited to one inch and each graduation represents

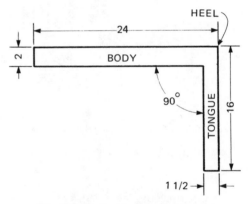

Fig. 3-1 Parts of a framing square

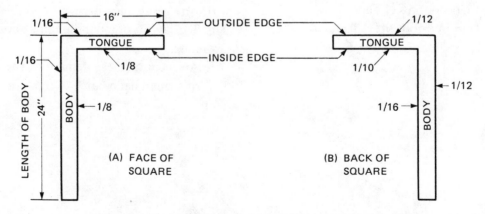

Fig. 3-2 Graduations found on a framing square

five one-hundredths of an inch. Directly below and in line with the hundredths scale is another scale graduated in sixteenths. Lining up these scales makes it possible to make conversions (changes) from either scale by observation.

Each scale shown on a framing square has a special use. The 1/16 and 1/8 scales are used for making conventional measurements and layouts. The 1/12 and 1/10 scales are used where multiples of tenths and twelfths help to simplify measuring and layout. The hundredths scale is used for laying out small precision measurements. This is done by placing dividers on the divisions of the scale, then transferring the measurement to the work.

Using the Square for Measuring a Width

Assume that the length of the tongue is 16 inches. The width to be measured is less than 16 inches.

1. Place the outside edge of the body of the square along, and even with, the edge of the board.

   NOTE: The tongue should be at the right. In this position, the sixteenth of an inch graduations can be read along the tongue since they are face up.

2. Read the graduation on the tongue which meets with the point of measurement. See figure 3-3.

3. For measuring a width which is greater than 16 inches, and less than 24 inches, the same process is used. But, the tongue is placed along the edge of the board and the body falls to the left. In this way, the sixteenth graduations, again, are face up.

   NOTE: Whenever possible, use a measuring tool that can be extended to the full length of the measurement.

Fig. 3-3 Measuring a width with the steel square

Using the Square for Spacing

1. To mark the spacing of studs or joists at 16-inch centers, place the end of the tongue of the square at a starting point along the edge that is to be laid out. Then mark a point at the heel of the tongue.

2. Move the tongue at full length intervals. Mark each interval until the layout is finished.

3. If a 24-inch spacing is required, the body of the square should be used for measuring the spacing. The same process is followed as described for the tongue.

THE RAFTER TABLE

The rafter table, figure 3-4, is on the face side of the body of the rafter and framing square. It is used to find the length of rafters and their cuts for roofs having standard pitches. Note that there are six lines of figures which make up this table.

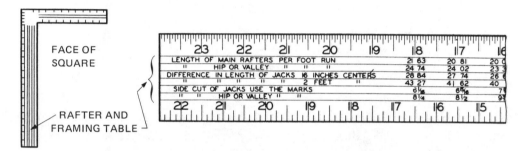

Fig. 3-4 Location of the rafter and framing table on the face side of the body

The figures represented by each line of the rafter table are as follows:

- The *first line* gives the lengths of common rafters per foot of run.

- The *second line* gives the lengths of hip and valley rafters per foot of run.

- The *third line* gives the length of the first jack rafter. It also gives the differences in length of the others centered at 16 inches.

- The *fourth line* gives the length of the first jack rafter. It also gives the differences in lengths of the others spaced at 24-inch centers.

- The *fifth line* gives the side cuts of jacks.

- The *sixth line* gives the side cuts of hip and valley rafters.

In order to use the framing table, one must know the meaning of the following terms: span, rise, run, and pitch. (See figure 3-5.)

- The *span* is that measurement which is the distance over the wall plates.

- The *rise* is that measurement which is the vertical height of the rafter above the top of the walls.

- The *run* is that measurement which is half the width span of the building.

- The *pitch* is a figure which represents the ratio of the rise to the total width (twice the run) of the building.

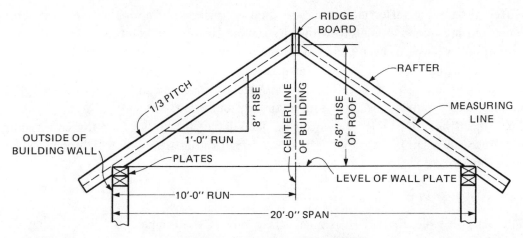

Fig. 3-5 Span, run, rise and pitch

The relationship of these terms is expressed by the following example. A house having a run of 10 feet and a rise of 6'-8" has a pitch of 6'-8"/20' or 1/3.

Using the Rafter Table for Finding the Length of a Common Rafter

Assume that the roof has a rise of 8 inches per foot of run or 1/3 pitch. The run is 10'-0".

1. Find on the inch line on the top edge of the body the number that is equal to the rise of the roof. In this case, the number is 8. See figure 3-6.

2. On the first line under the number 8, the number 14.42 is found. This is the length of the rafter in inches per foot run for this particular pitch.

3. Since the length of the rafter per foot run equals 14.42 inches, the total length of the rafter is 14.42 multiplied by 10. This equals 144.20 inches, or 144.20 ÷ 12 = 12.01 feet or, rounded off, 12 feet. See figure 3-7.

NOTE: To find the length of a common rafter, multiply the length given in the table by the number of feet of run.

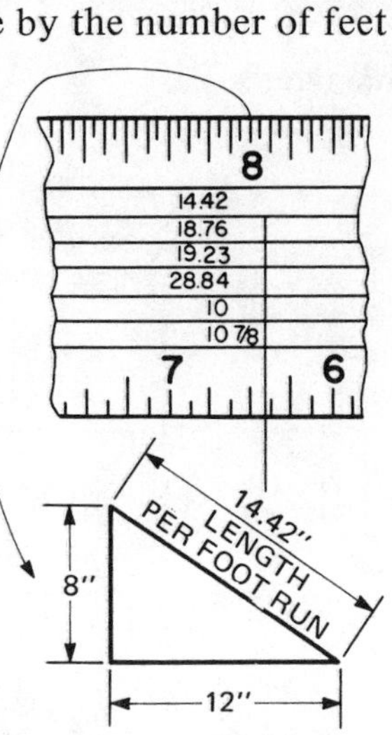

Fig. 3-6 Finding the rise figure on the inch line

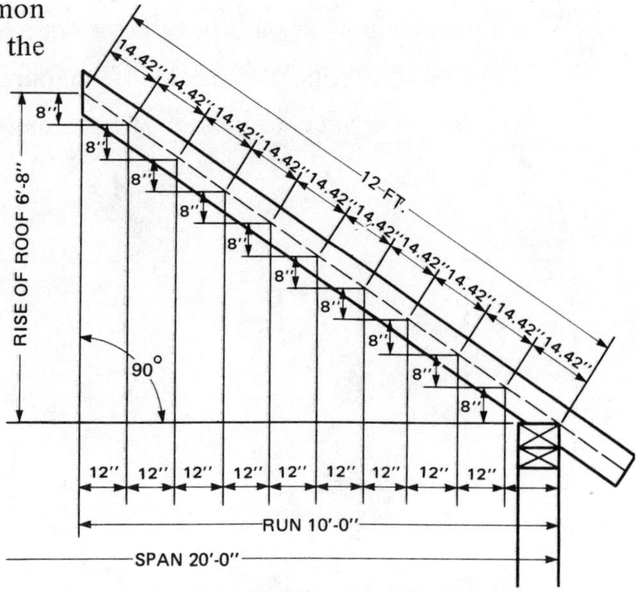

Fig. 3-7 Finding the total length of the rafter

19

Different forms of rafter tables are also used on rafter and framing squares. On some, all calculations are done completely within the table. However, when this is the case, some of the other tables have not been included on the square, and it is then referred to as a rafter square. Other squares do not include rafter tables, and these are referred to as framing squares. Thus, when a square is referred to as a steel square, it can be one of three types: a rafter and framing square, a framing square, or a rafter square.

The other five rafter tables shown on the face side of the body of a rafter and framing square are used in a similar manner. It is best to read the instructions which come with a square for detailed information on their use.

THE OCTAGON SCALE

The octagon scale, figure 3-8, is on the face side of the tongue. It is used to lay out octagonal (eight-sided) shapes. This scale is made up of a number of divisions marked along the center of the tongue.

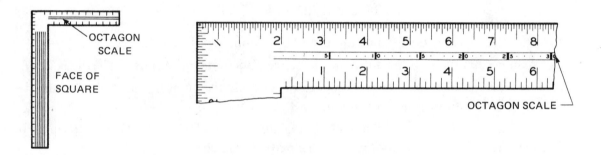

Fig. 3-8 Location of the octagon scale on the face of the tongue

Using the Octagon Scale

Assume that an octagon is to be made from a board 8 inches square.

1. Locate the center points on each of the four sides of the square as shown in A, figure 3-9.

2. Set a pair of dividers to a width of eight spaces on the octagon scale.

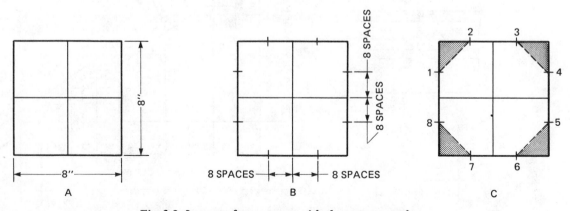

Fig. 3-9 Layout of an octagon with the octagon scale

3. Transfer this width to each side of each center point on the 8-inch square. See B, figure 3-9.

4. Connect points 1 through 8 as shown in C, figure 3-9.

THE ESSEX BOARD MEASURE TABLE

Before explaining the use of the next table, the meaning and calculation of board feet is reviewed. A *board foot* represents 144 cubic inches of lumber, or a piece of wood 1 inch thick, 12 inches wide, and 12 inches long, figure 3-10.

To calculate board feet, use the following formula:

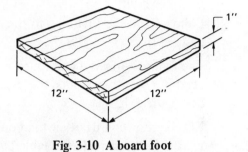

Fig. 3-10 A board foot

$$\frac{\text{No. of pcs. x thickness, in. x width, in. x length, in.}}{12 \text{ x } 12 \text{ (or 144)}}$$

When the length is given in running (linear) feet, use 12 (not 12 x 12) as the divisor.

The Essex board measure table, figure 3-11, is on the back of the body. It gives the contents in board measure of almost any size of board. Note that this table is made up of seven parallel lines of figures.

This table is used with the outer scale of the square. The twelve-inch graduation on the outer edge is the starting point for all calculations. It represents a one-inch board twelve inches wide. The meaning of the remaining figures is as follows:

- The column of figures under the figure 12 represents the lengths of boards to be calculated.

- The graduations to the right and to the left of the 12 (11, 13, etc.) represent the widths of the boards to be calculated.

- The column of figures under the graduations which represent the widths are the board measure values for one inch of thickness.

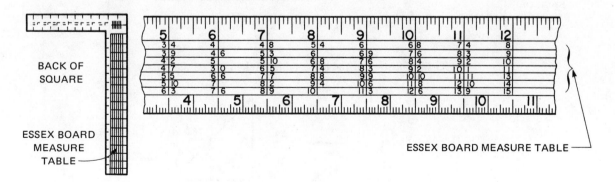

Fig. 3-11 Location of the Essex board measure on the back of the body

Using the Essex Board Measure Table

Assume it is necessary to find the number of board feet in a piece of lumber 1 inch thick, 11 inches wide, and 8 feet long.

1. In the column under figure 12, find figure 8.

2. Follow 8, on the first line, to the left and stop under 11.

3. The figure 7-4 (seven and four-twelfths) found at this point represents the board measure. See figure 3-12.

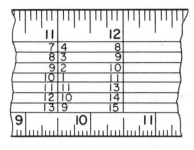

Fig. 3-12 Essex board measure table

NOTE: For boards other than one inch thick, the board measure is found by multiplying the figure given in the table by the thickness of the board in full inches. For boards longer than 15 feet, divide the length into several parts. Find the board measure for each length. Add these figures to get the total board measure. The six- and twelve-foot lengths have not been included in the column of figures under the figure 12. This is because a twelve-foot length of board contains as many board feet as it is inches wide. Similarly a board six feet long contains half as many board feet as it is inches wide.

THE BRACE MEASURE TABLE

The brace measure table is on the back of the tongue of the rafter and framing square. It gives the lengths of braces that are commonly used. See figure 3-13.

This table is made up of a row of three numbers grouped together. They are spaced at regular intervals. Two of the numbers are placed one over the other. They represent the measurements of the legs of a right angle. The third dimension directly following represents the diagonal measurement of the right angle formed by the first two measurements. See figure 3-14.

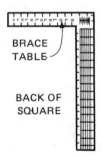

Fig. 3-13 Location of the brace table on the back of the tongue

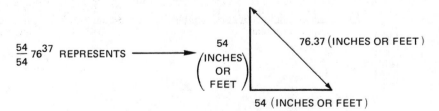

Fig. 3-14 Interpretation of figures from the brace table

Using the Brace Measure Table

Assume the run of a brace on a post and on a beam is to be 39 inches. See figure 3-15.

1. Refer to the brace table. Locate the figures $\frac{39}{39}$.

2. Read the figure which immediately follows: 55^{15}.

3. The length of the brace interpreted from this last figure is 55.15″.

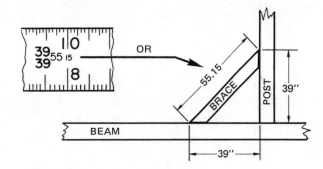

Fig. 3-15 **Application of figures from the brace table**

NOTE: Braces can be regarded as common rafters. Therefore, when the brace run on the post differs from the run on the beam, their lengths as well as top and bottom cuts can be determined from the figures given in the tables of common rafters.

REVIEW QUESTIONS

A. Short Answer or Discussion

1. Where is the rafter table located on the framing square?

2. Compare the terms *run* and *span*.

3. Describe the relationships of pitch, rise, and run.

4. To find the rise of a roof, multiply the _____ by the _____.

5. If the rise is 8 inches per foot run, the pitch is _____.

6. If the rise is 4 inches per foot run, the pitch is _____.

7. If the pitch is 1/3, the rise per foot run is _____.

8. If the pitch is 1/4 and the span is 20′-0″, the run is _____ and the rise is _____.

9. To find the length of a common rafter using the rafter table, multiply the _____ given in the table by the feet of _____.

10. Find the length per foot run of a common rafter if the pitch is 1/4 and the span is 20′-0″.

11. The steel square's construction and all its applications to roof framing are based on the mathematical principles of a _____ triangle.

12. Define a board foot. Give the formula for finding board feet.

13. Which table of the framing square gives board feet?

14. What is the starting point in the table for all board feet calculations? Explain why this starting point is used.

15. In the Brace Measure Table, what do the two figures placed one over the other always represent?

16. When the figures described in question 15 are not equal, the brace can be regarded as a _____.

17. The _____ scale is used to lay out eight-sided figures.

18. Using the proper table on the steel square, find the board measure of the following pieces of lumber.

   a. 1 pc. 2″ x 11″ x 8′-0″

   b. 2 pcs. 1″ x 9″ x 10′-0″

   c. 1 pc. 3/4″ x 10″ x 8′-0″

   d. 1 pc. 2″ x 4″ x 16′-0″

   e. 4 pcs. 1″ x 6″ x 10′-6″

   f. 7 pcs. 1/2″ x 8″ x 6′-3″

   g. 5 pcs. 2″ x 6″ x 12′-0″

   h. 14 pcs. 1 1/2″ x 1 1/2″ x 8′-0″

   i. 9 pcs. 1/4″ x 4′-0″ x 8′-0″

   j. 8 pcs. 2″ x 8″ x 16′-0″

   k. 11 pcs. 3/8″ x 2′-0″ x 8′-0″

   l. 3 pcs. 4″ x 4″ x 10′-6″

19. Find the board measure of the items in question 18 (a through f) by using the board feet formula.

20. Use of the hundredths graduations on the square is generally done by using _____ to transfer the measurement to the work.

21. From the information given in figure 3-16, use the steel square to find the length per foot run of common rafters, A through D.

	Rise	Pitch	Run	Span
A	10′		10′-0″	
B		1/3		24′-0″
C	7′			42′-0″
D		1/4	12′-0″	

Fig. 3-16 Rise, Pitch, Run and Span Table

22. Find the total length of common rafters A through D in figure 3-16.

B. Identification and Interpretation

1. In figure 3-17, identify the parts of the rafter and framing square. Complete the dimensions of each part.

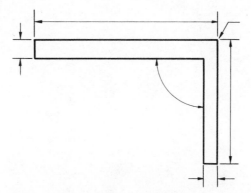

Fig. 3-17 Parts of a rafter and framing square

2. In figure 3-18, indicate the inch graduations found on the rafter and framing square.

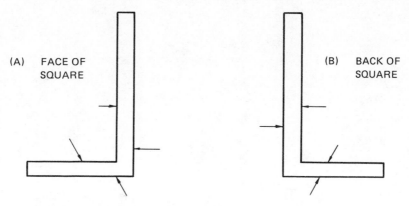

(A) FACE OF SQUARE

(B) BACK OF SQUARE

Fig. 3-18 Inch graduations on a rafter and framing square

3. Identify the tables which are indicated by the circled numbers in figure 3-19.

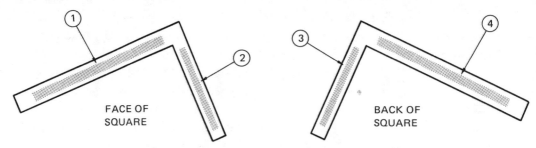

Fig. 3-19 **Tables on a rafter and framing square**

Unit 4 LAYOUT TOOLS

Layout work involves measuring and marking or scribing lines on materials that are used. These lines are taken from drawings or plans. The lines form an outline on the material. A machinist or carpenter follows the outline to shape the material to the correct size.

Distances are laid out with the measuring tools described in units 2 and 3. Discussed in this unit are the tools·and methods for the layout of:

- *Straight lines* — straightedge and pencil or knife, chalk line, layout (string) lines, and the use of builders' level and builders' transit-level.

- *Parallel lines* — marking gauge, mortise gauge, panel gauge, door butt gauge, and rough gauging.

- *Angles* — steel square, try square, try and miter square, sliding T bevel, combination square, and angle divider.

- *Circles, arcs, irregular contours* — scribers, dividers, and trammel points.

THE CARPENTER'S PENCIL

There are several types of carpenter's pencils (figure 4-1) used in carpentry work. A special type, made for rough layout work, has a soft rectangular-shaped lead. The lead is surrounded by a wooden case that is stronger than that of an ordinary pencil. For close layout work on smooth lumber, a regular pencil of hard lead should be used. When accurate work is to be laid out and fine joints are necessary, a knife should be used.

A STRAIGHTEDGE

Straight lines from 2 to 8 feet long are generally made by using a straightedge. This is done as one would use a rule to draw a straight line.

Fig. 4-1 Carpenter's pencil

A straightedge is made from a carefully selected piece of straight-grained clear pine or a piece of exterior grade 5-ply plywood. It is made from 1-inch or 1 1/4-inch stock about 5 inches wide and 6 feet to 8 feet long. The top edge (A, figure 4-2) is made about 30 inches long. It is parallel to and centered with the bottom edge. This section provides a surface on which a spirit level can be placed. This is done mainly when the straightedge is being used for plumbing or leveling.

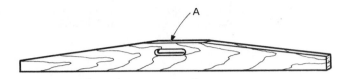

Fig. 4-2 Straightedge

Using the Straightedge to Form a Straight Line Between Two Points

1. Place the bottom edge of the straightedge in line with the given points.

2. Mark with a pencil along this edge, connecting the two points with the pencil line.

   NOTE: Any straightedge tool such as a framing square or rule can be used to scribe a straight line. However, keep in mind that the straightedged tool used should be long enough to reach the two points. Otherwise, the line can be scribed inaccurately.

GAUGES

   Marking gauges are tools designed for the accurate gauging of lines parallel to a planed edge or face of a board. They are made in two types: wood and metal.

   The wood marking gauge, figure 4-3, has a beam about 8 inches long. A scribing pin is clamped near one end of the beam. The pin is sharpened to a conical point. A sliding head, which has an inserted metal faceplate to prevent wear, is adjustable along the beam. It can be clamped to the beam at any distance from the scribing pin by tightening a thumbscrew.

   Wood marking gauges are commonly used in the shop or on the job where they are exposed to moisture and hard wear. Thus, when selecting a marking gauge, several points in its construction should be considered. The head should be protected with brass to guarantee long wear. The wood parts should be of a fine-grained hardwood. The thumbscrew and head should be provided with a coarse thread to resist stripping.

   Marking gauges are also made of metal. Their construction is the same as a wood marking gauge. However, the metal marking gauges are considered to be superior to the wood gauges, in terms of efficiency and wear. The surfaces of a metal marking gauge are

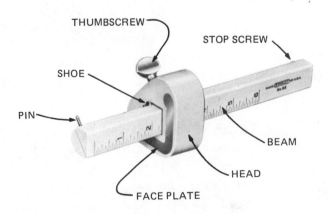

Fig. 4-3 Wood marking gauge

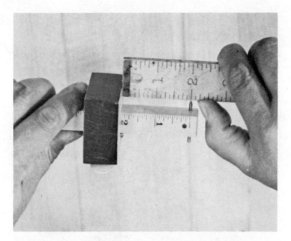

Fig. 4-4 Checking the setting of the gauge

Fig. 4-5 Proper method of holding the gauge for scribing

plated with a nonrusting material to prolong the life of the tool. The main difference between the wood and metal marking gauge is the device that marks the material. The metal marking gauge has a wheel (roller cutter). The wood marking gauge has a pin. The wheel-type scriber is easier to use when scribing across the grain and over knots.

Using a Marking Gauge

1. Adjust the head on the beam at the required distance. Measure the distance between the pin and the head with a rule as in figure 4-4.

2. Tighten the thumbscrew and measure again for correctness.

3. To gauge a line, grasp the gauge as shown in figure 4-5. The fingers should encircle the head and the thumb is on the beam and behind the pin.

4. Lay the bottom corner of the beam on the surface to be gauged. Allow the pin to touch the surface lightly.

5. Hold the face of the head firmly against the surface which is being used as the

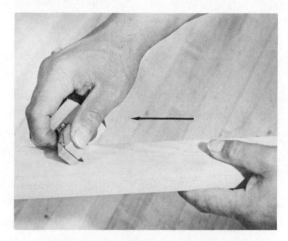

Fig. 4-6 Scribing a line with the gauge

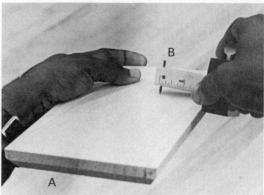

Fig. 4-7 Marking a short line

guiding edge. Move the gauge along this edge, marking the surface of the board as it is moved along.

NOTE: Distribute the hand pressure evenly over the head and the pin of the gauge. Do not bear down so heavily that the pin catches into the grain of the wood. Use enough pressure for the pin to ride smoothly over the surface, making a light mark.

6. To gauge a short board, as shown in figure 4-7, hold the gauge with the thumbscrew pointed toward end B. Start at end A. Work down the length of the board until the head of the gauge comes near end B.

7. Now reverse the direction of the thumbscrew so that it points to end A.

8. Hold the gauge in the same position. Start the pin at end B. Work back to where the gauge line stopped near end B.

THE DOUBLE BAR GAUGE

A double bar gauge (often referred to as a type of mortise gauge) is like the wood marking gauge. The difference is that the double bar gauge has two beams with a pin fastened to each beam, figure 4-8. The double bar gauge is used for marking a mortise.

Fig. 4-8 Double bar marking gauge

Various types of these gauges are made. Some have a head with a double face, with the beams located either side by side or one above the other. The beams can have a pair of cutter wheels at one end and a pair of pins at the other. These differences in the construction of the gauge allow for greater flexibility in its use. Whatever the difference, the basic use of the gauge is for scribing lines parallel to one another and to an edge.

Using a Mortise Gauge

Assume that the marking gauge to be used is one having beams located side by side. That is, the beams scribe both mortise lines at the same time.

1. Loosen the thumbscrew so that the beams slide easily through the head.

2. Set one pin from the face of the head at a distance desired for scribing the first mortise line from the edge of the board.

3. Set the other pin at a distance from the first pin equal to the width of the mortise.

   NOTE: The setting of the pins can be done by referring to the beams' graduation lines. However, pin settings should then be checked with a rule.

4. Lock the beams in position by tightening the thumbscrew.

5. Again, check the distances of the pins from the face with a rule.

6. Apply the gauge to the board in the same manner as described for the marking gauge. See figure 4-9.

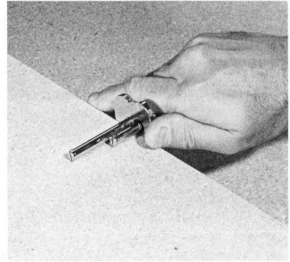

Fig. 4-9 Using the metal mortise gauge

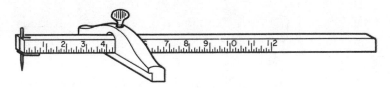

Fig. 4-10 Panel gauge

THE PANEL GAUGE

A panel gauge, figure 4-10, is used where the parallel lines are more than 6 inches from the edge of a board. This tool is like the marking gauge and is used in the same manner. The panel gauge is used in cases where the beam of the marking gauge is not long enough. It differs from the marking gauge in only one way. The head and beam are longer on the panel gauge, thus, the panel gauge covers more area.

THE BUTT GAUGE

The butt gauge, figure 4-11, is used to lay out the measurements for setting hinges on doors and door jambs. It is made of metal. The scribing cutters are located on the ends of the beams. These are adjusted by loosening or tightening thumbscrews fastened to the beams and fitted into slots in the body of the gauge.

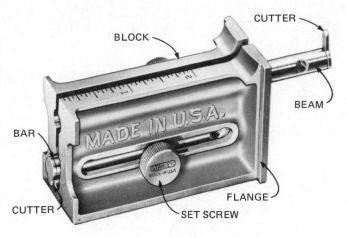

Fig. 4-11 Butt gauge

Using the Butt Gauge

1. To lay out lines for hinge locations on doors or jambs, first refer to figure 4-12. Learn the terms used to identify the butt layout.

   W = width of gain
   S = setback
   D = depth of gain (equal to thickness of hinge)

2. Decide where the gauge line is to begin and end. This is done by placing one of the hinges in its correct location on the door or jamb and marking its length with a sharp knife.

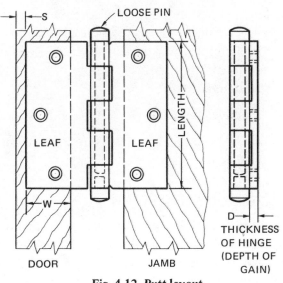

Fig. 4-12 Butt layout

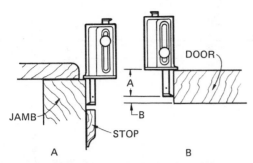

Fig. 4-13 Laying out the jamb and door

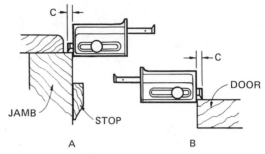

Fig. 4-14 Setting the gauge for depth of gain

3. Loosen the setscrew found on the block. Set the gauge for the width of the gain by referring to the graduation on the block (figure 4-11). Tighten the setscrew and check the cutter setting with a rule.

4. For laying out the door, place the gauge against the face of the door. Holding it square to the edge, move it along the edge using enough pressure so that a sharp mark is made (B, figure 4-13).

5. Set the gauge for the depth of the gain (B, figure 4-14). Mark the depth of the gain in the same manner as described for the width.

6. To square lines for the length of the hinge, hold the flange of the butt gauge against the side of the door. Slide it up to the knife mark (step 3) and mark the ends of the gains as shown in B, figure 4-15.

7. A completed layout is shown in figure 4-16.

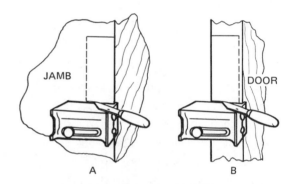

Fig. 4-15 Marking the ends of gains

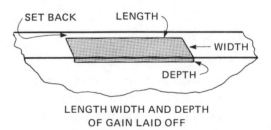

LENGTH WIDTH AND DEPTH
OF GAIN LAID OFF

Fig. 4-16 Completed layout

NOTE: The same process is used for laying out the jamb. See A, figures 4-13, 4-14, and 4-15.

FINGER (ROUGH) GAUGING

Rough gauging of parallel lines is often done by holding a pencil firmly with the fingers and using one finger as a guide along the edge of the board. The fingers are adjusted to hold the pencil at the required distance from the edge of the board. They are kept in this adjustment and moved along the board, thus making a line parallel to the edge.

Finger Gauging with a Pencil

1. Hold the pencil in the position shown in figure 4-17.

2. Adjust the pencil in the fingers so that the flat of the fingernail of the index finger or thumb rests against the edge of the board.

3. Either push or pull the pencil along the edge. Be careful to hold the pencil firmly to maintain the same width of space from the edge of the board.

   NOTE: Do not draw the edge of the fingernail against the grain of the board. It is easy to get a splinter under the fingernail if this is done.

Fig. 4-17 Finger gauging

ROUGH GAUGING WITH A BENCH RULE

Parallel lines can also be rough gauged by the use of a rule. This is a more accurate method of gauging lines because the rule, rather than the fingers, is used as the gauging device. With this method both hands are used: one to guide the rule and the other to guide the pencil. Therefore, the work must be held in place by a clamp or similar device while the lines are being laid out.

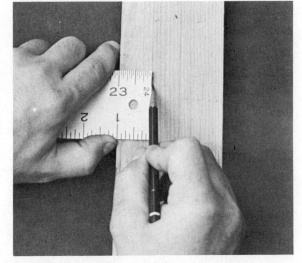

Fig. 4-18 Gauging with a rule

Gauging with a Rule and a Pencil

1. Adjust the thumb at the desired dimension on the rule.

2. Hold the pencil at the end of the rule.

3. Pull the rule and pencil back using the thumbnail as a guide for gauging, as shown in figure 4-18.

GAUGING WITH A BUTT SPACING RULE

The butt spacing rule is a zigzag type of rule often used for gauging 2 inch, 4 inch, 6 inch, 8 inch, and 10 inch widths. The construction of this rule is such that the first section extends 4 inches. Each following section adds six inches to the length of the rule. All sections have square ends. Joints open on even numbers only.

Figure 4-19 illustrates a butt spacing rule. In general, it looks like the standard spring-joint (zigzag) rule. Its name is derived from the manner in which it is used for gauging lines. It is also used for measuring like any other standard folding rule.

If a rule is opened from the long section end, it can be butted for gauging lines at six inch intervals. By alternating from the short section end to the long section end, a series of gauge marks can be made at either two or four inch intervals as shown in figure 4-20.

Fig. 4-19 Butt spacing rule

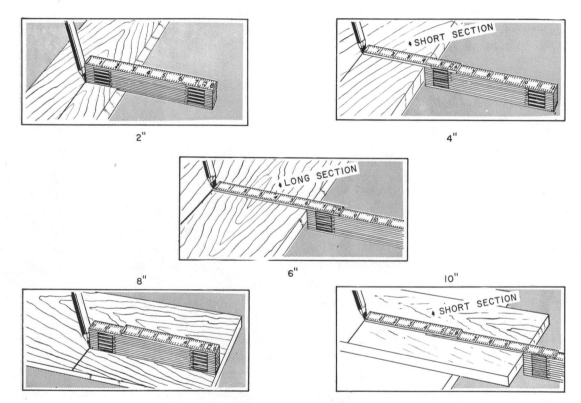

Fig. 4-20 Gauging with a butt spacing rule

THE STEEL SQUARE, TRY SQUARE, TRY AND MITER SQUARE

The steel square, try square, and try and miter square are used to lay out right (90-degree) angles. All three of these tools can be used to check the squareness of a board and the straightness of a surface. The try and miter square, figure 4-21, can be used to lay out 45-degree angles. The steel square can be used to lay out a range of angular measurements (see figure 4-24).

These tools are made with several features. The blade is made of steel to hold its shape. The blade is plated so that it does not corrode. The metal is polished and stamped so that inch graduations are easy to read. All edges are machined. Those edges that meet

Fig. 4-22 Laying out a 90-degree angle

Fig. 4-21 (A) Try square with metal handle, (B) Try square with wood handle, (C) Try and miter square with metal handle

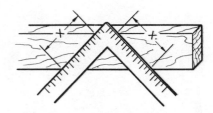

Fig. 4-23 Laying out a 45-degree angle

are machined so that they are square (90 degrees) to one another. The handles of a try square, and try and miter square, are made of either wood or metal and can be from 4 inches to 8 inches long. Those with metal handles wear better and keep their accuracy longer.

Using the Steel Square to Lay Out a 90-degree and a 45-degree Angle

1. To make a 90-degree or square mark, place the body of the square along or against one edge of the board. Mark along the outside edge of the tongue on the face of the board. See figure 4-22.

2. To lay out a 45-degree angle for making a right-angle miter, place the steel square on the face of the board so that an equal (X) number of graduations on the tongue and on the body fall on the board as shown in figure 4-23. Mark along the outer edges of the square. Mark along the inner edges if a 90-degree included angle is needed.

Angle	Tongue	Blade	Angle	Tongue	Blade
30°	12″	20 7/8″	72°	12″	3 7/8″
45°	12″	12″	73 7/11°	12″	3 17/32″
54°	12″	8 25/32″	75°	12″	3 7/32″
60°	12″	6 15/16″	77 1/8°	12″	2 3/4″
64 2/7°	12″	5 25/32″	78 3/4°	12″	2 13/32″
67 1/2°	12″	4 31/32″	80°	12″	2 1/8″
70°	12″	4 3/8″	81°	12″	1 29/32″

Table 4-1 Range of angles for the steel square

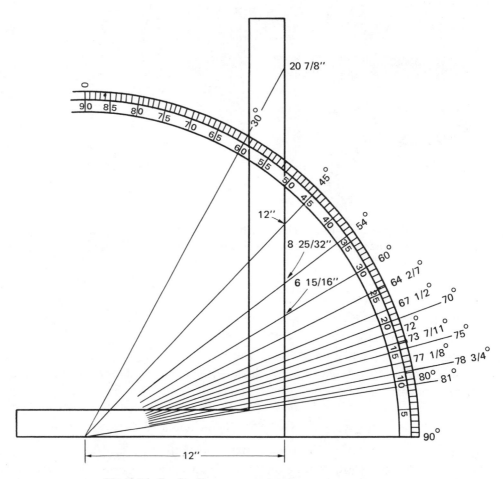

Fig. 4-24 Graduations on a protractor

NOTE: A range of other angles can be laid out with the steel square by referring to table 4-1. The angles given represent the included angle with reference to a vertical line. By referring to the graduations on the protractor (figure 4-24), the included angle can be found with reference to a horizontal line. This illustration is shown to help clarify table 4-1.

Using the Try Square

1. To square a mark across the face of a board, place the try square handle against the straight edge of the stock. The blade should be flat on the surface and extend across the stock.

2. Draw a line along the outer edge of the blade as shown in figure 4-25.

Fig. 4-25 Squaring a mark with the try square

Fig. 4-26 Squaring a line across the edge of a board

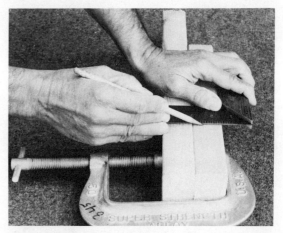

Fig. 4-27 Laying out similar locations of lines on duplicate parts

3. To square a line across the edge of a board, place the handle of the square firmly against the face of the board. Mark along the edge of the blade. See figure 4-26.

4. To lay out similar locations of lines on duplicate parts, hold the pieces together as one unit while marking. See figure 4-27.

Using the Try and Miter Square

1. To square a mark across the face of a board, use the square as shown in A, figure 4-28.

2. To lay out a 45-degree line, place the 45-degree shoulder against the working edge as shown in B, figure 4-28. Then draw the necessary line along the edge of the blade.

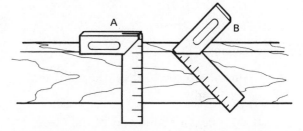

Fig. 4-28 Two applications of the try and miter square

THE COMBINATION SQUARE

The combination square has an adjustable head which can be clamped to the blade at any desired distance from the end of the blade, as shown in figure 4-29. The head, A, is made of cast iron with machined edges of 90 degrees and 45 degrees from the edge of the blade line.

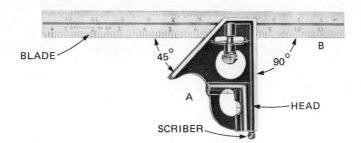

Fig. 4-29 Combination square

The blade, B, is made of tempered steel and is ground and polished. The blade is stamped in graduations of eighths, sixteenths, and thirty-seconds of an inch. The blade can be removed from the head and used as a short straightedge. The head is provided with a spirit level and a scriber, which is inserted in a hole made for this purpose, with the balled end protruding as shown in figure 4-29. A combination square can be used as an inside or outside try square, plumb and level, depth gauge, or marking gauge.

Fig. 4-30 Using the combination square as a straightedge

Using the Combination Square

• As a straightedge

1. Remove the blade from the head by depressing the thumbscrew and pulling the blade from the head.

2. Place the blade on a surface. Scribe a line along the edge as shown in figure 4-30.

• For gauging

1. Clamp the blade to the head set at the desired width.

2. Hold a pencil at the end of the blade. Move the combination square and pencil along the board, making the necessary gauge mark. See figure 4-31.

Fig. 4-31 Using the combination square for gauging

THE SLIDING T BEVEL

The sliding T bevel, figure 4-32, is like a try square with an adjustable blade. A slot in the blade allows the blade to slide or pivot to any desired angle. A thumbscrew at the end of the handle locks the blade in position. Angles can be taken from a protractor (A in figure 4-33), steel square (B), or a draftsman's triangle (C).

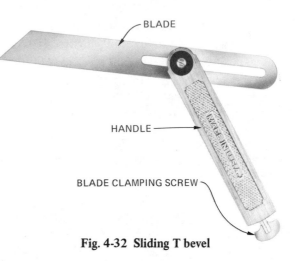

BLADE

HANDLE

BLADE CLAMPING SCREW

Fig. 4-32 Sliding T bevel

The parts of the sliding T bevel are shown in figure 4-32. Note that one portion of the blade is slotted. This permits the blade to slide so the angles of inside corners can be measured. The blade can retract into the slot in the handle when the tool is not being used.

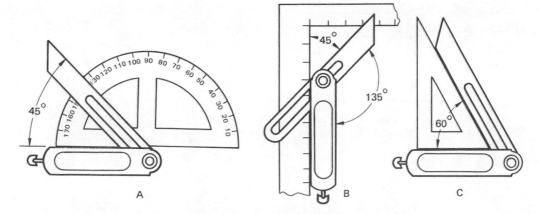

Fig. 4-33 Methods of setting the sliding T bevel to angles

Using the Sliding T Bevel

1. To transfer 90-degree angles, loosen the thumbscrew at the end of the handle. Adjust the blade to the required setting. Tighten the thumbscrew and use the sliding T bevel like a try square.

2. To set the blade at different angles, use the protractor as in A, figure 4-33. This shows the blade being set for 45 degrees.

3. At B, the steel square is being used. Notice that the same number of graduations are measured off on the tongue of the square as on the body. This gives a setting of 45 degrees.

4. At C, a 30°-60° triangle is being used to set a 60-degree angle.

5. To transfer the angle to a board, the sliding T bevel handle is placed against the edge of the board with the blade across the surface (figure 4-34). Mark a line along the edge of the blade.

6. For duplicating lines drawn at the same angle, such as laying off dovetails for a drawer, the sliding T bevel is used as shown in figure 4-35. Both sides of the dovetail can be laid out with one setting of the blade by alternately reversing the direction of the handle. See figure 4-36.

Fig. 4-34 Transferring an angle to a board

Fig. 4-35 Duplicating lines drawn at the same angle

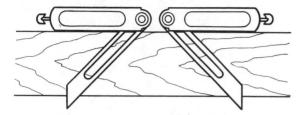

Fig. 4-36 Laying out both sides of the dovetail

THE ANGLE DIVIDER

The angle divider, figure 4-37, is a tool for bisecting angles. It can be adjusted so that the blades fit any angle from 45- to 90-degrees. Its main use is for transferring angles, such as in gable, frieze, or cornice work.

Using the Angle Divider

1. To set the angle divider, adjust the blades to the included angle. Clamp with the adjusting nut.

2. To lay out the miter of an angle, the body of the divider is held against the edge of the board, as shown in figure 4-38. The blade is used as a guide for marking.

WING DIVIDERS AND SCRIBERS

Curves, arcs, and circular lines are laid out by the use of a compass or wing dividers. Wing dividers look like a compass but have legs of solid metal which are ground to a point. The legs can be clamped with a thumbscrew (A, figure 4-39), to hold them at any desired distance apart. Micrometer adjustment is gotten by turning the thumb nut B. Clamp C is used to fasten a pencil or a scriber point to the leg of the divider as shown.

Dividers are used by carpenters for dividing a line or space into smaller spaces of equal length, such as spacing spindles in a railing. With the pencil attached, the dividers can also be used as a scriber.

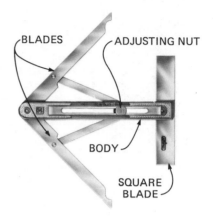

Fig. 4-37 Angle divider

Fig. 4-38 Laying out the miter of an angle

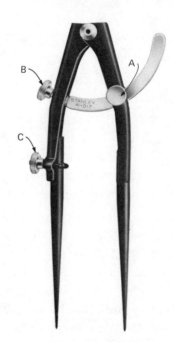

Fig. 4-39 Wing dividers

Fig. 4-40 Scriber

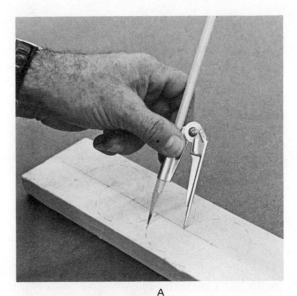

A

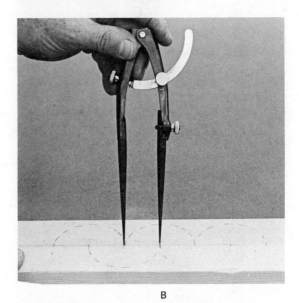

B

Ten-inch dividers are the average size used by the carpenter. When selecting dividers for use, the thread of the thumbscrews should be checked as this is generally the weak point of this type of tool.

A common scriber is made of pressed steel. One leg is formed to hold a short pencil. The other leg (B, figure 4-40), is fitted with an adjustable steel point. The spacing of the legs can be adjusted and tightened by means of a wing nut (A, figure 4-40). This tool is used for scribing an irregular line on the surface of a board, when the edge of the board is to fit against an irregular surface. An example is fitting a board to the face of an uneven stone or plastered wall, or to a clapboard siding.

Fig. 4-41 Laying out equal spaces: (A) with a scriber (B) with wing dividers

Laying Out Equal Spaces with Dividers

1. To mark off equal spaces, set the divider legs to the desired space by applying the dividers to a rule.

2. Loosen the thumbscrew, A, and adjust the legs. Then tighten the thumbscrew. If further adjustment is needed, regulate the knurled thumb nut, B, until the legs are in the exact position.

3. Step off the required number of spaces by rotating the dividers from leg to leg, holding it as shown in figure 4-41.

Laying Out a Rounded Corner

1. Measure an equal distance from the corner along the adjacent sides (A, figure 4-42).

2. Square in from these points, B and B.

3. The intersection of these lines locates the center of the arc, C.

4. Set one leg of the divider at C and the other leg at either B point. Rotate this leg to scribe the arc, B-B.

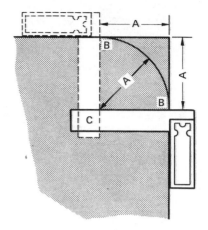

Fig. 4-42 Laying out a rounded corner

Scribing an Irregular Surface with Wing Dividers

1. To use the dividers as a scriber, set the piece of stock, figure 4-43, against the irregular surface W, to which the stock is to be fitted.

2. Set the piece of stock S, and plumb, holding it in position with a few nails or wedges if needed.

3. Set the divider points to a distance equal to the greatest space between the edge of the stock and the surface of the wall.

4. Start scribing at the top, holding one leg of the divider against surface W, and the other (penciled) leg in contact with surface S.

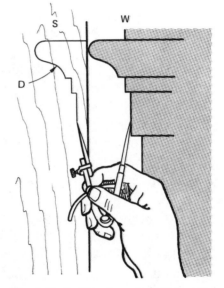

Fig. 4-43 Scribing in an irregular surface

5. Scribe the line D on the face of the board by following along the contour of surface W. This line is scribed down short of reaching the bottom. The dividers' points are constantly held in a level position and trailing as the line is being scribed.

6. Complete the scribing by positioning the scriber at the bottom in the same manner as described for starting at the top. Scribe the line upward until it joins the other line.

NOTE: The scriber point can be used in place of the pencil. When used, a scored line results. This line is then gone over with a pencil to make it show clearly. The scriber, figure 4-40, is specifically used for scribing in lines. It is used in the exact same manner as was described for the divider. The advantage of this layout is that its construction permits easier control than the divider.

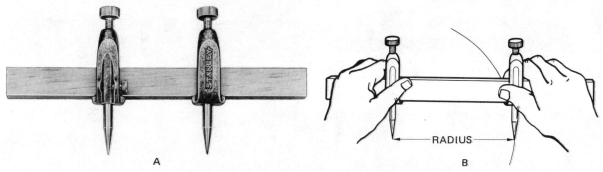

Fig. 4-44 Using trammel points to scribe an arc

TRAMMEL POINTS

Trammel points (A, figure 4-44), are metal points which can be clamped and adjusted on a wooden beam. A pencil can be fastened to one of the points by means of a clamping device. This tool is used for laying out and checking points, distances, and circles greater than the capacity of dividers or compasses.

Using Trammel Points to Scribe an Arc

1. Loosen the thumbscrews on the trammels to permit sliding them on the beam.
2. Set one trammel at a convenient distance (2 inches or 3 inches) from the right end of the beam. Lock it in place by tightening the thumbscrew.
3. Place this fixed trammel point on the one-inch graduation of the rule that is to be used for obtaining the measurement setting.
4. Slide the second trammel point to the graduation on the rule which will give the desired measurement setting. Lock it in place. This trammel point is set one inch beyond the reading on the rule as compared to the given measurement in order to compensate for the one-inch graduation.
5. Check the measurement by scribing an arc on scrap stock as shown in B, figure 4-44. Measure the arc on the material to be worked.

LAYOUT (STRING) LINES

Up to this point, the discussion has centered on tools and methods used for small-scale work. Large-scale operations such as the layout of building foundations on the site, laying out of partitions on the subflooring, and other large layout problems require different tools and methods.

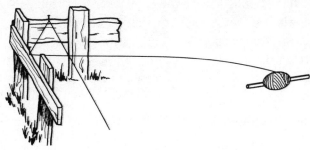

Fig. 4-45 Layout lines on batter boards at the corner of excavation

Strong white braided or twisted cotton mason's lines, about 200 feet long, are used for laying out outlines and elevations for walls and piers. These lines are wound on a stick or reel, as a kite string might be wound, for ease in handling. Layout lines are suspended on batter boards as shown in figure 4-45.

Using a Line as a Layout Line for Foundation Walls

1. Make a small loop with a half-hitch knot at one end of the line. See A, figure 4-46.

2. Hook this loop over the top of a nail partially driven into a stake or batter board.

3. Unwind the layout line. Stretch it to the opposite stake or batter board at the desired location. See B, figure 4-46.

4. Pull the line taut. Wind a few turns of the line around the nail, as at B. Fasten the line by looping a half-hitch knot over the nail.

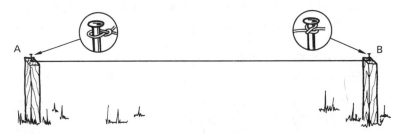

Fig. 4-46 Stretching a layout between stakes

CHALK LINE

A line can be laid out with a chalk line. A chalk line is not often used for distances greater than 50 feet. Chalk is rubbed on a line. The line is then stretched between two points and snapped. The snapping action sends the chalk to the surface being measured.

The chalk line can be used best for laying out lines on sub-floors for location of partitions, or for laying out lines for shingle and siding courses on the exterior of a house.

Some chalk lines are stored on a reel in a case, figure 4-47. A self-chalking chalk line reel stores the chalk line in a case like a tape measure. A handle on the case reels in the line. The line is chalked as it unreels. As the line is pulled from the case, it passes through a well of chalk dust contained in the case. A ring on the end of the chalk lines keeps the line from being reeled back into the case. This

Fig. 4-47 Chalk line case

ring is also used to attach the line to a nail or projection. The case of the chalk line reel is made so that it can be taken apart to replace the chalk line or opened to refill it with chalk dust.

Using the Self-Chalking Chalk Line Reel to Mark a Straight Line on a Surface

1. Hook the ring of the chalk line over a nail located at the point, or slightly beyond the point, where the chalk mark is to begin. Keep the ring close to the surface to be chalked.

Fig. 4-48 (A) Chalk line reel, and (B) chalk line and chalk

2. Pull the case outward at an angle from the horizontal so that the unreeling line does not contact the surface.

3. When the line has been unreeled to the length desired, grasp it with the index finger and thumb (of the hand holding the case). Pull the line taut, and lower it close to the surface. The line can be held against the surface with the thumb, if care is taken not to disturb the chalk on the line until it has been snapped.

4. With the free hand, grasp the chalk line as close to its center as possible. Lift it from the surface (at right angles to the surface) a few inches.

5. Release the line from the fingers, allowing it to snap on the surface. The result is a deposit of chalk on the surface in a straight line.

A chalk line reel (A, figure 4-48) with cupped ends is another type of arrangement used for holding, winding, and unwinding the line. Pressure can be applied by the thumb and finger to the cupped ends of the reel to provide enough tension to the line for chalking while unwinding the line. A hemispherical piece of chalk (generally blue in color) is used to charge the line with chalk.

Using the Chalk Line Reel to Mark a Straight Line on a Surface

1. Hook the loop of one end of the line over a nail at the layout point as at A, figure 4-49.

Fig. 4-49 Method of chalking line

2. Hold the chalk line reel in the left hand, pivoted between the thumb and forefinger. Keep the line taut. Apply the chalk to the line while moving toward the other layout point.

3. Keep the flat side of the chalk held upward in the right hand while applying it to the line. Turn it in the hand while chalking the line. This helps the chalk to wear evenly.

4. After the line has been chalked, stretch it taut between the nail, A, and point B, figure 4-50, with the thumb holding the line tight and close to the surface, as at B.

5. Lift the line a few inches from the surface between points A and B, as at C.

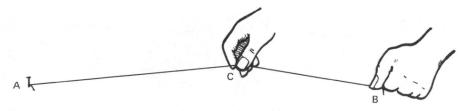

Fig. 4-50 Snapping a line

6. Release the line from the fingers, allowing it to snap back to the surface.

Horizontal chalk lines that are to be snapped over a long span on a vertical surface are sometimes a problem because of the tendency of the line to sag in the middle. This problem is common in snapping chalk lines for siding on a house or building. A method used to overcome this problem is described.

Laying Out Horizontal Chalk Lines on a Vertical Surface Over a Long Span

1. Attach one end of the chalk line to a terminal point.

2. Extend the line to the desired length. Pull it taut and attach it to the other terminal point. (Driven nails can serve as terminal points.)

3. Note the amount of sag in the line by inspection. (View the line squarely.) At the center of the sag, raise the amount that it appears to sag and drive a nail in under the line to support it. See figure 4-51.

4. From either terminal point, sight the chalk line. Make any necessary adjustments in the location of the center nail until the entire length of the line appears to be level.

5. Position yourself at the center nail. Hold the line to the wall at this point. Snap one half the length of the chalk line. Then, snap the other half. This step is illustrated by the broken lines in figure 4-51.

NOTE: When snapping a chalk line, be sure the line is well chalked. However, be careful that it is not overchalked. If overchalked, a fuzzy line results.

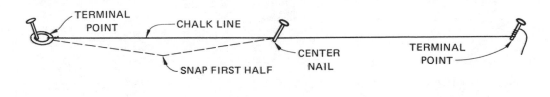

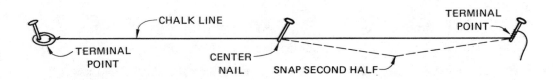

Fig. 4-51 Snapping a chalk line over a long span

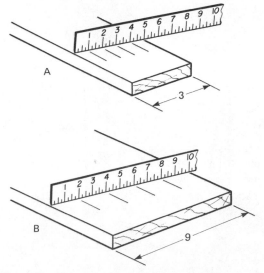

Fig. 4-52 Using a rule to divide boards into equal parts.

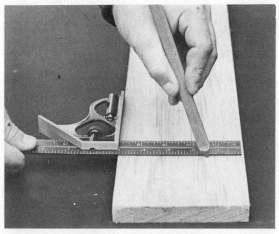

Fig. 4-53 Laying out rough work with a heavy carpenter's pencil

Care must be taken to draw the line so that it has a proper tension.

The line should be lifted at right angles to the surface and released from the fingers in the same manner as drawing a bow.

THE BUILDERS' LEVEL AND BUILDER'S TRANSIT-LEVEL

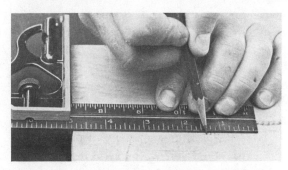

Fig. 4-54 Laying out lines for finish carpentry with a hard lead pencil

Building lines are also laid out by sighting either through a builders' level or builders' transit-level. These instruments are testing instruments and are discussed in unit 5.

MISCELLANEOUS LAYOUT TECHNIQUES

Dividing a Board into a Number of Equal Parts with a Rule

1. Place the rule diagonally across the surface of the stock so that the distance from edge to edge can be evenly divided by the number of desired parts. Figure 4-52, A, shows a 3-inch board divided into 5 equal widths. To divide a 9-inch board into 5 equal parts, place the rule diagonally across the surface as at B, figure 4-52. Since the diagonal is 10 inches, and 5 parts are desired, mark along the diagonal at each 2 inch interval.

2. After marking the distances along the diagonal, gauge lines through the marks parallel to the edge of the board.

Selecting the Scribing Device

1. To lay out rough work, a heavy carpenter's pencil can be used. See figure 4-53.

2. To lay out lines for finish carpentry, a regular hard lead pencil sharpened to a conical point is used. See figure 4-54.

Fig. 4-55 Using a knife for very accurate work.

3. For very accurate work, use a knife line for layout work, as shown in figure 4-55.

Using a Plumb Bob and Square for Laying Out a Level Line

1. Attach a plumb line with plumb bob to the wall on which the level line is to be scribed as shown in figure 4-56.

2. Place the body of the square in line with the suspended plumb line. Mark a line across the outside edge of the tongue.

3. If necessary, extend the marked line by using the body of the square or another type of straightedge in place of the tongue. The straightedge selected is placed so that it is in line with the mark that was made with the tongue.

Techniques for Laying Out Duplicate Parts

1. Figures 4-57 through 4-60 illustrate methods for laying out duplicate parts with a pattern, template, or an actual part.

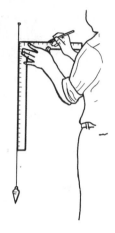

Fig. 4-56 Attaching a plumb line with plumb bob to the wall and marking a line

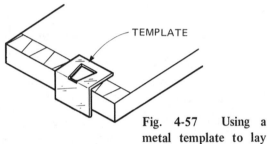

Fig. 4-57 Using a metal template to lay out duplicate parts

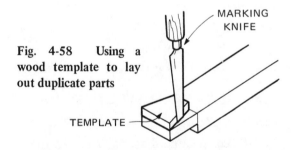

Fig. 4-58 Using a wood template to lay out duplicate parts

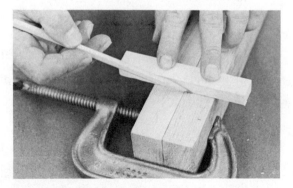

Fig. 4-59 Marking the width of a cutout on duplicate parts

2. When marking duplicate parts with an actual part (figure 4-60) use the same piece for the pattern for all layouts, thus cumulative error is avoided.

3. Marking the width of a cutout on duplicate parts is shown in figure 4-59. The material to be used to fit into the cutouts is placed on top of the clamped duplicate parts. Each edge, representing the width, is used as the guide for marking the necessary layout lines.

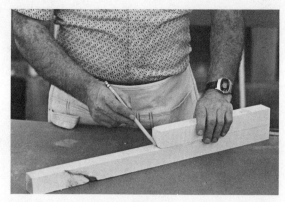

Fig. 4-60 Using an actual part to mark duplicate parts

REVIEW QUESTIONS

A. Name the tool best suited to perform the following operations.

1. Lay out a curve with a radius of 3 inches.
2. Scribe a line 2 inches from and parallel to a planed edge.
3. Lay out a mortise 1 1/2 inches wide.
4. Scribe a line 9 inches from and parallel to the edge of a table.
5. Lay out hinge locations on a door jamb.
6. Lay out a series of parallel lines 4 inches apart.
7. Lay out a crosscut line at 90 degrees to a 4-inch wide board.
8. Lay out a 45-degree angle on a 4-inch wide board.
9. Lay out a 45-degree angle on a 10-inch wide board.
10. Transfer a 55-degree angle from a protractor to a board.
11. Transfer a cornice angle to a piece of stock.
12. Lay out equal spaces 1 7/8 inches apart.
13. Scribe a board to fit an irregular contour.
14. Lay out a curve with a radius of 9 inches.
15. Mark a line 14 feet long on the subflooring.
16. Lay out a rounded corner with a radius of 12 inches.

B. Short Answer or Discussion

1. What is the difference between a panel gauge and a marking gauge?

2. How does a mortise gauge differ from a double-bar gauge?

3. What is the advantage of a marking gauge with a wheel rather than a pin for scribing the line?

4. How should the pin settings be checked before scribing parallel lines with the mortise gauge?

5. Show by a simple sketch how the steel square can be used to lay out a 45-degree angle on a 6-inch wide board.

6. What tool can more easily be used for question 5?

7. Describe four different uses for the combination square.

8. What is the advantage of a sliding T bevel over other angle measuring tools?

9. What tool can be used in the same manner as the sliding T bevel although it is limited to angles between 45 degrees and 90 degrees?

10. To lay out a corner with a radius of 4 inches, what tools are used?

11. Suppose question 10 involved a radius of 11 inches; what tools can be used?

12. If a swimming pool layout required a rounded corner with a radius of 10 feet, what tools can be used?

13. What device is used to mark a straight line 20 feet long on subflooring?

14. From most accurate to least accurate, list three scribing devices the carpenter uses.

15. On the sketch of a butt layout shown in figure 4-61, label the width of gain, A, the set-back, B, and the depth of gain, C. With necessary extension lines show clearly what these terms mean.

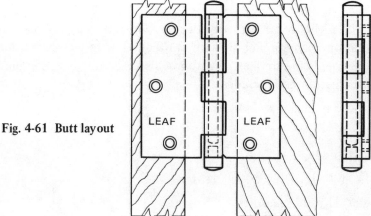

Fig. 4-61 Butt layout

16. Why is a knife rather than a pencil used for marking butt layouts?

17. When gauging with a rule and a pencil, how are the rule and pencil guided parallel to the board's edge?

18. What tool is best for gauging widths from 2 inches to 10 inches in multiples of 2 inches?

19. Show by a simple sketch how a 4-inch wide board can be divided into seven equal widths.

20. Describe two methods for dividing an 8-inch board into five equal widths.

21. How far should the pin of the marking gauge project beyond the beam?

22. How does the carpenter lay out 30-degree and 60-degree angles on a board? Show this by sketches.

Unit 5 TESTING TOOLS

Testing tools are used to check the accuracy of a layout. They are also used to check the accuracy of one operation before going on with another. The tools used for measuring and layout work also serve as testing devices. This unit discusses the common methods of testing as done by the woodworker and includes:

- Testing for levelness and plumbness.
- Testing for straightness.
- Testing for squareness and bevels.
- Checking the lengths and widths already measured.
- Checking the thickness already measured.

THE SPIRIT LEVEL

The spirit level is a very important testing tool for the carpenter. It is used to determine whether or not a surface is level or plumb. The term *level* means any straight line or place that is horizontal or parallel to the surface of a body of still water. The term *plumb* means a line or plane surface that stands upright or at right angles to a level surface. The spirit level is based on the principle that an air bubble in a glass filled with liquid will rise to the highest point.

The glass tube, as shown in figure 5-1, is slightly crowned. It is partly filled with alcohol and sealed. This provides a small air bubble in the tube. When the tube is held in a horizontal position, the air bubble rises to the highest part of the glass tube.

The highest part of the tube is shown by lines marked on the tube. The distance between these lines is generally equal to the length of the bubble. This makes it easy to read the location of the bubble.

The construction of the level uses the glass leveling tube in pairs or singly. The mountings are either fixed or adjustable. These are located at various points within the body of the level. The level is made from such materials as wood and metal, in lengths from one to four feet. The two-foot length is the most popular for carpenters' use.

Figure 5-2 shows a common wood level. Three pairs of tubes are located within the body of the level: two pairs at each end, and one pair in the center.

In testing for levelness, the two glass tubes located at B, figure 5-2, are used. The pairs of tubes at each end, located at A and C, are used for testing plumbness. Some levels

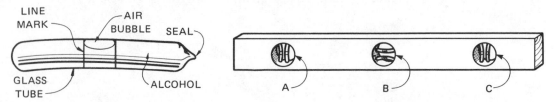

Fig. 5-1 Glass leveling tube   Fig. 5-2 Common wood level — solid mountings

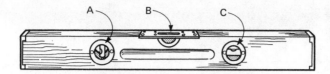

Fig. 5-3 Common wood level — adjustable mountings

have different arrangements of tubes. However, whatever the arrangement, tubes that are in a vertical position with relation to the long edges of the level are used for checking plumbness. Those which are parallel to these edges are used for checking levelness. The pairs of tubes at A and C act as a check for each other. Note that they are in solid mountings and therefore cannot be adjusted.

Figure 5-3 shows another type of common wood level. In this type, windows are used to protect the tubes. The construction of this level allows the tubes, A and C, to be adjusted if inaccurate. Note that in this case the tubes at B and C are used for checking levelness and A, alone, is used for checking plumbness.

The adjustment of the tubes of the level shown in figure 5-3 is done by first loosening the screws at the mountings. The tube is then rotated until the proper settings are made. If it becomes necessary to adjust the level, refer to the manufacturer's directions. These directions usually come with the level and are very complete.

The quality of a level can be determined from the material from which it is made. Materials used for the construction of the body include fine-quality woods, aluminum, magnesium, and various alloys.

The laminated or built-up type levels are preferred by most carpenters. This is because they do not warp. Solid wood levels can warp. The ends of the wood levels should be completely covered with a hard, noncorrosive material to protect them from splitting. This also prevents moisture from getting into the end grain. There should be a good protective coat of spar varnish or other sealing and waterproof material covering the entire wood surface. The leveling tubes should be enclosed in adjustable mountings. With adjustable mountings the level can be corrected if it becomes out of true.

The aluminum level, figure 5-4, is lightweight, rustproof, and does not warp or twist. It is, perhaps, the best type for carpentry work, as it is generally provided with several adjustable glass tubes. These are located so that one or more glasses can be read, no matter how the level is placed. Both sides of the windows are enclosed with heavy glass to protect the tubes from dust and dirt. By using pairs of tubes in the construction of the level, they can be used as a check for each other. Also, in the event that one of the tubes is broken, the level can still be used.

Magnesium levels have the same characteristics as aluminum levels but are one-third lighter in weight.

Fig. 5-4 Aluminum level

Fig. 5-5 Testing for levelness

Using the Spirit Level to Test a Horizontal Plane for Levelness

1. Place the level on the surface to be tested as shown in figure 5-5. Be sure that the body of the level is parallel with the edge of the surface being tested. There should be no particles of dirt or any irregular surfaces between the bottom of the level and the board.

2. Refer to the bottom tube located in the center of the level. Observe the position of the bubble. Note that this tube has the crowned side up. If the bubble rests to the right or left of the center of the lines on the tube, the surface is not level.

3. To level the surface, raise or lower one end of the surface until the bubble is centered between the lines.

4. To level or plumb a long surface, always use a straightedge with the spirit level. If the long surface is crowned, place the straightedge against the opposite or hollow side of the board. See figure 5-6.

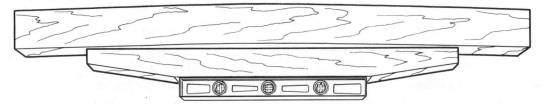

Fig. 5-6 Testing a crowned board with a straightedge and spirit level

Using the Spirit Level to Test a Vertical Plane

1. Place the level against one side of the surface to be tested as shown in figure 5-7.

2. Observe the position of the bubble in the crowned tube, A. If the bubble rests to the right or left of the center lines, the surface being tested is not plumb.

3. Check the accuracy of the level by observing the bubble in the lower tube, B. The bubble should be in the same position in tube B as is the bubble in tube A. If it is not, the level is out of adjustment.

4. Place the level on the opposite side of the surface being tested. If the top bubble, A, does not rest in the center as before, the surface is not plumb.

   NOTE: It is assumed that the side opposite to the one being tested is parallel to it.

5. In order to plumb the surface with the level, it is necessary to tilt the surface until the bubble appears centered on the level when the level is placed on the side (and opposite side) of the surface being tested.

   NOTE: Adjusting the surface to a plumb position is often done with the aid of shims or some other wedging device.

   Another method for checking the level when plumbing is to reverse the level so that its opposite edge is against the surface to be checked. Then if tubes A and B read the same as before, the level is true.

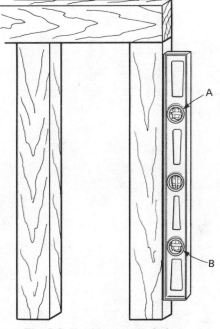

Fig. 5-7 **Testing a vertical plane**

Using the Spirit Level to Test the Pitch of an Inclined Surface

Assume that the pitch of the surface should be 1/4 inch per foot. The length of the level is 24 inches.

1. Determine what the pitch should be for two feet. Since it is 1/4 inch per foot, it is 1/2 inch for two feet.

2. At one end of the level, tape a block of wood so that it projects 1/2 inch beyond the bottom edge as shown in figure 5-8. If only an approximate check is necessary, the block can be placed under the extreme end of the level. It is then held in place by hand until the reading is taken. See B, figure 5-8.

3. Place the level on the inclined surface so that the end of the level with the taped block rests on the lower end of the incline.

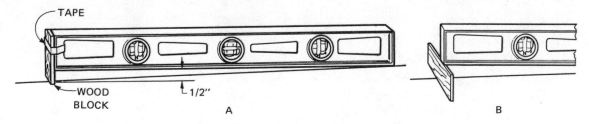

Fig. 5-8 **Testing pitch with a spirit level**

4. Read the level. If the bubble is centered, the pitch is correct. If not, the pitch can be determined by sliding the taped block (up or down) to a position which gives a level reading of the bubble. The amount of the block projecting beyond the lower edge of the level is then measured to determine the pitch. If the measurement should be 5/8 inch, the pitch is 5/16 inch per foot. (Keep in mind that the level spans two feet.)

THE LINE LEVEL

The line level, figure 5-9, is a short and very light level. It has hooks at each end so it can be hung on a line. It is used to test the approximate levelness of a stretched line for excavation and elevation guidelines.

Fig. 5-9 Line level

Using the Line Level

1. Stretch a layout line taut between two terminal points of the span to be checked.

2. Locate the center of the layout lines. Attach the level at this point by means of the hooks found at each end of the level so that the bubble is face up.

3. Read the level. If the bubble is not centered, first check to see if the level is centered on the layout line. Next, check the line for sag. This can be done by sighting down the line. Only a minimum amount of sag is allowed for accurate results.

4. Make the necessary adjustments at one of the terminal points so that the bubble is centered.

5. Check the levelness by unhooking the level and reversing the ends. Then hook it again to the line at midpoint. The bubble should be centered as before.

THE PLUMB BOB

The plumb bob, figure 5-10, is a tool used to test or establish vertical lines. Its principle of operation is based on the fact that when a weight is suspended from a line, it will cause the line to fall vertically (90 degrees) to a horizontal.

The common type of plumb bob is made of iron or steel. It is ground and polished to a point at the lower end. The top is provided with a round cap screw through which a chalk line is threaded. The chalk line is used to suspend the plumb line.

The more costly type plumb bob is hollow in the middle. This provides a

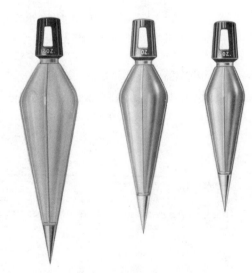

Fig. 5-10 Plumb bobs

chamber in which the mercury is placed. The mercury adds weight without enlarging the size of the plumb bob. This makes it come to rest more quickly than the lighter, common plumb bob. This type is also provided with replaceable points. The plumb bob is often used in connection with a builder's level.

Using a Plumb and Line to Plumb a Surface

1. Tack a block of wood on the upper side of the surface to be plumbed. Fasten the block with a nail that projects beyond the face of the block. A line can then be suspended from the nail.

2. Hang the plumb line on the nail. Be sure the line touches the outside face of the block. The block should be tight to the surface to be plumbed.

3. Prepare another block the same thickness as at A in figure 5-11. Use the block to gauge the distance at point B.

4. Move the upper end of the surface to be plumbed in or out until the line shows the same distances from the face of the surface at points A and B.

5. When these distances are the same, brace the surface. It should be plumb.

THE PLUMB RULE

The plumb bob and line is sometimes used with a straightedge called a plumb rule. This device is made from a board about 1 inch thick, 4 inches wide, and 6 feet long, with the bottom portion cut out as shown in A, figure 5-12. A pencil line, B, is drawn in the middle of one face. It is parallel to the edges and extends the length of the board. Saw kerfs, cut into the end of the board as at C, provide a convenient method of fastening the top end of the plumb line.

A small block about 1/4 inch thick and 3/8 inch wide is nailed across the board as at D. A shallow saw kerf, E, is made at the top of the board directly over the pencil line, B. The plumb line, when fastened to the top of the board, passes through the kerf at E, and hangs freely from the face of the board.

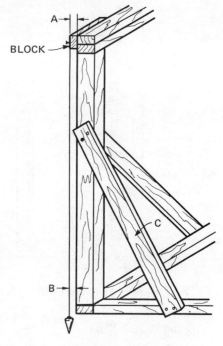

Fig. 5-11 Plumbing a surface

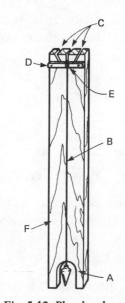

Fig. 5-12 Plumb rule

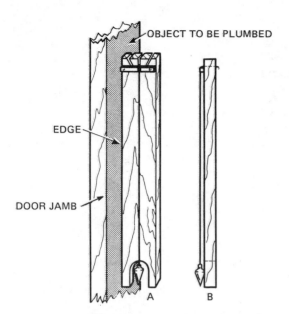

Fig. 5-13 Plumbing an object with a plumb rule

Fig. 5-14 Using a plumb rule to align the plumb line with the pencil line.

Using the Plumb Rule

1. Hold the edge of the plumb rule against the surface to be plumbed (see A, figure 5-13), so that the plumb line hangs uniformly about 1/4 inch from the surface of the plumb rule. See B, figure 5-13.

2. Adjust the surface to be plumbed so that the plumb line lies directly over the pencil line scribed on the plumb rule.

Fig. 5-15 Testing the face for straightness across the width.

3. If the plumb line is in line with the pencil line, the edge of the plumb rule is plumbed.

4. If the plumb line is not in line with the pencil line, it must be brought into line by moving the top or bottom of the plumb rule sideways. See figure 5-14.

THE TRY SQUARE

The try square is used for testing the straightness and squareness of faces, edges, and ends of small boards. It can also be used in testing 45-degree angles.

Using the Try Square to Test for Straightness of a Surface

1. Place the outer edge of the blade on the surface as shown in figure 5-15.

2. Move the square, in this position, along the surface. Note the parts that do not touch the edge of the blade. These parts are low in relation to the parts that touch. These high and low spots show that the surface is not flat. Mark the high spots.

3. Lay the try square along the length and then across the surface diagonally to test further for straightness (figure 5-16). Mark the high spots.

4. The high spots must be planed down until the entire surface of the board touches the full length of the try square blade when the try square is placed upon the board as explained in steps 1, 2, and 3.

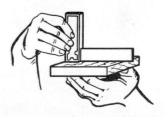

Fig. 5-16 Testing the face for straightness across width

Using the Try Square to Test for Squareness

1. Remember that before testing a surface for squareness, the surface must be flat. Therefore, first test the working face for straightness.

2. Place the handle of the try square firmly against the working face as in figure 5-17. Test for squareness of the edge by noting the high or low spots between the lower edge of the blade and the top surface of the edge of the board. Mark the high spots.

3. Move the square in this position along the face of the board, noting the high and low spots on the top edge of the board. Mark these high spots.

   The same process for testing the edge is used to test the end of the board for squareness. The only difference is that the handle of the square should be held against the straight edge of the board as shown in figure 5-18.

   Observe that the blade of the try square extends beyond the full width of the board. This is as it should be for making an accurate test.

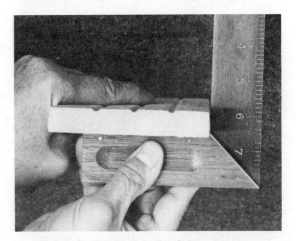

Fig. 5-17 Testing an edge for squareness

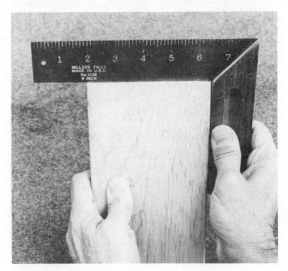

Fig. 5-18 Testing an end for squareness

THE FRAMING SQUARE

When testing the squareness of the wide boards, the framing square is used. It is often used for testing the squareness of inside and outside corners. It can also be used as a straightedge for testing the wind, warp, and straightness of boards.

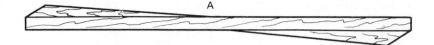

Fig. 5-19 Warp of a board: (A) wind and (B) cup

NOTE: The term *wind* refers to the surface of a board which has taken on a twist due to careless piling or faulty seasoning. See A, figure 5-19.

The term *cup* refers to the surface of a board which has taken on either a concave or convex cross section. See B, figure 5-19. Boards cup as a result of uneven evaporation or moisture during seasoning.

Using the Framing Square for Testing

1. For testing the squareness of wide boards, the steel square can be used in the same manner as the try square is used for small boards.

2. To test for straightness on surfaces and edges, the steel square blade can be used as a straightedge.

3. To test for wind with a framing square, place the outer edge of the blade on both diagonals of the surface to be tested. See figure 5-20.

   NOTE: If the surface is not a plane surface, but has a twist or wind, the edge of the framing square does not rest flat on the surface when placed diagonally.

THE SLIDING T BEVEL

The sliding T bevel, besides being used as a layout tool, is often used for checking and testing chamfer, bevel, and miter cuts.

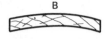

Fig. 5-20 Testing for wind with a framing square.

Using the Sliding T Bevel for Testing Angular Cuts

1. Set the sliding T bevel to the required bevel with the aid of the protractor, steel square, or draftsman's triangle.

2. Use the sliding T bevel as one would a try square when testing the angles of an edge or end as shown in figure 5-21.

THE USE OF RULES AS TESTING TOOLS

Rules are used as testing tools in the same manner in which they are used as measuring tools. See unit 2. In addition, they can be used to check right angles.

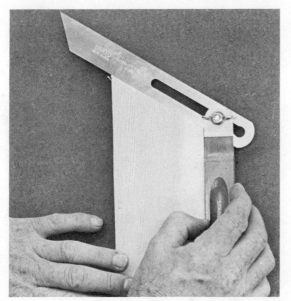 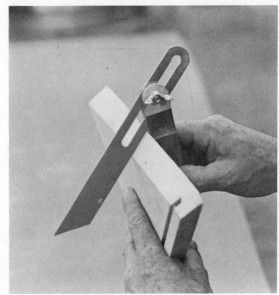

Fig. 5-21 Testing angular cuts with a sliding T bevel

THE 6-8-10 TRIANGLE

While not a testing instrument in itself, knowledge of the 6-8-10 mathematical rule can aid in determining a 90-degree or right angle. The rule is based on the fact that any triangle whose sides are 6, 8, and 10 inches, feet, yards, etc. in length, is a right triangle. This information can be used in testing for squareness of door and window jambs, layout of building lines, and similar uses where it is necessary to have a 90-degree angle. Since 3-4-5 is exactly half of 6-8-10, these dimensions can also be used.

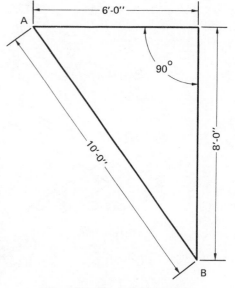

Fig. 5-22 The 6-8-10 triangle

Checking a 90-Degree Angle

1. Measure a distance of 6-feet along one side of the object. See figure 5-22. (If the 3-4-5 method is used, measure 3 feet.)

   NOTE: The unit of measure selected depends on the size of the object. If small, the inch unit is used; if large, the foot or yard unit is used. Each side of the triangle must be measured using the same unit of measure.

2. Measure 8 feet along the adjacent side of the object. (For the 3-4-5 method, measure 4 feet.)

3. Measure the distance between points A and B. It must equal 10 feet to have a right angle. (Measure 5 feet if using the 3-4-5 method.)

**Laying Out Building Lines
with the 6-8-10 Triangle**

1. Measure 30 feet along side A-B. See figure 5-23.

2. Measure 40 feet along side A-D.

3. Measure diagonal distance between points E-F. This should be 50 feet.

4. Check the other corners in a similar manner.

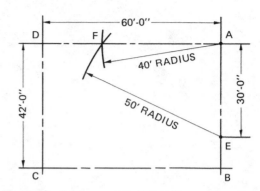

Fig. 5-23 Laying out building lines with a 3-4-5 triangle.

**Testing the Squareness of a Layout
with the 6-8-10 Triangle**

1. Square the corners of the building lines as shown in figure 5-23.

2. Drive stakes A, B, C, and D, 4 to 10 feet from A′, B′, C′, and D′. See figure 5-24.

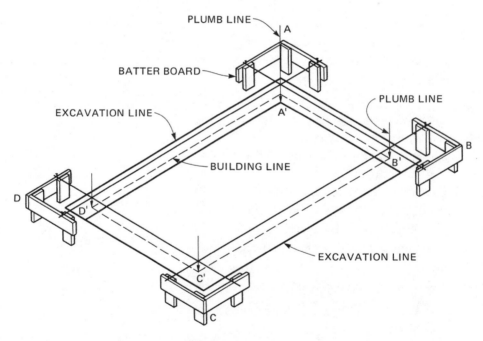

Fig. 5-24 Testing the squareness of a layout with a 6-8-10 triangle.

3. Place batter boards at corners A, B, C, and D. To construct the batter boards at the same level, sight them with a builders' level.

4. String building lines so that they pass directly over points A′, B′, C′, and D′. A plumb line can be used for this purpose as shown. Tie the building lines in place to the batter boards.

5. Establish the excavation and foundation lines from the building lines.

THE BUILDERS' LEVEL AND BUILDERS' TRANSIT LEVEL

The builders' level and builders' transit-level, although similar looking, are two different instruments. Both are considered to be testing tools and are also used for layout and measuring purposes. The two instruments differ in that the builders' level is limited to measurements on a horizontal plane, whereas the builders' transit-level can be used for measurements on both a horizontal and vertical plane.

THE BUILDERS' LEVEL

The builders' level is an instrument used mainly for testing levelness and for transferring points and measuring angles on a horizontal plane. However, it is not as accurate or convenient as the transit-level when used for this purpose.

The parts of a builder's level are shown in figures 5-25 and 5-26. A tripod is also shown attached to the trivet. The tripod is not an integral part of the level, rather, it is an attachment which serves as an adjustable base for the level.

The uses of the parts of the level are as follows:

- The *telescope* contains the lens and focus adjustment for sighting.

- The *telescope level* is mounted beneath the telescope and is used as an indicator for leveling the instrument.

- The *clamp screw* is used to firmly hold horizontal settings.

- The *tangent screw* is used for making fine horizontal adjustments.

- The *leveling head* acts as a support. It is attached to a half ball joint which permits universal movement for leveling adjustment.

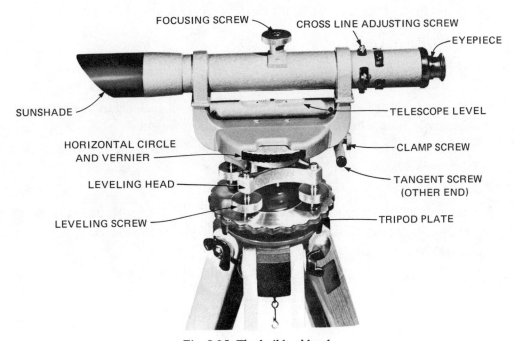

Fig. 5-25 The builders' level

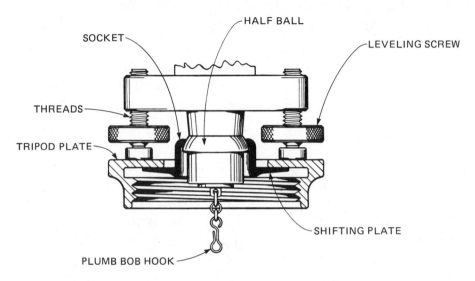

Fig. 5-26 Details of selected components of a builders' level.

- The *horizontal circle and vernier* is a horizontal circle graduated into degrees with a vernier calibration. This divides the degrees into minutes. It is used for checking or laying out angles on a horizontal plane. (See figures 5-36 through 5-42, and accompanying material, for a detailed discussion.)

- The *leveling screws* are used for leveling the instrument by causing movement of the leveling head.

- The *tripod plate* acts as a support for the leveling screws.

- The *trivet points* are projections extending from the trivet plate. They act as legs (nonadjustable) of the level when the instrument is not used with a tripod.

Preparing the Builders' Level for Use

Assume a tripod is to be used with the level.

1. Adjust the tripod as follows:

   a. Either tighten or loosen the wing nut at the top of each leg to a point where the leg falls slowly from a horizontal position by its own weight.

   b. Spread the legs about three feet apart. Arrange their positions so that the head of the tripod is nearly level.

   c. Push the legs firmly into the ground.

   d. Unscrew the tripod cap. The cap is simply a device for protecting the threads on the head of the tripod which screw into the tripod plate of the level.

2. Adjust the clamp screw on the level so that it is loose.

3. Place the instrument on the tripod so that the plumb bob hangs through the tripod head. Screw the instrument firmly into place.

4. Pull off the dust cap on the front of the telescope. Slide the sunshade on (if needed) in place of the dust cap.

Setting Up, Leveling, and Sighting

1. To set up:

   a. If a tripod is to be used, and the ground is irregular, face uphill.

   b. Hold a tripod leg in each hand. Place the third leg on higher ground.

   c. Pull the two legs outward and backward. Place them on the ground so that they are well spread out and so that the tripod plate is nearly level.

   d. Push each leg firmly into the ground. Some tripod legs have spurs attached. These permit using the heel for pressing the legs into the ground.

   NOTE: There are times when the instrument cannot be used with a tripod. When this is the case, the trivets act as the legs of the level and are placed on a steady, firm support. The limitation of the trivet application is that no provision is made for leg adjustment. Therefore, the supporting surface must be fairly level. Also, since the trivets do not span as great an area as the tripod legs, the instrument is likely to be less stable. Therefore, greater care should be taken to avoid knocking it over.

2. Level the instrument by adjusting the leveling screws. This should be done as follows:

   a. Loosen two adjacent screws. See A, figure 5-27. This frees both pairs of opposite screws.

   b. Turn the telescope until it is lined up over a pair of opposite leveling screws (figure 5-27, B and C.)

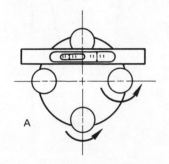

FIRST LOOSEN ADJACENT SCREWS

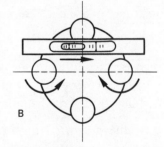

TO MOVE BUBBLE TO THE RIGHT

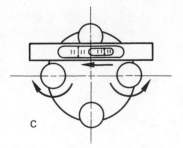

TO MOVE BUBBLE TO THE LEFT

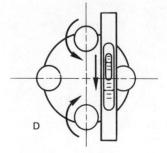

REPEAT OVER SECOND PAIR

Fig. 5-27 Procedure for centering the bubble on the telescope level.

c. Center the bubble of the telescope, using the leveling screws. This is done by loosening one screw and tightening the opposite screw. If one screw is tightened more than the opposite one is loosened, the pair press harder and harder on the tripod plate until it is very difficult to turn them. Thus, they should be turned equal amounts. This regulates them so that the pressure is very light while the instrument is being leveled and slightly firmer when it is brought to its final position. Note that the bubble moves toward the screw being tightened.

d. Turn the telescope 90 degrees. Repeat leveling over the other pair of screws. See D, figure 5-27.

e. Continue with alternate pairs until the bubble is exactly centered over both pairs. The screw pressure is light but firm.

3. To set up over a point, use the following procedure. Assume the point is represented by a driven stake.

a. Place the tripod on the ground so that the level is nearly over the point.

b. Pass the plumb bob cord over the plumb hook (figure 5-26). Tie the end around the middle of the cord with a single slip knot. See figure 5-28. The bob can then be raised or lowered by sliding the knot along the cord.

c. Move the instrument until the bob hangs not more than two inches to one side of the point.

d. Push the feet firmly into the ground.

e. Adjust the positions of the tripod feet by pushing them further into the ground until the bob is within 1/4 inch of the point.

f. Adjust the height of the bob so that it is not more than 1/8 inch above the point.

g. Loosen two adjacent leveling screws. This frees the shifting plate and makes it possible to slide the instrument over the tripod plate. Place the bob exactly over the point by this means.

h. Level the instrument.

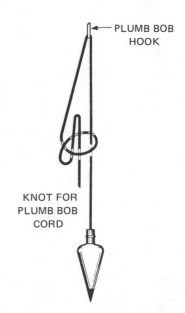

Fig. 5-28 Tying the end around the middle of the cord with a single slip knot

4. Focus the eyepiece. The eyepiece must be focused for the particular eyesight of the person using the instrument. The focusing should be done as follows:

a. Aim the telescope at a bright surface which should not be in focus.

b. Adjust the focus by rotating the eyepiece focusing ring by the knurling at the very end of the telescope (see figure 5-25) until the cross lines appear clear-cut. Once the eyepiece focus has been set, it need not be changed.

5. Sight the instrument as follows:

   a. To find the object to be sighted, first aim the telescope by looking along the top of the barrel.

   b. Focus the scope by turning the focusing screw until the cross lines appear clear-cut against the object. The intersection of the cross lines marks the line of sight which is a straight line extending from the scope. When the telescope is level, this line is truly horizontal (level) in whatever direction the instrument is turned.

   NOTE: Sighting is often done on leveling rods or on a target type of rod held in a vertical position at points to be sighted.

   A portion of a leveling rod is shown in figure 5-29. Rods of this type are made in various lengths.

Fig. 5-29 Leveling rod

Measuring a Difference in Elevation (See figures 5-30 and 5-31.)

1. Set up and level the instrument.

2. Hold a white finish folding rule or a leveling rod at each point in order. The rod (or rule) must be held truly vertical.

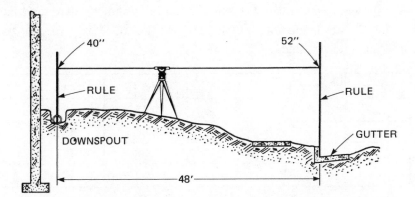

FALL FROM DOWNSPOUT DRAIN TO GUTTER 12″ IN 48′ OR 1/4″ PER FOOT

Fig. 5-30 Measuring the difference in elevation between two points below the level

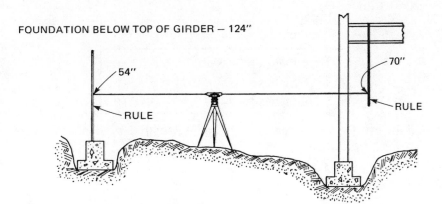

Fig. 5-31 Measuring the difference in elevation between a point above the level and a point below the level

3. Turn the telescope toward the rule at each point. Read the position of the horizontal cross line on the rule, thus measuring the vertical distance from each point to the line of sight.

4. Compute the difference in elevation as required.

    NOTE: When two points cannot be viewed from one position of the instrument, set an intermediate point (called a turning point or TP) as shown in figure 5-32. Any number of TP's can be used and the same process is thereby continued.

Setting a Grade Mark

Assume that the four corner stakes have been established. It is desired to set the line wires 20 inches above the top of stake A, figure 5-33.

1. Set up the instrument near the center of the area.

2. Sight the rule on A as shown in figure 5-34. If this reading should be 34 inches, have the rule held at each batter board so that the 14-inch mark comes on the line of sight.

3. Mark the position of the end of the rule at each batter board.

    NOTE: Elevations are usually given in feet and hundredths instead of feet and inches. To avoid errors in arithmetic all leveling should be done in hundredths and changed to inches only when necessary. Folding pocket rules and standard graduated leveling rods in hundredths are made for this purpose. If it is necessary to change from inches to hundredths, refer to table 5-1.

Inches	Hund. Ft.	Inches	Hund. Ft.	Inches	Hund. Ft.
1	0.08	5	0.42	9	0.75
2	0.17	6	0.50	10	0.83
3	0.25	7	0.58	11	0.92
4	0.33	8	0.67	12	1.00

Table 5-1 Conversion table: inches to hundredths of feet

To compute fractions of an inch use the relationship 1/8 inch equals approximately 1/100 foot or 0.01 foot.

Examples

> 7 1/2 inches = 0.58 + 0.04 = 0.62 ft.
> 3 7/8 inches = 0.33 − 0.01 = 0.32 ft.
> 5 3/4 inches = 0.50 − 0.02 = 0.48 ft.

By this method the error is never greater than, and is usually less than, 1/16 inch.

Setting Marks in a Line (See figure 5-35.)

1. Set up and level over A.

2. Have a plumb bob held over B.

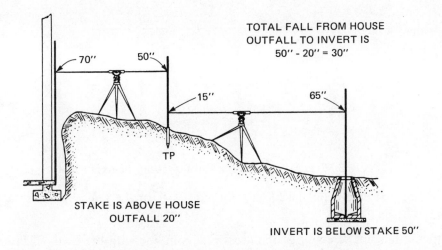

TOTAL FALL FROM HOUSE
OUTFALL TO INVERT IS
50″ - 20″ = 30″

70″

50″

15″

65″

TP

STAKE IS ABOVE HOUSE
OUTFALL 20″

INVERT IS BELOW STAKE 50″

Fig. 5-32 Measuring difference in elevation with an intermediate point (TP) as a reference

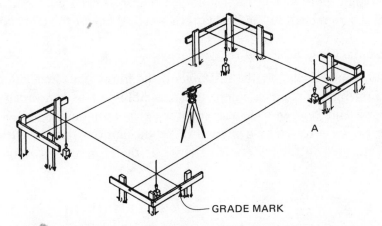

A

GRADE MARK

Fig. 5-33 Location of the instrument for setting a grade mark

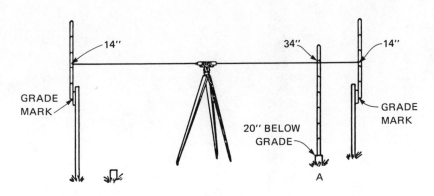

14″

34″

14″

GRADE
MARK

20″ BELOW
GRADE

GRADE
MARK

A

Fig. 5-34 Sighting for setting a grade mark

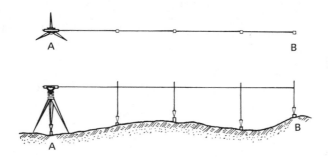

Fig. 5-35 Location of instrument for setting marks in a line

3. Sight approximately on the plumb bob cord. Turn the telescope so that the vertical line nearly meets with it.

4. Turn the tangent screw until the cross line is in line with the cord. Tighten the clamp screw to hold the telescope in the direction it is pointed. The tangent screw now acts as a fine adjustment to set the direction of the line of sight precisely.

5. Have the plumb bob held at each point desired. At each point, directions must be given until the plumb cord is on line with the vertical line of the cross line.

Using the Horizontal Circle Scale and Its Vernier

To read horizontal angles on the instrument, the horizontal circle and its vernier must be used. The horizontal circle is a complete circle, only part of which can be seen at one time. It is marked in degrees which are numbered in four quadrants. See figure 5-36.

The circle can be revolved by hand, but it does not move when the telescope is turned. The vernier is attached to the instrument frame. It therefore moves around the inside of

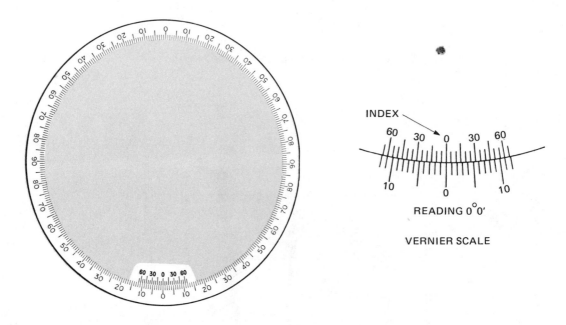

Fig. 5-36 Horizontal circle scale and vernier

LEFT VERNIER   RIGHT VERNIER

Fig. 5-37 Reading
0° 5′ clockwise.

LEFT VERNIER   RIGHT VERNIER

Fig. 5-38 Reading
0° 30′ clockwise

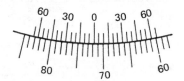
LEFT VERNIER   RIGHT VERNIER

Fig. 5-39 Reading
71° 40′ clockwise

the circle as the telescope is turned left or right. The graduation marked 0 on the vernier is the index. That is, the position of this 0 mark on the horizontal circle gives the angle reading. The rest of the vernier is used only when angles are expressed in degrees and minutes instead of in degrees only.

The vernier on the builders' level is a scale that is graduated in fractions of a degree. These fractions are called minutes. Twelve graduations numbered from 0 to 60 are found on each side of the vernier index. The left hand set is used for reading clockwise angles. The right hand set is used for reading counterclockwise angles. To turn the telescope 1/12 of a degree or 5 minutes: (1) the index is placed opposite the zero on the circle as shown in figure 5-36; and (2) then the instrument is turned slightly clockwise until the first mark to the left of the index is made to meet with the 1 degree mark to the left of zero on the circle (figure 5-37).

If the telescope is again turned so that the second vernier mark meets with the second mark on the circle, the telescope will have been turned 2/12 of a degree or 10 minutes, and so on. In figure 5-38, the 6th mark (30 minutes) meets with a mark on the circle. This indicates that the angle is zero degrees and thirty minutes (0° 30′).

To read an angle to the nearest five minutes, first find the degree mark which is just short of the index. Then find the five minute mark that most closely meets with a mark on the circle. The number of minutes indicated is the distance the index lies beyond the degree mark (figures 5-39 through 5-42).

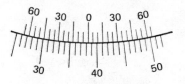
LEFT VERNIER   RIGHT VERNIER

Fig. 5-40 Reading
38° 25′ counterclockwise

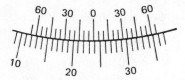
LEFT VERNIER RIGHT VERNIER

Fig. 5-41 Reading
23° 50′ counterclockwise

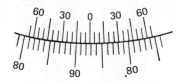
LEFT VERNIER   RIGHT VERNIER

Fig. 5-42 Reading
87° 15′ clockwise

When the degree numbers run to the left, clockwise angles are read and the left vernier is used. When the degree numbers run to the right, counterclockwise angles are read and the right vernier is used. In other words, always use the side of the vernier in which the numbers are increasing in the same direction as those on the circle.

Measuring an Angle

1. Set up and level at A. See figure 5-43.

2. Sight B accurately with the tangent screw.

3. Turn the horizontal circle with the fingers so that the reading is zero.

4. Using the clamp and tangent screws, sight C. Read the angle.

5. If the angle is greater than 90°, the vernier will travel out of the original quadrant as shown in figure 5-44. The reading 20° shown is measured from the direction opposite to B. Thus, the angle is 90° + 90° − 20° = 160°. If the reading were 21° 35′, the angle would be computed as follows: 90° + 90° − 21° 35′ = 158° 25′.

Marking a Grade Line

The tops of stakes A and B mark the two ends of a grade line. It is desired to set stakes at 50 feet intervals between them to mark the grade line, figure 5-45.

1. Find the difference in elevation between A and B (4.25 ft.).

2. Measure from A to B (817 ft.).

3. Compute the rate of fall: 4.25/817 = 0.0052 ft. per foot.

4. Set up at C and read the rule on A (3.35 ft.).

5. Compute the fall in 50 ft.: 50 x 0.0052 = 0.26 ft.

6. Compute the readings for each stake:

Stake		Reading
A 0 + 0		3.35
		+0.26
0 + 50		3.61
		+0.26
1 + 0		3.87
		+0.26
1 + 50		4.13
4 + 0	etc.	5.43

7. Drive in each stake between A and 4 + 0 until the proper reading is obtained.

8. Set up at D and proceed as before, sighting first on 4 + 0.

Stake	Reading	Stake	Reading	The fall from 8 + 0 to
4 + 0	2.95	8 + 0	5.03	8 + 17 is computed
	+0.26		+0.09	as follows:
4 + 50	3.21	B 8 + 17	5.12	17 x 0.0052 = 0.09 ft.
	+0.26			
5 + 0 etc.	3.47			

NOTE: To check the work, have the rule held on B and see if the reading is 5.12 ft.

Testing and Adjusting the Instrument

NOTE: Two tests should be made, one for the bubble and one for the cross lines. The tests must be carried out in the shade or on a cloudy day. The setup must be absolutely

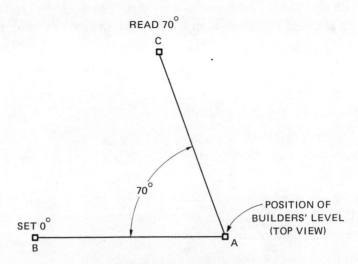

Fig. 5-43 Measuring an angle

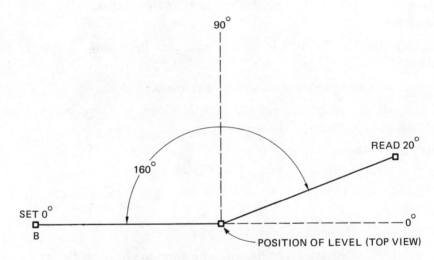

Fig. 5-44 Measuring an angle greater than 90 degrees

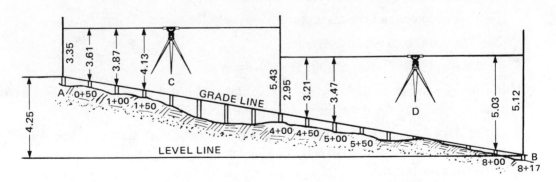

Fig. 5-45 Location of instruments for marking a grade line

firm. Each test should be made at least three times. If the results are not consistent it must be assumed that there is an error in the method of testing, not in the instrument.

1. To set up the instrument for testing:

   a. The ground must be hard, firm earth. Set up in the usual way. Then loosen all three tripod wing nuts.

   b. Retighten them and level carefully.

2. To test the telescope level:

   a. Level carefully over both pairs of opposite leveling screws, and finally very carefully over one pair.

   b. Turn the telescope through 180 degrees. The bubble should come to rest at the center. If each time this is tried the bubble comes to rest more than one division from the center, an adjustment is required.

3. To adjust the telescope level:

   a. Estimate where the bubble would stand if half the error were eliminated. With the adjusting pin, loosen the two capstan nuts at the eyepiece end of the bubble tube (figure 5-46).

   b. Gradually tighten the nuts in such a way that the bubble comes to the position estimated.

   c. Repeat the test as needed until a perfect adjustment is made.

   NOTE: If the telescope level has been adjusted, it is important to test the cross lines and to adjust them if necessary.

4. To test the cross lines:

   a. Select a 100-foot stretch of level, firm, shaded ground. Set three stakes, A, B, and C, in line, the distances A to B and B to C each measuring exactly 50 feet. See figure 5-47.

   b. Drive stake C only lightly.

   c. Set up the instrument over stake B. Revolve the head so that a pair of opposite leveling screws is on line A, B, C. Level carefully.

   d. Read a leveling rod held on stake A, being careful that:

      (1) The telescope bubble is exactly centered.

      (2) The eyepiece and the telescope are precisely focused.

      (3) The rod is held exactly vertical.

   e. Read the rod to the nearest 0.001 ft. or 1/64 inch.

   f. Revolve the telescope 180 degrees. Drive stake C until the rod reads the same as on stake A, again observing the three precautions in step d.

   g. Check stake A to make sure the rod reads the same on both stakes. A line from the top of stake C will now be exactly horizontal no matter how far the cross lines may be out of adjustment.

   h. Set up the instrument on line and about 8 feet behind stake A, as shown in figure 5-48.

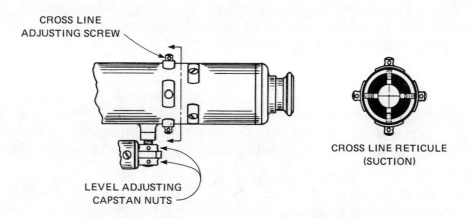

CROSS LINE
ADJUSTING SCREW

LEVEL ADJUSTING
CAPSTAN NUTS

CROSS LINE RETICULE
(SUCTION)

Fig. 5-46 Adjusting the telescope level.

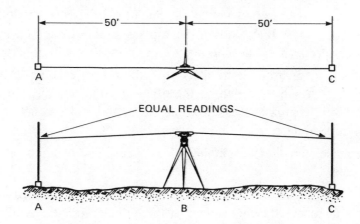

50'

50'

A

C

EQUAL READINGS

A

B

C

Fig. 5-47 Setting the stakes for cross line reading.

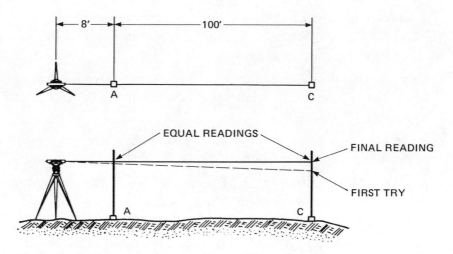

8'

100'

A

C

EQUAL READINGS

FINAL READING

FIRST TRY

A

C

Fig. 5-48 Finding proper readings for adjusting cross lines.

i. Level carefully and take a reading on stakes A and C (figure 5-48). As before, make sure the level is exactly centered each time, just before the reading is taken. The readings on the two stakes should be the same.

j. If after several trials it is found that the readings differ by 0.01 ft. or 1/8 inch, an adjustment is necessary.

5. To adjust the cross lines:

The cross lines must be adjusted until the same reading is obtained on both stakes when the instrument is level. The reading on the far rod must be brought to that of the near rod.

The cross lines are mounted on a ring or reticule which is held in place by four capstan headed screws threaded to the reticule. See figure 5-46. The positions of the lines determine the direction of the line of sight. To make it point further upward, for example, the cross lines must be lowered, and therefore moved in the opposite direction to that which would normally be expected.

a. Assume that after careful leveling, the line of sight strikes below the desired reading. To lower the cross lines, loosen the top screw about one quarter turn and tighten the lower screw an equal amount. The cross lines will apparently move upward.

b. By trial and error bring them exactly on the proper reading. Always loosen one of the screws first and then tighten the other an equal amount. In that way when this adjustment is complete the screws are firm, but not so tight as to risk distorting the telescope barrel.

c. Finally make sure that the bubble is centered. The readings on both stakes should be the same.

NOTE: For slight cross line adjustment as just described, it is not necessary or desirable to relieve the side screws of the reticule. If a major adjustment is required as a result of an accident, it is best to call in a competent instrument repairer.

CARE OF THE BUILDERS' LEVEL

A builders' level needs particular care. Continual exposure to rain and dust can cloud the optics and wear the bearings. A slight blow or continual vibration can ruin the instrument. The following rules are suggested.

- Keep the instrument in the box when not in use. Have the dust cap in place over the lens. The vertical clamp screw should be loose and the lock-release lever should be disengaged.

- Protect the instrument with the waterproof cloth cover if it must remain standing for any considerable amount of time in rain or heavy dust.

- Never set up the instrument, even temporarily, without spreading the tripod legs wide and pressing the shoes firmly into the ground.

- Never rub dust or dirt off a lens. Blow or brush it off lightly. If the view through the instrument becomes dark, take it to a competent instrument repairer for cleaning. The dirt is probably in the eyepiece.

- When the instrument must be set up on a smooth surface, cut notches for the tripod shoes to prevent slipping.
- When transporting the instrument in a car, carry it on a seat or protect the box from contact with vibrating parts.
- As the tripod gets older see that the shoes remain firmly screwed to the legs.

BUILDERS' TRANSIT-LEVEL

The builders' transit-level is a more versatile instrument than the builders' level. It can be used to perform all of the functions previously described for a builders' level. In addition, it can be used for plumbing and laying out or measuring angles on a vertical plane.

The parts of a builders' transit-level are shown in figure 5-49. The uses of the parts are the same as those described for the builders' level. Additional parts and their uses are as follows:

- The *vertical arc and vernier* is a device with a graduated arc for reading vertical angles.
- The *lock-release lever* is an arrangement to allow for setting and locking the telescope at a range of angles on a vertical plane.
- The *vertical tangent screw* is a part which allows for making fine adjustments of the horizontal cross line (vertical angles) with relation to a point.
- The *vertical clamp screw* is a device which locks the telescope setting that is controlled by the vertical tangent screw.

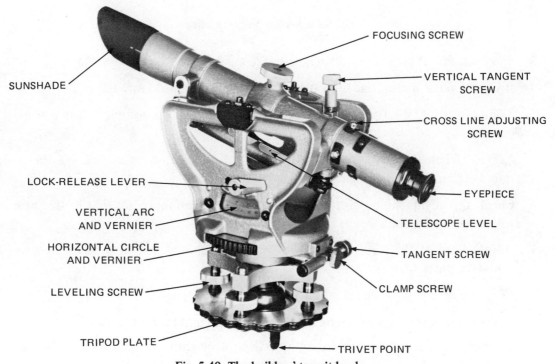

Fig. 5-49 The builders' transit-level

Preparing the Transit-Level for Use

1. Follow the same procedure as described for the builders' level.

2. The following should also be observed: Never tighten the vertical clamp screw (figure 5-49) when the lock-release lever is engaged (with the lever pointing toward the objective end). Always disengage the lock when returning the instrument to its box. After the instrument is in the box, tighten the vertical clamp screw lightly.

Setting Up, Leveling, and Sighting

1. Make sure that the lock-release lever is engaged so that the telescope is held horizontally and the vertical clamp screw is loose.

2. Follow the same procedure as described for the builders' level.

Setting Marks in a Line

1. Disengage the lock-release lever. Make sure the vertical clamp screw is loose.

2. Set up at point A (figure 5-50).

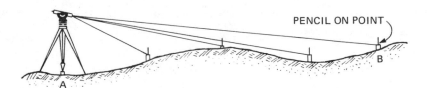

Fig. 5-50 Setting points in a line.

3. Sight directly at point B by tilting the telescope downward.

4. Bring the vertical cross line on B using the clamp and tangent screws.

5. Sight directly at each point. Often a pencil point held on a point will make sighting easier.

   NOTE: When the point to be sighted is out of sight below an object, use the plumb bob, holding the cord as near the bob as possible.

6. Check the alignment by sighting in the reverse direction. Note that in this case the telescope will be tilted upward.

7. Another use of the transit-level for alignment is shown in figure 5-51. Observe the following procedure:

   a. Set up over point A and sight directly at point B.

   b. Bring the vertical cross line on B using the clamp and tangent screws.

   c. Swing the telescope in an arc on a vertical plane through the center of the drainage tile.

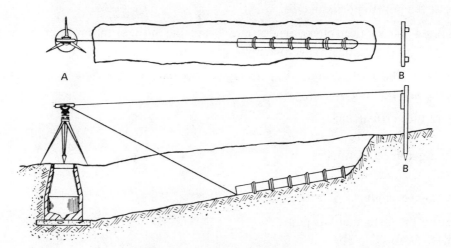

Fig. 5-51 Aligning drainage tile

Plumbing

Assume a column is to be plumbed, figure 5-52.

1. Set up nearby.

2. Level carefully.

3. Raise the telescope and have a vertical edge at the top of the column put on line with the vertical cross line.

4. Sight for plumbness by swinging the telescope in an arc on a vertical plane using the selected vertical edge for reference.

5. Set up at about 90 degrees from the original position and repeat.

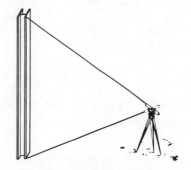

Fig. 5-52 Plumbing a column

Measuring a Vertical Angle

NOTE: Vertical angles are mainly used for determining rates of grade and approximate differences in elevation. A plus vertical angle is measured upward and a minus vertical angle is measured downward from a horizontal line. The values can be read with the vertical arc and vernier just as horizontal angles are read. The right-hand vernier is used for plus angles and the left-hand vernier is used for minus angles. (See figure 5-53.)

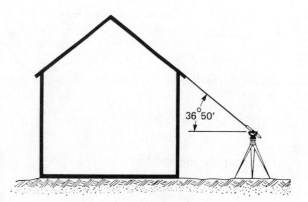

Fig. 5-53 Measuring a roof slope

1. Disengage the lock-release lever. The vertical clamp screw should be loose:

2. Sight the point approximately.

3. Tighten the vertical clamp screw and bring the horizontal cross lines exactly on the point with the vertical tangent screw.

   NOTE: The vertical and tangent screws operate in the same way as the horizontal clamp and tangent screws.

4. Read the vertical angle.

Establishing a Vertical Angle

Assume a pipe hanger is to be set at a 30-degree angle to a horizontal.

1. Set up the instrument at point A, figure 5-54.

2. Using the vertical clamp screw, set the vertical angle according to the vertical arc and vernier.

3. Line in the point.

   NOTE: Always disengage the lock-release lever before attempting to use the vertical clamp and tangent screws.

Measuring an Approximate Difference in Elevation

1. Set up over point A, figure 5-55.

2. Measure the vertical angle from A to B.

3. Find the fall per foot which is equal to the tangent of 5° 20′ = 0.093.

4. Measure the horizontal distance from A to B (300 feet).

5. Compute the total fall:

   300 x 0.093 = 27.9 ft.

   The difference in the elevation is 27.9 feet.

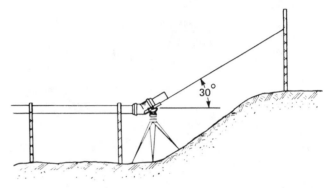

Fig. 5-54 Setting a pipe hanger

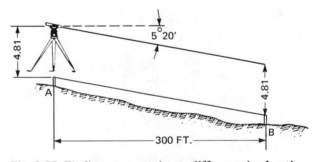

Fig. 5-55 Finding an approximate difference in elevation

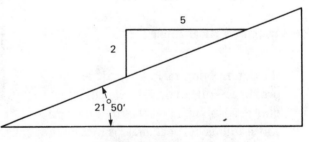

Fig. 5-56 A 5 to 2 slope

Shooting in a Grade Line

NOTE: Any slope can be specified by four different methods. Figure 5-56 shows a 5 to 2 slope. It can be expressed as follows:

- By slope − 5 horizontal to 2 vertical.
- By rate of fall or rise − 0.40 feet per foot or 3/4″ per foot.
- By percent of grade − 40% of grade.
- By vertical angle − 21° 50′.

The rate of rise or fall per foot is the most useful way of expressing the slope. It can be obtained from the other three as follows:

- *From the slope.* Divide the vertical distance by the corresponding horizontal.
- *From the percent of grade.* Divide the percent of grade by 100: 40/100 = 0.40.
- *From the vertical angle.* Look up the tangent of the vertical angles. It is the same as the rise of fall per foot: Tangent 21° 50′ = 0.40.

The tangent of an angle can be found in table 5-2, page 82.

The method to be described for shooting in a grade line is a quicker but less accurate method of setting grade stakes than had been previously described with the builders' level.

1. Set up over A, figure 5-57.

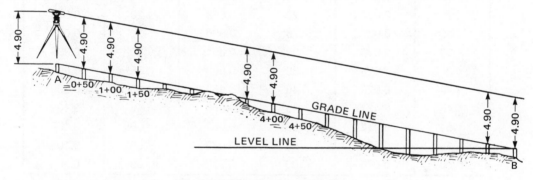

Fig. 5-57 Shooting in a grade line

2. Measure the height of the telescope above A (4.90 ft.).
3. Tilt the telescope with the vertical tangent screw or with leveling screws until the line of sight strikes the 4.90 mark on a rule held at B.

   NOTE: For long sights a pencil must be held across the rule at 4.90.

4. Drive all stakes so that the reading will be 4.90.
5. Once in a while sight the rule on B to make sure the line of sight still points at 4.90.

Shooting a Desired Rate of Grade

Assume it is desired to run a 2 percent grade up from the top of stake A, figure 5-58.

1. Compute the rise per foot: 2/100 = 0.02 ft. per foot.

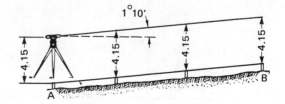

Fig. 5-58 Establishing a 2% grade

Angle	Tangent	Angle	Tangent	Angle	Tangent
0° 00′	0.000	2° 00′	0.035	4° 00′	0.070
05′	0.001	05′	0.036	05′	0.071
10′	0.003	10′	0.038	10′	0.073
15′	0.004	15′	0.039	15′	0.074
20′	0.006	20′	0.041	20′	0.076
25′	0.007	25′	0.042	25′	0.077
30′	0.009	30′	0.044	30′	0.079
35′	0.010	35′	0.045	35′	0.080
40′	0.012	40′	0.047	40′	0.082
45′	0.013	45′	0.048	45′	0.083
50′	0.015	50′	0.049	50′	0.085
55′	0.016	55′	0.051	55′	0.086
1° 00′	0.017	3° 00′	0.052	5° 00′	0.087
05′	0.019	05′	0.054	05′	0.089
10′	0.020	10′	0.055	10′	0.090
15′	0.022	15′	0.057	15′	0.092
20′	0.023	20′	0.058	20′	0.093
25′	0.025	25′	0.060	25′	0.095
30′	0.026	30′	0.061	30′	0.096
35′	0.028	35′	0.063	35′	0.098
40′	0.029	40′	0.064	40′	0.099
45′	0.031	45′	0.066	45′	0.101
50′	0.032	50′	0.067	50′	0.102
55′	0.033	55′	0.068	55′	0.104
2° 00′	0.035	4° 00′	0.070	6° 00′	0.105

Angle	Tangent	Angle	Tangent	Angle	Tangent
5° 45′	0.101	13° 30′	0.240	20° 50′	0.381
6° 15′	0.110	14° 00′	0.249	21° 20′	0.391
6° 50′	0.120	14° 35′	0.260	21° 50′	0.401
7° 25′	0.130	15° 05′	0.270	22° 20′	0.411
8° 00′	0.141	15° 40′	0.280	22° 45′	0.419
8° 30′	0.149	16° 10′	0.290	23° 15′	0.430
9° 05′	0.160	16° 40′	0.299	23° 45′	0.440
9° 40′	0.170	17° 15′	0.311	24° 15′	0.450
10° 10′	0.179	17° 45′	0.320	24° 40′	0.459
10° 45′	0.190	18° 15′	0.330	25° 10′	0.470
11° 20′	0.200	18° 45′	0.339	25° 40′	0.481
11° 50′	0.210	19° 15′	0.349	26° 05′	0.490
12° 25′	0.220	19° 50′	0.361	26° 35′	0.500
12° 55′	0.229	20° 20′	0.371	27° 00′	0.510

Table 5-2 Tangents of angles

2. Look up the angle whose tangent is 0.02; it is 1° 10′.

3. Set up over A. Level carefully.

4. Measure the height of the telescope center above A (4.15).

5. Tilt up the telescope so that the vertical angle is 12° 10′.

6. Set the stakes so that the reading on each is 4.15.

To find a value other than those listed, use combinations of listed values. For example, for 11° 30′, use 11° 20′ (0.200) plus 10′ (0.003) = 0.203.

REVIEW QUESTIONS

A. Short Answer or Discussion

1. For plumbing or leveling a long surface, why is it desirable to use a straightedge with the spirit level?

2. Referring to figure 5-8, explain why the method shown at B is less accurate than that shown at A.

3. If the pitch of a porch floor is specified at 1/8 inch per foot, how could a 4-foot level be used to test this pitch?

4. An overhead girder is specified to rise 1/4 inch per foot. Show by a sketch how the spirit level can be used to test this pitch.

5. How are excavation and elevation guidelines checked for levelness?

6. On what principle does the plumb bob operate?

7. What is the advantage of using a mercury-filled plumb bob?

8. When testing surfaces for straightness and squareness, at what level should the try square or steel square be held? Why?

9. What do the terms wind and cup mean? What causes them?

10. Why is a steel square rather than a try square generally used to test for wind?

11. What tool is used to check the diameter of a dowel?

12. Describe a method of checking the rough framing of a window for squareness using only a zigzag rule.

13. Suggest a method of applying the 6-8-10 rule to small applications such as a desk top, and another for large applications such as a batter board layout.

14. What tool would be used to test a 42.5-degree angle?

15. Describe three tools that can be used to test the depth of a tenon or a dowel hole.

16. What is the difference between a builders' level and a transit-level?

17. Describe the procedure for finding the difference in elevation of points A and B in figure 5-59.

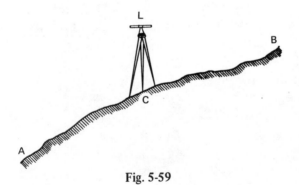

Fig. 5-59

18. Describe a simple procedure for obtaining a uniform drop in any given distance.

B. Identification and Interpretation

Describe exactly the tools used and the correct procedure for checking the specific information required on the following work:

For 1 through 4, refer to figure 5-60.

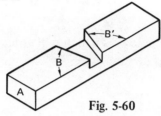

Fig. 5-60

1. Test end A for squareness.

2. Be sure angles B and B′ are equal.

3. Check the depth of the dovetail.

4. Check the length of the work.

For 5 through 9 refer to figure 5-61.

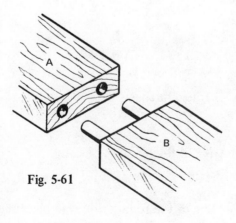

Fig. 5-61

5. Test surfaces A and B for wind and cup.

6. Check the diameter of the dowels.

7.   Check the diameter of the dowel holes.

8.   Test the depth of the dowel holes.

9.   Check the length of the dowels which will enter the dowel holes.

For 10 through 13 refer to figure 5-62.

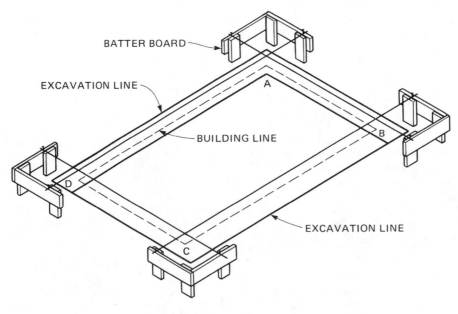

Fig. 5-62

10.   Test rectangle A-B-C-D for squareness.

11.   Check the distances A-B and B-C.

12.   Make sure the outside line of the foundation wall lies directly under the suspended lines.

13.   Test the levelness of all excavation guidelines.

Unit 6 SAWING TOOLS

Many types of saws are used to cut materials by hand. This unit describes those which the beginner in woodworking is most likely to use: the handsaw, compass and keyhole saws, the coping saw, and the backsaw.

HANDSAW

The term, *handsaw,* usually refers to either a crosscut saw or ripsaw. These two types of handsaws are identified by the shape of their teeth. The names of these handsaws tell their use. The crosscut saw has teeth that are designed to cut across the grain. The ripsaw is designed to cut with the grain. Neither should be used to do both types of cutting. Figure 6-1 shows several views of both types of handsaw teeth.

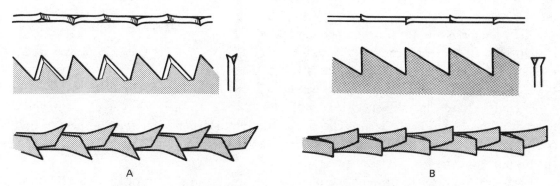

Fig. 6-1 Selected views of (A) crosscut teeth and (B) ripsaw teeth.

Saw blades are made in different shapes and lengths. The blade shown in figure 6-2 is a skewback blade. It has a slight curve toward the toe of the blade. The curved construction gives greater flexibility to the toe end of the blade, thus lending this part of the blade for use in cutting slight curves. Also, the top corner of the toe is easily found for sighting when starting a cut.

Figure 6-3 shows a handsaw with a straight-back blade. This type of saw is not as flexible as the skewback. However, it does have the advantage of a straight back edge which can be used as a straightedge for laying out lines.

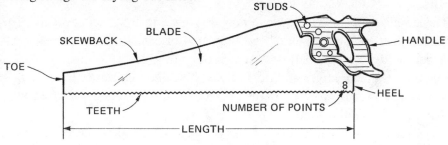

Fig. 6-2 Skewback handsaw

Fig. 6-3 Straight-back handsaw

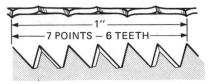

Fig. 6-4 Number of points stamped on the face of the blade.

The blade of a saw is made of spring steel. It is tempered so that it can be filed and set, and yet keep its shape and hold its cutting edge.

The face of the blade is ground and polished. The edge on which the teeth are cut is, in most cases, thicker than the back of the blade. This gives strength to the cutting edge and clearance to the back edge. Because the teeth edge of the blade is thicker than the back edge, a great deal of setting of the teeth is not needed.

The handle is made of fine-grained hardwood. It is shaped to fit the hand comfortably and finished to protect it from moisture. The handle is fastened to the blade with brass studs. These studs can be tightened if they become loose.

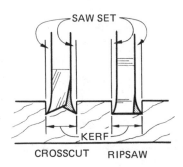

Fig. 6-5 Set applied to handsaw teeth.

Handsaws are generally specified by the length of the blade, the type of teeth, and the number of teeth points per inch. The size of the teeth depends on the numbers of points per inch. This number is often found stamped on the face of the blade at the heel. See figures 6-2 and 6-4.

Saw teeth are set to prevent the blade from binding in the cut or kerf. Each alternate tooth is set in opposite directions so that when the cut is made in the wood, the kerf is wider than the thickness of the saw blade. See figure 6-5.

The amount of set or bending of each tooth is determined by the type of wood that is to be cut. Wet, green, or soft lumber needs more set than dry or hard lumber. A special tool called a *saw set* is used for setting the teeth. The saw set is discussed in more detail in unit 7.

THE HAND CROSSCUT SAW

Crosscut saws are made in lengths from 20 inches to 28 inches. The lengths most commonly used are 24 inches and 26 inches.

The points on a crosscut saw can range from six to fourteen per inch. There are special saws having finer and coarser teeth, but they are not often used by carpenters.

A coarse-tooth saw cuts faster. It is better suited to thicker material because the gullets between the teeth are larger and do not easily become clogged. Saws with seven or eight points per inch are preferred by carpenters for general use and for crosscutting on heavier materials, such as framing lumber.

The crosscut saw for joinery can be one with finer teeth, such as 10 points per inch, and 22 inches long. This size is more suitable for making square, precise cuts on flooring,

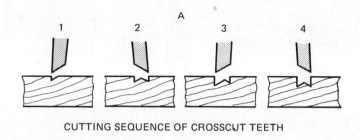

CUTTING SEQUENCE OF CROSSCUT TEETH

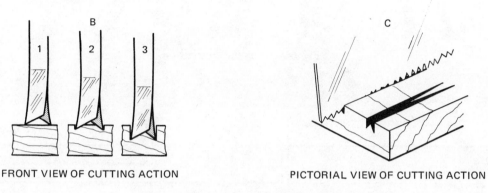

FRONT VIEW OF CUTTING ACTION   PICTORIAL VIEW OF CUTTING ACTION

Fig. 6-6 Cutting action of a crosscut saw

inside trim, and general joinery work. Short fine-tooth crosscut saws are called *panel saws.* They are very good for cutting thin plywood panels.

Crosscut teeth are shaped to produce scoring and cutting action across the grain on either the push or pull stroke. About 75 percent of the cutting is done on the push strokes. Figure 6-6 shows several views of the cutting action of a crosscut saw. Figure 6-6, A and B, shows the progress of the cut by numerical order.

Using the Crosscut Saw

1. Choose a saw with six or eight points to the inch. This number is usually stamped on the heel of the blade.

2. Mark the board where it is to be cut. Use a square or sliding T bevel. Always have a guideline to follow when sawing.

3. If the board is long, place it on two saw horses; if short, place it on one. Hold it firmly with one knee placed on the board as shown at B in figure 6-7.

4. Hold the saw so that it is in line with the shoulder joint and also in line with the mark on the board. Slant the saw on the surface of the wood at about a 45-degree angle as shown at B in figure 6-7. The face of the blade should be held square with the board. See A, figure 6-7.

5. Place the teeth at the heel of the saw against the starting edge of the board at the side of the mark nearest the waste stock. See figure 6-8.

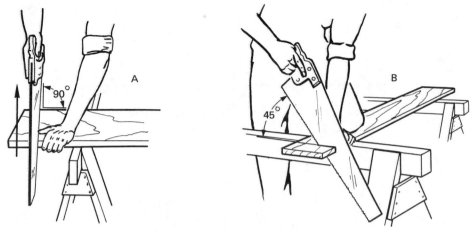

Fig. 6-7 Using the crosscut saw.

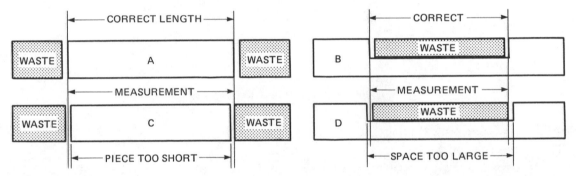

Fig. 6-8 Be sure to saw carefully on the waste side of the line as at A and B. Sawing on the line or on the wrong side of the line makes the stock too short as at C or the opening too large as shown at D.

6. Sight along the side of the blade. Position it so that it lines up with the mark on the board.

7. Place the thumb against the side of the blade to guide the saw to the mark. See A, figure 6-7. Be sure to hold the thumb above the teeth to avoid cutting it. Draw the saw lightly over the wood toward the shoulder with a short stroke until a saw kerf is made.

8. Gently push the saw down and deepen the saw kerf. Throughout the cut, keep the position for holding the board down, as shown at B in figure 6-7. Always keep the saw blade lined up with the mark on the board.

   NOTE: If the saw teeth are large and too much pressure is applied when starting the saw, it can buckle and jump. This can cause cuts on the fingers of the operator.

9. Use successive upward and downward strokes. As the saw kerf deepens, lengthen the strokes and use an even pressure on the saw. Guide the length of the stroke by the length of the saw. That is, the toe of the saw should be about 3 inches below the wood at the end of the upward stroke. If the toe is pulled up further, it is likely to buckle on the downward stroke.

10. Do not force the saw. The saw is made to cut at a certain speed. If it is forced to cut faster, it buckles.

11. Support the waste stock as the end of the cut nears. This prevents splitting the wood. Shorten the length of stroke toward the end of the cut.

THE RIPSAW

Ripsaw teeth generally run from four to eight points per inch. A coarse-tooth saw is usually selected for ripping thick stock and a fine-tooth saw for thin stock.

The ripsaw cuts in the same manner as the crosscut saw. However, sawing lumber with the grain is easier than sawing across the grain. Therefore, ripsaw teeth can be shaped with a slant of almost 90 degrees at the front of the teeth and a gradual slant at the back of the teeth. This is because the tooth rips the fibers of the wood more than it cuts them. No bevel is needed on the edge of the tooth because each tooth rips the grain rather than cutting it.

The cutting action of a ripsaw can be compared to a row of wood chisels being pushed forward with the bevel edges trailing. Figure 6-9 shows several views of the cutting action of a ripsaw.

Using a Ripsaw

1. Begin in the same way as described for crosscutting. However, be more careful in forming the saw kerf because the teeth of the ripsaw are larger than those of the cross-cut saw. They are more likely to catch in the wood and cause the saw to buckle.

2. When the kerf is well formed, apply more pressure on the downward stroke of the saw than on the upward stroke.

3. If the saw jams or buckles in the wood, it is being held at too steep an angle.

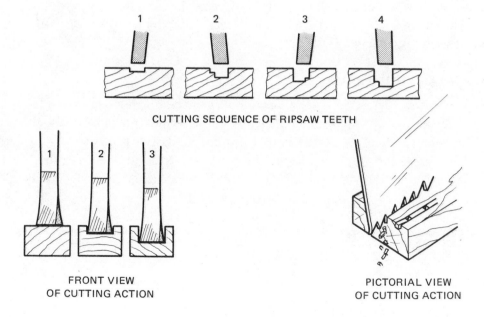

CUTTING SEQUENCE OF RIPSAW TEETH

FRONT VIEW
OF CUTTING ACTION

PICTORIAL VIEW
OF CUTTING ACTION

Fig. 6-9 Cutting action of a ripsaw.

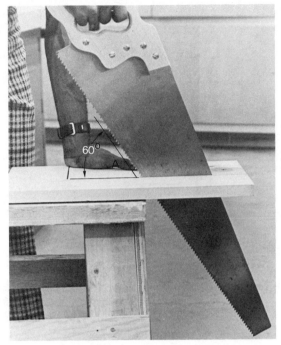

Fig. 6-10 Sawing with a ripsaw.

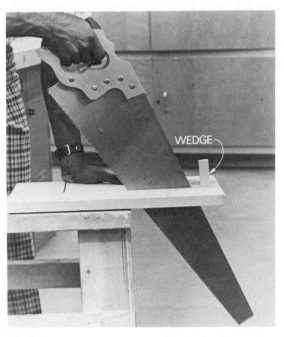

Fig. 6-11 A wedge is inserted in the kerf to prevent binding.

4. In ripping soft wood, the saw runs smoothly when held at an angle as great as 60 degrees, as shown in figure 6-10. However, if it jerks through the board under the pressure of the downward stroke, decrease the angle (A, figure 6-10), until the saw cuts smoothly.

5. If the saw binds when making long cuts, it might be necessary to force a small wooden wedge into the cut and spread it. See figure 6-11.

   NOTE: Oil or wax can be applied to the surface of the blade to reduce friction in cutting. This treatment also helps to protect the blade from rusting when the saw is stored or used for cutting wet lumber.

COMPASS AND KEYHOLE SAWS

   The compass saw, figure 6-12, has a tapered blade made to cut along curved lines. It is used for sawing out various shaped holes, such as those needed for plumbing and lighting fixtures. The wider part of the blade is used for cutting large open curves. The narrow part is used for small cutouts. Care should be taken not to bend or buckle the blade by applying too much pressure when cutting. The compass saw handle is provided with a wing

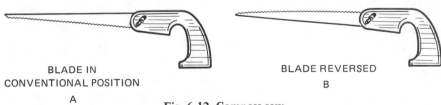

BLADE IN
CONVENTIONAL POSITION
A

BLADE REVERSED
B

Fig. 6-12 Compass saw

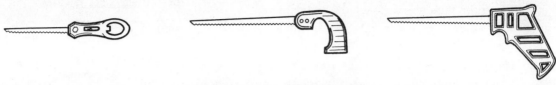

Fig. 6-13 Styles of keyhole saws

nut and bolt which fit into a slot in the blade. This allows reversing the blade as shown at B in figure 6-12. Positioning the blade in this way is sometimes done when an undercut is to be made. The teeth are filed in such a way that the saw can be used for crosscutting or ripping. Blades can vary from ten to fourteen inches in length. They can be purchased in nests of two or three saws, one of which is specially tempered for cutting nails and light metals.

A keyhole saw, figure 6-13, is very similar to a compass saw. It can have either a straight or curved handle. It differs from the compass saw in that its blade is narrower and shorter, and its teeth are finer. It is mainly used for small work such as cutting sharp curves and openings not possible with a compass saw.

Using the Compass or Keyhole Saw

1. Follow the same procedure for cross-cutting or ripping.

2. Use the wider section of the blade when following long curved guide-lines. For abrupt or small curves, use the narrow section of the blade. Remember that the smaller the section of the blade that is being used, the less pressure is to be put on the blade.

3. When cutting out sections within the material where the saw cannot be started on an outside edge, bore holes inside the guidelines. Place the top of the blade in a bored hole and cut along the guidelines. See figure 6-14.

Fig. 6-14 Cutting an inside hole with a compass saw.

THE COPING SAW

The coping saw is used for forming the ends of molding for coped joints and for other types of fine irregular sawing. It has a spring steel frame with a wood handle. The frame is provided with pawls having slots in which the blade is held. The saw

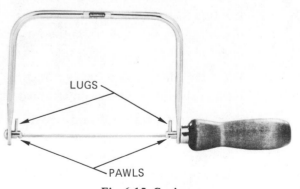

LUGS

PAWLS

Fig. 6-15 Coping saw

blade is secured in proper tension by turning the wood handle. The blade can be
turned at various angles in relation to the
frame with lugs as shown in figure 6-15.

The blades used for coping saws can
have a flat or spiral shape. Flat blades cut
in one direction only (like a ripsaw),
whereas spiral blades cut in any direction.
The ends of blades have a loop, pin, or
bend for attaching the blade to the saw.
See figure 6-16.

The blade can be put in the frame
with the teeth pointing toward or away
from the operator. The direction is determined by the type of cutting to be done
and the type of holding device to be used
for supporting the work. If a v-block
arrangement is used (see figure 6-18), the
blade is put in with the teeth pointing
toward the handle. If the work is to be
held in a vise, figure 6-17, or supported
on a saw horse, the blade is put in with the
teeth pointing away from the handle. The
pressure applied to get the cutting action is
in the direction in which the teeth point.

Using the Coping Saw

Assume that a flat blade is to be used,
the work is to be held in a bench vise, and
a short external curve cut is to be made.

1. Secure the work in the vise with the
   guidelines facing the operator.

   NOTE: Guidelines should be made on
   the face side of the material because
   the cutting action will be on the forward stroke. Thus any splintering or tearing of the
   material will be on the back side.

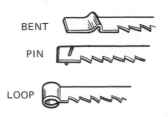

Fig. 6-16 Types of flat coping saw blades.

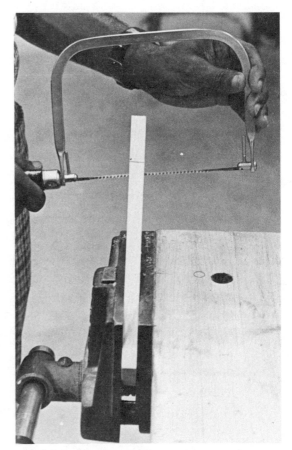

Fig. 6-17 Using a coping saw with the work held
in a bench vise.

2. Place the blade in the frame with the teeth pointing away from the handle. Enough
   tension should be placed on the blade so that it does not buckle under normal cutting.

3. Start the cut with a forward stroke to avoid splintering the face. If the cut is to start
   on a sharp corner, notch the starting point with a knife so that the cut starts easily.
   The beginning strokes should be short and light to avoid buckling the blade. This also
   allows the blade ot make a kerf. Both hands can be used to guide the saw as shown in
   figure 6-17.

NOTE: If small, accurate curves are to be cut, use the section of the blade nearest the supporting parts (pawls). These sections of the blade have less give, and thus a more accurate cut results.

4. After a deep enough kerf has been made, continue cutting using a longer stroke. Avoid striking the pawls of the saw against either face of the material. Guide the saw so that it cuts along the waste side of the material. To get cutting action, apply pressure only on the forward stroke.

NOTE: When following a curved line with the coping saw, keep one eye sighted about one-half inch in front of the cutting teeth and on the guide mark. Gradually turn the blade in this direction while making the cutting strokes. This keeps the saw blade from twisting and allows it to make smoother curves. If the blade becomes bound in the cut, carefully back it out by taking short back-and-forth strokes. Gently pull it out of the cut far enough for it to get free. The enlarged saw cut allows the blade to move freely and follow the guideline. Never force the blade.

5. On nearing the end of the cut, reduce the cutting pressure and the length of the stroke. Support the waste end of the material with one hand to avoid splintering the finished end.

When curves are to be cut in thin material, the support arrangement shown in figure 6-18 is desirable. The work, rather than being fixed, is gradually moved so that the guideline at the point of cutting falls within the v-cutout of the support. For this type of cutting, the blade is inserted with the teeth pointing toward the handle. Note that one hand is used to hold the work down and that the blade is held in a vertical position in relation to the surface of the work. Cutting with the saw in a straight up-and-down movement helps to lessen binding and buckling. Always face in the direction of cutting. This assures better control of the saw and avoids awkward cutting positions.

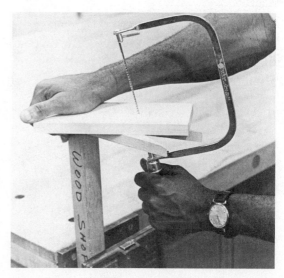

Fig. 6-18   Support for cutting curves in thin material.

Another method of using the coping saw is shown in figure 6-19. This method is used for cutting curves beyond the depth of the frame. An operation of this kind requires that the blade be put in at right angles to the frame and with the teeth pointing toward the handle. To insert the blade in such a position, the pawls must be rotated 90 degrees. This is done by grasping and rotating the lugs. Many coping saws have grooves cut in the frame so that the lugs can be seated in line with or at right angles to it.

Note that the work is held in a fixed position for this type of cutting. The blade is at right angles to the frame with the teeth pointing toward the handle. The layout line shown on the upper surface with the handle of the saw below means that the cutting should take place on the down or pull stroke. Note also that the blade stays square to the upper surface.

THE BACKSAW

The backsaw is a crosscut type of saw with ten to fourteen teeth per inch. Sometimes carpenters have backsaws filed so that they can be used for ripping. The blades have reinforced backs for rigidity and range in lengths from ten to twenty-six inches. Short backsaws are used for precision cutting for joinery work, and long saws (often called *miter saws*) are used with a miter frame for making angle and square cuts.

The backsaw is used in much the same way as a crosscut or ripsaw (depending on the type used). The main difference is that the angle between the teeth and work surface is slowly reduced until the saw is cutting parallel to or level with the surface. See figures 6-21 and 6-22.

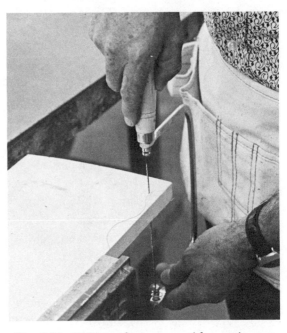

Fig. 6-19 Cutting a long curve with a coping saw.

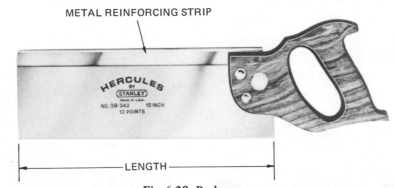

METAL REINFORCING STRIP

HERCULES BY STANLEY
MADE IN U.S.A.
NO. 39-342 12 INCH
12 POINTS

LENGTH

Fig. 6-20 Backsaw

Fig. 6-21 Starting the cut.

Fig. 6-22 Using the backsaw.

The layout lines for cutting with a backsaw should be made with a sharp pointed knife. Both the face and the edge of the material to be cut should be scored. In this way guidelines are provided assuring a square cut (figure 6-21). The cut should be made slightly outside (toward the waste side) the knife line, and should leave no wood projecting beyond this line when the cut is completed. A method used for starting a backsaw cut accurately is to cut a triangular groove at the starting point on the waste side of the scored line with a knife or wood chisel.

Using the Backsaw

1. Make a saw kerf on the waste side of the guideline and over its full length.
2. After this kerf is made, keep the saw in the full length of the kerf by using long, horizontal strokes.
3. Keep the saw positioned in the kerf so that the face of the blade is square with the surface being cut. This can be done by sighting the blade so that it appears to be vertical to the surface.
4. Do not force the saw. Pay close attention to holding the saw in the kerf and in a vertical position while taking long, even strokes.

   NOTE: If the board is held on a surface that should not be marred by saw cuts, be sure to place a scrap board or bench hook under the board being cut.

THE IRON MITER BOX

The iron miter box is a device for guiding a large backsaw (crosscut type) for making square and angular cuts on narrow stock or moldings. It is commonly used for cutting joints for moldings to fit around cornices, panels, windows, and door trim.

The miter box frame is made with guides into which the saw fits. The guides can be adjusted so that the saw can cut angles from 90 degrees to 45 degrees. Stops can be adjusted so that the saw cuts to a certain depth. Stock guides are made in the frame to hold the stock tightly against the back of the frame. A stop is also provided so that duplicate lengths of stocks can be cut.

Figure 6-23 shows the lock lever, A, that holds the saw guides at any desired angle around the quadrant, B. The graduations on B show the degree of the cut when an identifying mark on A meets with the graduation mark. In this figure a piece of molding is shown held in place by a stock guide, C. The molding is also placed against the adjustable length stop, D.

Making a Square Cut

1. Fasten the legs of the frame to the bench so that it will not shift when the stock is being sawed.

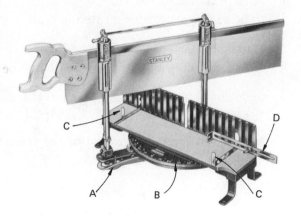

Fig. 6-23 Iron miter box

2. Check each component of the miter box to see if it is in proper working order.

3. Place the saw in the guides of the box. Lower the guides by releasing the automatic catches (E, figure 6-24). Pull the saw carefully back and forth in the guides until it touches the top of the baseboard. Adjust the fixed stops, F, on the uprights, so that the saw cuts into the baseboard about 1/16 of an inch.

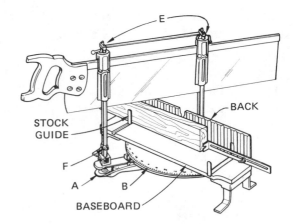

Fig. 6-24 Using the miter box to make a square cut.

4. Depress the lock lever, A. Swing the guide so that the witness mark on the frame plate lines up with the witness mark of 90 degrees which is marked on quadrant B.

5. Place the board with the dressed edge toward the back of the frame and on top of the baseboard of the frame. Adjust the board under the saw so that the saw teeth lie on the mark where the board is to be cut.

6. Adjust the stock guides up against the stock to be cut. Fasten them so that they hold the stock firmly to the back of the frame.

7. Saw the stock through by pulling and pushing the saw through the guides. The weight of the saw and the guides provides enough downward pressure for cutting.

   NOTE: The length of the strokes should be controlled so that the handle of the saw does not hit the front stop, and so that the saw is not pulled through the rear guide.

8. Loosen the stock guides and remove the stock.

Cutting Stock into Duplicate Lengths

1. Attach the length stop to the frame in a position that will clear the length of the board to be cut. Lock the length stop in place.

2. Mark the stock where it is to be cut. Place it under the saw so that the saw rests to the left of the guideline. An allowance must be made for the set of the teeth.

3. Slide the length rod until it touches the end of the piece to be cut. Lock it in place by tightening the thumbscrew at the top of the length stop.

   NOTE: Be sure that the end of the stock which is against the length rod is cut square or has the required finished cut.

4. Hold the stock firmly against the length stop. Saw it off in this position.

5. Cut each succeeding length of stock by placing it against the length stop. Care should be taken not to slam the stock into the stop as this can move it out of adjustment.

Cutting Mitered Joints for Frames

NOTE: Some miter boxes have numbers marked on top of the quadrant which represent guide settings for the number of sides that will make up a frame. The proper angle of cut for frames ranging from four to twenty-four sides can be made by positioning the saw guides with respect to these numbers.

1. Adjust the saw guides at the proper cutting angle by setting them in line with the number on the top of the quadrant which represents the number of sides of the frame to be made. This setting is made by lining up the witness mark on the frameplate with the number on top of the quadrant.

2. Proceed to cut as described for making a square cut.

Adjusting the Guides to Hold the Maximum Width Board

1. Loosen the front guidepost by unscrewing the fastener at the bottom of the post under the frame.

2. Loosen the setscrew at the top of the guidepost that holds the bar at the top of the post.

3. Remove the front post and put it in the end hole of the guideframe.

4. Line up the guideposts with those of the rear post. Tighten the screw at the bottom of the post and also the setscrew at the top of the post.

SELECTION AND CARE OF SAWS

In selecting saws it is best to buy them from reliable manufacturers. Make sure that the name and grade are stamped on the blade. A good saw, handled with care, lasts for about fifteen years. Poor quality saws cannot do satisfactory work.

In the selection of handsaws, there are some rule-of-thumb methods to judge the quality of the blade. There are also exceptions to the rules, but, in general, they aid in the selection of a good saw.

The following rules apply more to ripsaws and crosscut saws, but some can be applied to compass and keyhole saws.

- To test the quality of steel in the saw blade, hold the saw tightly in one hand, by its handle. With the other hand, catch the toe of the blade under the thumbnail and snap the blade. The blade should give a clear, lasting ring. The clearer the ring, the better the blade. A dull, short ring indicates inferior spring steel. In some cases, the steel can be of good quality, but it is too thick for carpentry use.

- Bend the blade toward the handle. If it snaps back to its former shape quickly, it is made of good spring steel.

- Check to see if the edge where the teeth are located is thicker than the back edge. If it is, this is a sign that the saw blade has been ground and that the saw is designed well.

- Examine the surface of the blade. Good saws have surfaces which are finely ground and polished.

- Examine the handle to see that it is made of hard, close-grain wood and finished to protect it from moisture.

- Note whether there are brass studs in the handle and that there are enough to hold the handle firmly to the blade.

For carpentry, a miter box like that shown in figure 6-23 should be selected. The miter box saw and frame, properly used, should last a long time. However, care should be taken to select the complete saw and frame from the same manufacturer and to use only the saw specified by that manufacturer. The type chosen should be one for which worn out parts can be easily replaced.

A frame of an iron miter box should be mounted on a board so that it can be screwed or clamped to a bench. When making any adjustment on the saw frame where slotted screws are involved, use a screwdriver that properly fits the slots in the screws. Do not use pliers or a wrench to tighten the thumbscrews on the miter saw frame.

All types of saw blades should be wiped off with an oily rag after they have been used. If once allowed to rust or stain, their efficiency is lessened and more setting of the teeth will be needed to allow easy travel through the wood.

Avoid sawing nails with a handsaw as this damages the teeth of the saw. If sawing through a nail is necessary, use a keyhole saw with a metal cutting blade to cut through the nail. Then proceed to cut with the handsaw.

Do not cut sheetrock or painted lumber with handsaws as this dulls the saw rapidly. An old saw should be used for cutting such materials.

Remember that saw handles can break when dropped. Be sure that the handle of a saw is fastened securely to the blade when in use, otherwise damage to parts of the saw and poor cutting can result.

Store saws so that their teeth are protected from contact with other metal tools. A special rack is usually made for this purpose within the tool box.

REVIEW QUESTIONS

A. Short Answer or Discussion

1. How does the thickness of the saw blade on the teeth edge differ from the thickness on the back edge? Why?

2. What is meant by the term, set?

3. Why does the saw blade require set?

4. Which requires more set, soft or hard lumber? Explain.

5. What does the number stamped on the heel of the saw blade indicate?

6. How does the number in question 5 indicate the use for which the saw is intended?

7. What is meant by sawing to the line? Where should the saw kerf be?

8. From observation of the blades, what is the difference between a crosscut saw and a ripsaw?

9. Sketch front views of (a) a crosscut kerf and (b) a rip kerf. Explain the cutting action of the blade in each case.

10. How can binding of the saw blade be avoided when ripping a long cut?

11. If the blade buckles or jams while cutting, how can this be corrected?

12. Describe six checks to be made in selecting a good quality crosscut saw or ripsaw.

13. For what purpose is the compass saw designed? How are its teeth shaped to serve this purpose?

14. How does the keyhole saw differ from the compass saw?

15. For what purposes is the coping saw used?

16. What determines the way the blade is placed in the coping saw? Explain the answer by examples.

17. For what uses is the backsaw intended?

18. Why not use a fine-tooth crosscut saw instead of a backsaw for precise cutting jobs?

19. Describe a good technique to ensure starting the backsaw cut accurately.

20. Describe the adjustments that are possible on the iron miter box.

B. Completion

1. The _____ the number on the heel, the coarser the saw blade.

2. A handsaw which has a slightly curved back is called a _____ handsaw.

3. The _____ is used for bending alternate saw teeth left and right.

4. The points of crosscut blades generally run from _____ to _____ while ripsaw points range from _____ to _____.

5. The front edges are beveled on _____ teeth, but are not on _____ teeth.

6. The crosscut saw should generally be held at an angle of _____ with the surface of the wood.

7. The ripsaw should generally be held at an angle of _____ with the surface of the wood.

8. If the saw blade tends to buckle using the angles in question 7, the angles should be _____.

9. The backsaw should be held at an angle of _____ with the surface of the wood.

10. The miter box provides for cuts from _____ to _____ degrees.

C. Identification and Interpretation

1. Identify the parts indicated on the saw shown in figure 6-25.

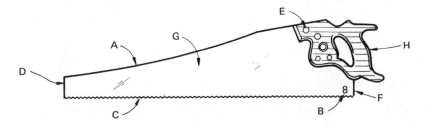

Fig. 6-25

2. How many points are shown on the saw in figure 6-25? How many teeth are shown? Are there always more points per inch than teeth? Explain.

3. Name the saws in figure 6-26 and give the main use for each saw.

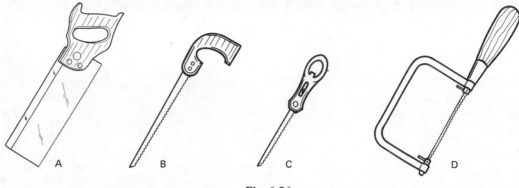

Fig. 6-26

4. Identify the type of saw teeth shown in sketches A and B, figure 6-27. Explain why each type is shaped as illustrated.

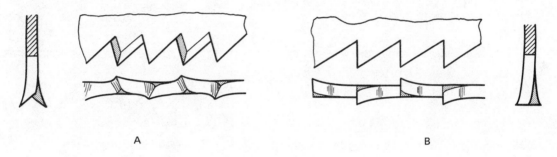

Fig. 6-27

Unit 7 REFITTING HANDSAWS

Preparing a saw so that it cuts easily and smoothly is termed *saw fitting*. Saw fitting involves six operations: jointing, shaping, dressing, rejointing, setting, and re-shaping (sharpening) of jointed and set teeth. Each operation is performed in the order listed.

A saw does not cut effectively with teeth that are uneven or irregular in size or shape. When in this condition, the teeth should be jointed, figure 7-1. This opera-tion is done with a tool called a *handsaw jointer* or with a mill file. The purpose is to prepare the teeth so that they are even in height.

As a result of jointing, the teeth must be reshaped. This is often called *rough shaping*. It is done with a triangular file as shown in figure 7-2.

After reshaping the teeth, a burr is usually formed on the faces of the teeth due to the filing. Since burrs lessen the effectiveness of cutting edges, the burrs should be removed. This is done by lightly rubbing (dressing) the faces of the teeth with an oilstone. Following the dressing operation, the teeth are then rejointed, figure 7-3, to correct any slight error which might have resulted from filing the shapes.

At this point the teeth are ready to be set. See figure 7-4. This operation involves offsetting a part of each tooth alternately to the left and to the right by means of a saw set. The saw kerf formed by the cut-ting of the teeth is then wider than the thickness of the blade. Offsetting the teeth in this way lessens the amount of friction in cutting, thus resulting in an easier cut. Both ripsaws and crosscut saws need set. Setting is not required each time that a saw

TEETH UNEVEN BEFORE JOINTING

TEETH LEVEL AFTER JOINTING

Fig. 7-1 Teeth before and after jointing.

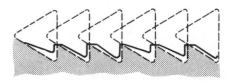
ROUGH LAYOUT OF NEW POINT POSITIONS

TEETH ROUGH SHAPED

Fig. 7-2 Reshaping teeth.

Fig. 7-3 Teeth rejointed.

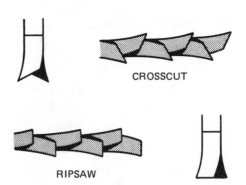
CROSSCUT

RIPSAW

Fig. 7-4 Appearance of saw teeth that have been set.

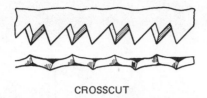
CROSSCUT

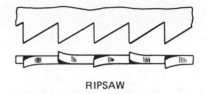
RIPSAW

Fig. 7-5 Appearance of saw teeth after sharpening.

is filed. It is usually done after the saw has been filed four or five times. However, this can best be determined by inspecting the teeth or by the action of the saw when cutting. If the saw tends to bind, it is a sign that setting is needed. The number of times which a saw must be set depends upon how sharp the saw is kept. If the saw is retouched regularly, just as a wood chisel is whetted prior to use, setting is not required as often.

The amount of set is determined by the type of material to be cut. When cutting soft wood or wet wood, saws with coarse teeth having a great amount of set are used. For hardwoods, fine-tooth saws with very little set to the teeth are preferred. Every tooth should be offset an equal amount (alternating the direction of each), to give the same width of cutting edge throughout the length of the blade. When set in this way, the saw is more likely to make a true cut.

The last operation in saw fitting is sharpening the teeth, figure 7-5. A triangular file is used for filing both rip and crosscut teeth. However, the manner of filing differs for each. A detailed explanation for this operation is given later in this unit.

EQUIPMENT REQUIRED FOR SAW FITTING

The equipment required for saw setting is as follows: saw clamp or vise, flat mill file (or handsaw jointer), tapered triangular file, and saw set.

Saw clamps are made in several different styles. Figure 7-6 shows one type of clamp which can be folded when not in use. This permits them to be carried in a carpenter's tool

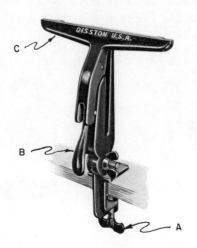

Fig. 7-6 One type of saw clamp.

box. The clamp screw, A, provides a means of clamping the vise to a support. It is built at a good height for filing. The lever, B, moves the jaw, C, so that it holds the saw blade in place against the fixed jaw.

A serviceable vise can be made of hardwood as shown in figure 7-7. The uprights, A, are made of stock 1 5/8 inches by 3 5/8 inches. The stretchers, B, are 1 1/4 inches by 2 1/2 inches.

The outside of each crosspiece, C, is beveled about 1/16 inch toward the lower edge. The slots in the top of the uprights are also beveled slightly toward the bottom. When the saw blade is placed between the top pieces, these bevels have a tightening effect on the blade as they are forced into the uprights.

Because of its long clamping area, this type of saw vise has the advantage of lessening the number of times that the saw must be changed in the vise. It is suited for shop use whereas the short, folding type is satisfactory for carrying in a tool box.

When saw clamps are not handy, a machinist's vise and two strips of hardwood about 3/4 inch by 2 inches by 12

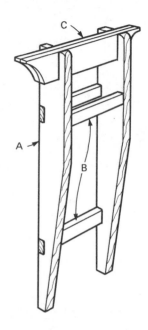

Fig. 7-7 Hardwood saw vise

inches can be used instead. With this arrangement, the blade is placed between the wood strips and clamped in the vise. The strips are held firmly in the vise parallel to the toothed edge of the saw. The teeth project above the strips high enough to permit filing.

A handsaw jointer, figure 7-8, is the preferred tool for jointing the teeth. However, a smooth-cut mill file can also be used for this purpose. The mill file has fine, serrated cuts on both surfaces and edges. The flat surfaces are used for jointing. Cutting by the file is done on the forward stroke. In this type of filing a handle is not used because the full length of the file must lay flat on the teeth.

Triangular files of various sizes, figure 7-9, are used for shaping the teeth after jointing. In selecting a file for shaping, the size of the file is an important factor and should conform to the points of a saw as follows:

- For 4 1/2-, 5-, and 6-point saws use a 7-inch slim taper file.

- For 7- and 8-point saws use a 6-inch slim taper file or 7-inch extra slim taper file.

- For 9- and 10-point saws use a 5-inch slim taper file.

HANDSAW JOINTER

FLAT MILL FILE

Fig. 7-8 Tools for jointing handsaw blades.

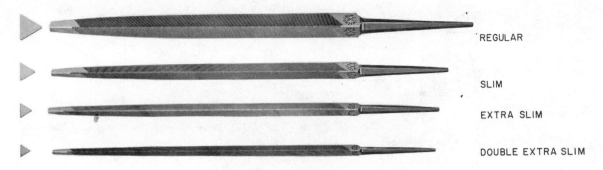

REGULAR

SLIM

EXTRA SLIM

DOUBLE EXTRA SLIM

Fig. 7-9 Types of triangular files.

- For 11-, 12-, 13-, 14-, and 15-point saws use a 4-inch to 4 1/2-inch slim taper file.
- For 16-point saws and finer, use a 4 1/2-inch to 5-inch number 2 cut slim taper file.

A fine grit oilstone is used for dressing the faces of the teeth. A 1-inch by 2-inch by 8-inch oilstone with flat faces and edges is desirable for this operation.

Two types of saw sets are shown in figure 7-10. The function of this tool is to set each alternate tooth of the saw to a certain degree beyond the face of the saw blade.

To do this properly, two adjustments are provided in the saw set: one provides for the depth to which the saw tooth can be set, and the other provides for the amount of set to be given each tooth. The action of the saw set is to cause a plunger, which is started by pressing the handles together, to press the upper part of a tooth against a beveled surface or anvil.

Some sets have several beveled faces located on a disc. The disc can be rotated for selecting the desired amount of set. The disc is usually numbered to correspond to the number of teeth points commonly found on handsaws. These numbers act as a guide for selecting the particular bevel to be used. Triangular files used for sharpening the teeth are the same type as those used for shaping the teeth.

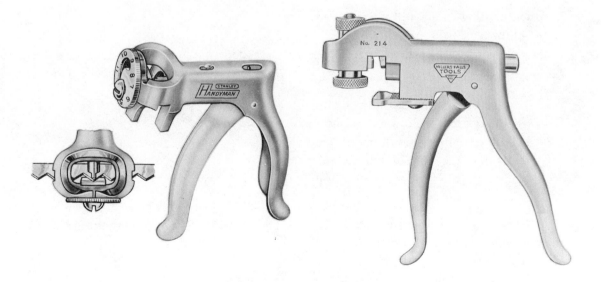

Fig. 7-10 Two types of saw sets.

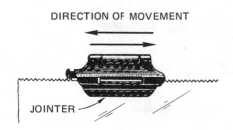

DIRECTION OF MOVEMENT

JOINTER

Fig. 7-11 Jointing with a handsaw jointer

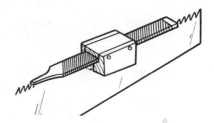

Fig. 7-12 Jointing with an improvised handsaw jointer

Jointing a Handsaw

1. When jointing with a handsaw jointer, proceed as follows:

   a. Secure the saw blade firmly in the saw vise with the blade protruding enough above the vise so that the jointer clears the jaws when placed in position over the blade. The handle of the saw can be placed either to the right or to the left.

   b. Fit the saw jointer over the teeth of the blade as shown in figure 7-11.

   NOTE: The jointer opens and closes like a hinge so that it can be slipped over the toothed edge of the blade. A file, figure 7-12, is incorporated in the construction of the jointer for doing the jointing.

   c. Run the jointer back and forth over the teeth until the blade has been jointed down to its shortest tooth. It is desirable to slightly crown the teeth with the high point located at the center of the blade.

   NOTE: Do not try to joint teeth that are very uneven with one jointing. Rather, joint only the highest teeth and file these into shape. Then joint the teeth a second time and shape as required.

   d. Sight the teeth to check on the completion of the jointing.

2. When jointing with a mill file, proceed as follows:

   a. Secure the blade in the vise so that the teeth clear the vise jaws.

   b. Lay the file lengthwise on the teeth, as in figure 7-13. File lightly lengthwise along the tops of the teeth for the full length of the blade until the file touches the top of every tooth.

   NOTE: Hold the file flat when jointing. It should not be allowed

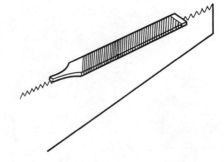

Fig. 7-13 Jointing with a flat file

to tip or rock from one side to the other as this creates a bevel on the tooth point. Do not joint more than is necessary, or else greater effort will be required to reshape the teeth.

Reshaping Ripsaw Teeth

1. Clamp the saw in the vise with the handle positioned to the right or to the left.

2. Choose a proper type and size triangular file. A 6-inch slim taper file is suitable for the average handsaw.

3. Determine which tooth most closely resembles the original shape of the saw tooth. Use this as a guide for filing the shapes of the others. Generally, a tooth having its original shape is found at the heel of the saw.

4. Begin filing in the gullet nearest the handle or at the toe. Hold the file at right angles (90 degrees) to the blade as shown in figure 7-14, and file straight across.

   NOTE: Do not bevel the teeth when filing them to shape.

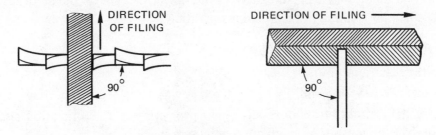

Fig. 7-14 Views showing the position of the file when reshaping ripsaw teeth.

5. The broken lines in figure 7-15 indicate the position of the file for shaping each tooth. Use a light controlled forward stroke to shape each tooth. Do not pull the file back through the teeth; rather, lift it clear after each forward stroke.

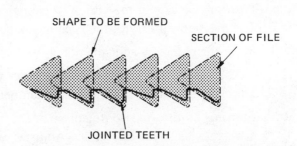

Fig. 7-15 Rough layout of new point positions.

6. Repeat the stroke in the same tooth, holding the file in the same position. The tooth, if badly out of shape, may require several strokes to form it properly. When this is finished, move the file to the third tooth and file in the same manner.

7. Do not try to file the teeth down to a point at this time, but file the alternate teeth in a similar manner until the end of the clamp is reached.

8. Return to the first tooth and, with the file adjusted to the bed that was formed in the tooth, take a full stroke with the file as before. Using a little pressure on the file, bring the tooth to a rough shape. Continue in this manner with the teeth previously filed.

9. Move the blade forward in the clamp and file the remaining alternate teeth.

10. Reverse the saw in the clamp and file the alternate teeth in the same way.

Dressing a Handsaw

1. Place the blade of the saw on a flat surface as shown in figure 7-16.

2. Apply a film of oil to the long edge of an oilstone. Rub the stone lightly over the face of the teeth for the length of the blade until the burr is removed.

    NOTE: Do not use the face of the stone for this purpose as it will damage the stone for other tool sharpening.

3. Turn the saw over and dress the opposite face.

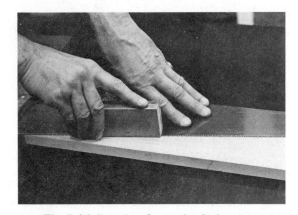

Fig. 7-16 Dressing the teeth of a handsaw.

4. Wipe any residue of oil from the faces of the saw blade. Oil on the teeth tends to clog the file when performing the sharpening operation.

Rejointing Ripsaw Teeth

1. Clamp the saw in the vise.

2. Apply a saw jointer or a mill file to the teeth as was described for jointing.

3. Use very light strokes to remove any slight projections. This operation also removes any burrs on the tops of the teeth created by shaping.

Setting Ripsaw Teeth

1. Position the saw in the vise with enough room for applying the saw set to the blade. The position varies with the type of saw set used.

2. Make the necessary adjustments on the saw set for the amount of bend desired.

    NOTE: If several anvils (disc-type saw set) are provided, use the one whose number corresponds to the points per inch stamped on the heel of the saw.

3. Starting at the first tooth, place the saw set against the side of it. Adjust the depth gauge of the saw set so that the plunger and anvil bend only about one-half of the upper part of the tooth. Then set the tooth.

4. Set each alternate tooth in the same way. See the shaded portion of teeth in A, figure 7-18.

5. Reverse the saw clamp and set the other alternate teeth. When all of the teeth on both sides of the saw are set, they should look like those shown in C, figure 7-18.

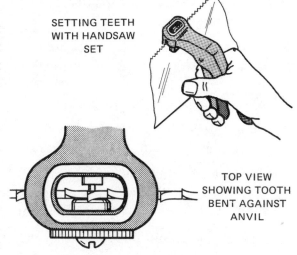

SETTING TEETH WITH HANDSAW SET

TOP VIEW SHOWING TOOTH BENT AGAINST ANVIL

Fig. 7-17 Using the saw set.

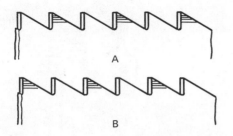

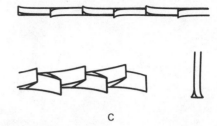

Fig. 7-18 Setting ripsaw teeth.

6. Examine the teeth to see that they are uniformly set. If they are not uniform, reset them properly before starting the final pointing of the teeth.

Sharpening a Ripsaw

1. Clamp the blade in the saw vise so that the bottom of the gullets of the teeth are 1/8 inch above the vise jaws.

2. Apply a triangular slim tapered file to the gullet of the first tooth at the heel or toe of the saw, figure 7-19. File in the same manner as described for shaping the teeth. Carefully bring each tooth to a finished point. Maintain the angles and shape of the teeth as shown in figure 7-20.

NOTE: When the teeth are uniform in shape and the small, flat spots on the points are about the same size, it is usually the best practice to disregard the shape of the individual teeth and take a uniform stroke of the file for each tooth. This means that it

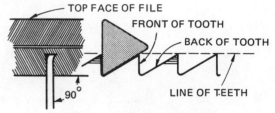

Fig. 7-19 Position of the file.

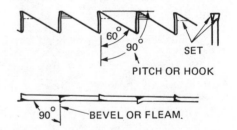

Fig. 7-20   Angles and shape of the teeth while sharpening.

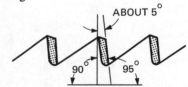

Fig. 7-21 Sloping front shoulder of ripsaw toward the handle.

is better practice to file the teeth uniformly over the length of the blade by taking the same number of strokes on each tooth, rather than file on one series of teeth more than another series. Skilled carpenters who do a lot of sawing that is diagonal to the grain of the wood, such as cutting roof rafters, often use a ripsaw and slope the front shoulder of the ripsaw tooth slightly toward the handle. See figure 7-21.

REFITTING HAND CROSSCUT SAWS

The procedures described for jointing, dressing, rejointing, and setting the teeth for a ripsaw are the same for performing similar operations on a crosscut saw. However, the shaping and sharpening operations differ. A detailed description of these two operations follows.

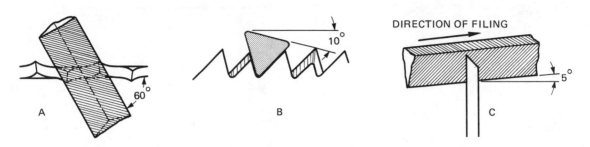

Fig. 7-22 Views showing the position of the file when reshaping crosscut teeth.

Shaping Crosscut Teeth

1. Clamp the blade in the vise so that the gullets of the teeth are 1/8 inch above the jaws of the vise.

2. Choose a tooth which most closely resembles the original shape of the teeth as a guide for reshaping the teeth.

3. Select the proper type of triangular file. Position the file in the gullet of the first tooth and be sure that:

    a. The file is held at an angle from 60 degrees to 80 degrees to the blade (A, figure 7-22).

    b. The top side of the file tips about 10 degrees to 15 degrees off the horizontal toward the toe of the saw (B, figure 7-22).

    c. The handle of the file is lowered from 5 degrees to 10 degrees from the horizontal (C, figure 7-22). The purpose of this is to form a point on the top of the tooth.

    NOTE: Positioning the file at the three different angles shown in figure 7-22 is not possible if much shaping is required. If this is the case, hold the file level and at 90 degrees to the blade as though shaping ripsaw teeth. Keep the file positioned as shown at C. Rough shape the teeth in this manner, disregarding the forming of bevels until the final shaping.

4. File every other tooth from one side to shape, holding the file at the correct angles. Remember that cutting is done with a forward stroke of the file.

5. Reverse the saw from position A, figure 7-23, to position B and file the alternate teeth to shape. Keep the file at the same angles with respect to the tooth and blade as described before.

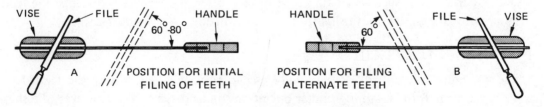

Fig. 7-23 Positions for filing teeth.

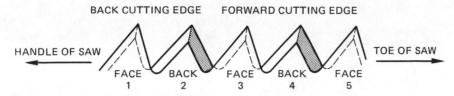

Fig. 7-24 **Filing the face and back of the tooth.**

Sharpening a Crosscut Saw

1. Clamp the toe end of the blade in the vise so that the bottom of the gullets of the teeth are about 1/8 inch above the vise jaws.

2. Choose a proper type of triangular file.

3. Stand directly in front of the teeth to be filed.

4. Carefully align the file in the first tooth at the toe end to the correct angles as described for shaping the teeth (figure 7-22).

    a. Hold the file at an angle from 60 degrees to 80 degrees to the blade.

    b. Drop the handle end of the file about 5 degrees to 10 degrees to the horizontal.

    c. Tilt the face of the file at 10 degrees to 15 degrees from the horizontal.

    NOTE: If the teeth have been properly shaped, the file easily seats itself at the correct angles.

5. Start the tip of the file in the first tooth bed at the toe end of the saw and take a light, full stroke.

    NOTE: The direction and amount of cutting is regulated by the pressure applied with the fingers holding the tip of the file. Remember that cutting is done on the forward stroke and that the file should be lifted clear of the tooth on the return stroke. Use the same number of file strokes for each tooth so that the size of the teeth stay uniform throughout the length of the blade.

    The file points toward the handle for this method of sharpening. It is pressed more firmly against the back edge of the teeth as at teeth 2 and 4, figure 7-24. The forward cutting edge of teeth 1 and 3 are filed lightly. If too much pressure is used against the forward edge of teeth 1 and 3, the saw chatters.

6. Continue the strokes until a bevel and point are formed on the tooth.

7. Move the file to the alternate (third) tooth and file as before. Do this until every tooth within the span of the vise jaws is sharpened.

8. Move the saw in the vise to a position for filing the next series of teeth. Line up the file and continue to file until all of the alternate teeth on one side of the blade are filed.

9. Reverse the saw in the clamp and file the other alternate teeth in the same way.

    NOTE: The filing is started with the second tooth at the toe end. Again, the direction of filing is toward the handle of the saw.

Fig. 7-25 How teeth should appear when completed.

10. Inspect the completed job. The teeth should look like those shown in A and B, figure 7-25.

REVIEW QUESTIONS

A. Completion

1. Preparing saw teeth to be even in height is called _____ and is performed with a _____.

2. _____ the teeth removes burrs caused by shaping them with a _____.

3. The burrs of reshaped teeth are removed by using _____.

4. Bending each alternate tooth a specified degree beyond the face of the blade is called _____ and is performed with a _____.

5. In reshaping ripsaw teeth, the file should be held at _____ degrees to the face of the blade.

6. In reshaping crosscut teeth, the file should be held at _____ degrees to the face of the blade.

7. A saw set can be adjusted for _____ and _____.

8. Filing with the triangular file is done on the _____ stroke.

9. An indication that a saw needs setting is shown by the tendency of the blade to _____.

10. _____ a saw blade regularly avoids excessive setting.

B. Short Answer or Discussion

1. Describe, in their proper order, the six operations involved in fitting a saw.

2. When reshaping teeth, where is the most likely place to find a tooth in its original shape to be used as a guide? Why here?

3. Why is the selection of the proper size triangular file important in shaping or sharpening the teeth?

4. How much of the tooth is set? How is this adjustment done in the saw set?

5. In clamping the saw blade in the vise before shaping or sharpening, how far above the top of the vise should the gullets of the teeth be? What is the effect of greatly increasing or decreasing the distance?

6. On the return stroke of the triangular file, what precaution should be taken?

7. The procedures for fitting crosscut blades and ripsaw blades are the same with two exceptions. Name these exceptions and explain why the procedures must differ with each type of blade.

8. What tools are used for jointing?

9. What is the main precaution that must be taken in jointing?

10. On the two views of ripsaw teeth, figure 7-26, a file is shown in the correct position for reshaping the teeth. Indicate the angles of the file with the blade and the direction of filing.

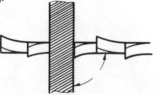 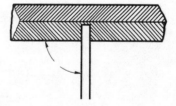

Fig. 7-26

11. On the three views of crosscut teeth in figure 7-27, a file is shown in the correct position for reshaping the teeth. Indicate the angles of the file with the blade and the direction of filing.

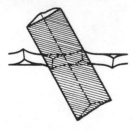  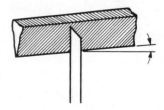

Fig. 7-27

12. The sketch in figure 7-28 shows teeth which require jointing. By another sketch show
     how these teeth should appear after they have been jointed.

Fig. 7-28

13. Refer to figure 7-29. At A, ripsaw, and at B, crosscut, indicate the proper angles of
     the saw teeth when fitting has been completed.

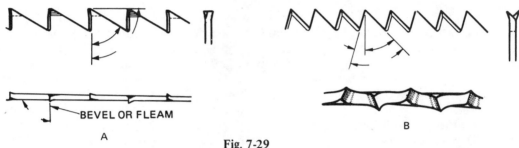

BEVEL OR FLEAM

A

Fig. 7-29

B

14. Refer to sketches A and B in figure 7-29 and identify the *pitch* or *hook* and *set.*

Unit 8 BENCH PLANES AND SPECIAL PLANES

Bench planes are cutting tools used for smoothing rough surfaces. They also bring woodwork down to a desired finished size after it has been rough-cut close to the finished size.

A number of bench planes are made. All types use the same principle of cutting. However, the difference in construction (weight, length, width, and type of blade) determines the type of work they are able to do. The main types of bench planes described in this unit are the jointer, fore, jack, smooth, and block planes.

THE JOINTER PLANE

The jointer plane, figure 8-1, is the largest of the planes. Its size ranges from 20 inches to 24 inches in length, with blade widths from 2 3/8 inches to 2 5/8 inches. This type of plane is made long and heavy because it is used on long boards. It produces long, straight edges, performing like a power jointer. It is used mainly for fitting doors and making the edges straight and true. The jointer plane also joints boards which are to be joined (fitted) together.

THE FORE PLANE

The fore plane looks the same as the jointer plane except that it is shorter in length — 18 inches. The blade is usually 2 3/8 inches wide. This type of plane is used to do the same work as a jointer plane. However, since it is lighter in weight, carpenters prefer to carry the fore plane in their tool chest.

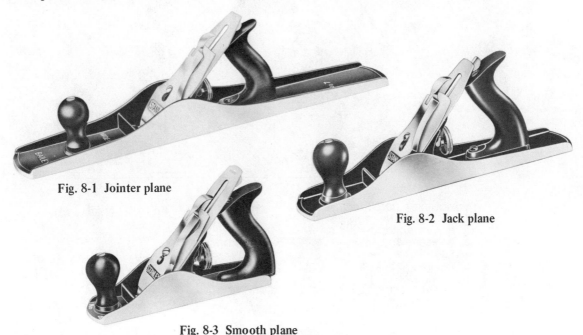

Fig. 8-1 Jointer plane

Fig. 8-2 Jack plane

Fig. 8-3 Smooth plane

THE JACK PLANE

The jack plane, figure 8-2, has the same features as the jointer and fore planes. Although made in several sizes, the 14-inch length with a 2-inch blade is the most popular. It is used as a general purpose plane — for smoothing and jointing boards and doing all around work.

THE SMOOTH PLANE

The smooth plane, figure 8-3, is built like the jack plane, but it is smaller and lighter. It comes in a limited range of lengths. However, the 8-inch size with a 1 3/4-inch blade is recommended. Smooth planes are used to smooth a surface after the rough surface has been removed. This type of plane produces a smooth but not necessarily true surface.

PARTS OF A PLANE

The parts of a jointer, fore, jack, and smooth plane are all alike except for the length of the *sole* (plane bottom). In figure 8-4, the parts of a plane are labeled and their relationship to one another is shown.

ADJUSTING MECHANISMS OF PLANES

Planes have adjustments for the throat opening, depth of cut, and lateral movement of the blade. The purpose of each of these adjustments should be understood so that they can be used to align and set the blade for the cut desired.

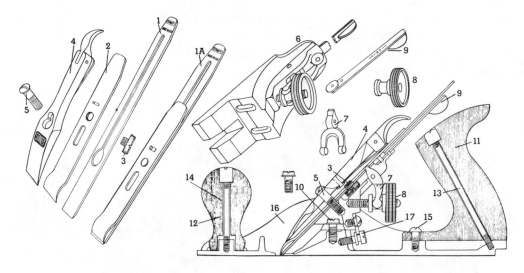

1A	DOUBLE PLANE IRON	9	LATERAL ADJUSTING LEVER
1	SINGLE PLANE IRON	10	FROG SCREW
2	PLANE IRON CAP	11	HANDLE
3	CAP SCREW	12	KNOB
4	LEVER CAP	13	HANDLE BOLT & NUT
5	LEVER CAP SCREW	14	KNOB BOLT & NUT
6	FROG COMPLETE	15	HANDLE SCREW
7	"Y" ADJUSTING LEVER	16	BOTTOM
8	ADJUSTING NUT	17	FROG ADJUSTING SCREW

Fig. 8-4 Parts of a plane.

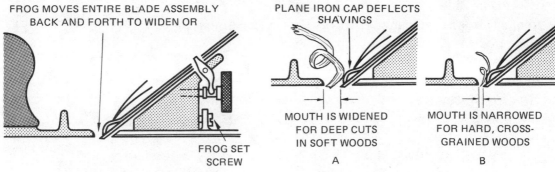

FROG MOVES ENTIRE BLADE ASSEMBLY
BACK AND FORTH TO WIDEN OR

FROG SET
SCREW

Fig. 8-5 Throat adjustment

PLANE IRON CAP DEFLECTS
SHAVINGS

MOUTH IS WIDENED
FOR DEEP CUTS
IN SOFT WOODS
A

MOUTH IS NARROWED
FOR HARD, CROSS-
GRAINED WOODS
B

Fig. 8-6 Effects of throat adjustment

Throat and Mouth Adjustment

The throat adjustment in the jointer, fore, jack, or smooth plane is made by moving the frog, figure 8-5, forward or backward on the plane bed. The throat adjustment makes it possible to change the distance between the cutting edge of the plane iron and the front edge of the opening. The smaller the opening, the more often the shaving will be broken (A, figure 8-6). This produces a smoother cut on curly- or wavy-grained wood. For fine planing, a close throat adjustment is recommended, but for coarser planing and on pitchy and resinous woods, the throat opening should be greater to allow for thicker shavings and to prevent clogging.

Depth Adjustment

The depth adjusting mechanism as shown in figure 8-4, and in detail in figure 8-7, has a lug (A, figure 8-7), which engages the slot of the chip breaker. The double plane iron is moved up or down by turning the thumbscrew, B, to the right or left, thus changing the depth of the cut.

Lateral Adjustment

The lateral adjusting lever shown in figure 8-4 is riveted to the frog. At the lower end of the lever, a round washer is riveted. This engages the slot in the plane iron blade. Moving the lever shifts the plane iron to the left or right, thus adjusting the cutting edge. Figure 8-8, B, shows the correct alignment of the blade, whereas A and C illustrate a blade that is poorly adjusted.

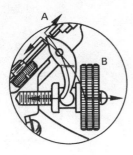

Fig. 8-7 Depth adjusting mechanism

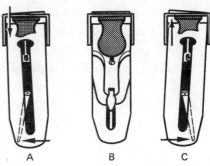

A   B   C

Fig. 8-8 Knob, lever cap and plane iron cap removed
to show the action of the lateral adjusting lever.

Figure 8-9 shows a double plane iron. This is an assembly of the single plane iron and the plane iron cap which acts as a chip breaker. Note the curved surface at the bottom of the plane iron cap. This surface is formed on the cap so that a tight spring joint is made between the plane iron, or blade, and the plane iron cap at the cutting edge. This prevents the shavings from lodging between these two surfaces and choking the throat of the plane.

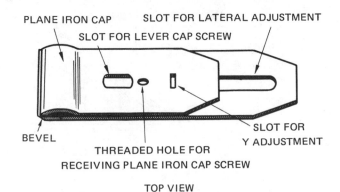

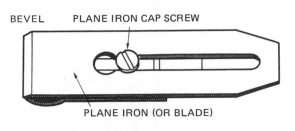

Fig. 8-9 Double plane iron

The plane iron cap screw passes through the slot in the blade and screws into a threaded hole in the cap, figure 8-9, fastening the blade and cap together. The slot for the Y adjustment engages the Y adjusting lever. The lever is moved up or down as the adjusting nut is turned toward or away from the frog. This causes the plane iron to be raised or lowered in the throat of the plane bed. The thickness of the shavings is regulated by this adjustment.

The slot for the lateral or side adjustment is engaged by a knob fastened to the end of the lateral adjusting lever. When this lever is moved from side to side, it moves the cutting edge of the blade from side to side in the mouth opening at the bottom of the plane.

The lever cap shown in figure 8-4, number 4, is a cap that is held in place by the lever cap screw, figure 8-4, number 5. This screw is threaded into the frog, passes through the slot for the lever cap screw, and is adjusted to hold the lever cap closely over the plane iron and plane iron cap. The cam, located at the upper end of the lever, is locked into place to firmly tighten the lever cap against the double plane iron.

THE BLOCK PLANE

The block plane, figure 8-10, is the smallest and least complex of the common type planes. Several types are made. Some include special features for making throat and lateral adjustments.

The block plane is used to plane small pieces of wood as well as end grain of molding and trim. It is also used to make chamfers and bevels. Because the blade is set at a lower angle than other planes, end grain is easier to cut.

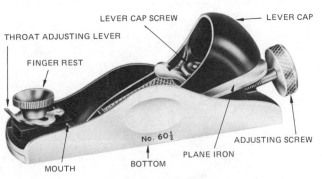

Fig. 8-10 Block plane

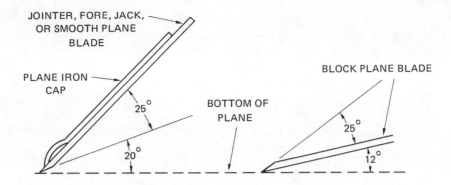

Fig. 8-11 Comparison of plane blades.

Unlike other planes, the block plane is held in one hand for planing. Its small size permits easy and accurate control when properly held.

An assembled block plane is shown in figure 8-10. The adjusting screw controls the movement of the blade for depth of cut. The lever cap screw and lever cap hold the blade firmly in place. No provision is made for lateral adjustment by mechanical means in the plane shown. Throat adjustment is accomplished by moving the throat adjusting lever under the finger rest. Lateral adjustment of the blade for the plane shown is done by loosening the lever cap and then putting the blade in the desired position by hand.

No chip breaker is required in the block plane because when end grain is cut, it is sheared from the wood, in most cases, in a powder form. When cutting with the grain, the blade is usually set for a fine shaving; again, there is little danger of clogging the throat opening.

The cutting angle and the position of the face of the bevel (which forms the cutting edge) on the blade of a block plane is shown in figure 8-11. Note the difference as compared to the position of a jointer, fore, jack, or smooth plane blade. For those blades, the bevel is face down, whereas for the block plane the bevel is face up. Positioning the bevel of the block plane face up provides for enough back clearance, whereas if it is placed face down, there is little or no clearance.

The bevel setting of the plane blade shows that the lower the angle the cutting tool is ground, the less is the resistance to cutting. A higher angle increases cutting resistance. However, blades with lower angles do not wear as well and must be sharpened more often. This principle applies to all cutting tools.

Larger planes are also used for end-grain planing if the bevel of the cutter blade is ground with a long bevel to reduce the angle between the cutter and the wood surface. This is done when the area of end grain to be planed is large, or where the face grain is very irregular.

Larger planes generally have fixed angle blade settings or frog beds. Block planes can be obtained with blade angle frogs of various angle settings.

PROCEDURES FOR USING BENCH PLANES

The following procedures apply to the jointer, fore, jack, and smooth planes. These planes have the same construction and therefore are adjusted and handled in the same manner.

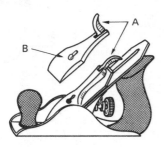

Fig. 8-12 Removing the lever cap.

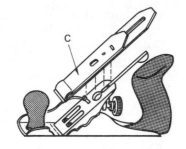

Fig. 8-13 Removing the double plane iron.

Disassembling a Plane

Lift the cam lever (A, figure 8-12), and remove the lever cap B. This permits removal of the double plane iron (C, figure 8-13).

Adjusting the Plane Frog

1. Loosen the bed screws (A, figure 8-14), and turn the frog adjusting screw B to the right or left.

2. After the adjustment is made, tighten the bed screws.

   NOTE: In a solid-bottom plane, the frog should be adjusted only when the size of the throat needs to be changed.

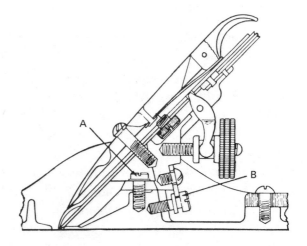

Fig. 8-14 Adjusting frog.

Assembling the Double Plane Iron

1. Lay the plane iron cap on the flat side of the plane iron as in step 1, figure 8-15, with the screw in the slot.

2. Draw the plane iron cap back to a point where it clears the cutting edge when revolved into place. See step 2, figure 8-15.

3. Turn it so that it lines up with the edges of the plane iron, step 3, figure 8-16.

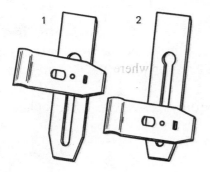

Fig. 8-15 Assembling the double plane iron (steps 1 and 2).

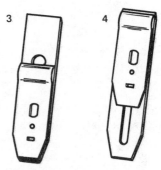

Fig. 8-16 Assembling the double plane iron (steps 3 and 4).

4. Advance the plane iron cap until the edge is just back of the cutting edge of the plane iron as shown in step 4, figure 8-16. Do not drag the plane iron cap across the cutting edge or the blade can become dulled.

5. Place the plane iron cap 1/16 inch back of the cutting edge for general work. On cross-grained or curly wood it should be about 1/32 inch from the cutting edge.

6. Fasten the plane iron cap to the plane iron by tightening the plane iron cap screw. The lower edge of the lever cap is used for this purpose instead of a screwdriver.

Placing the Double Plane Iron in the Plane Bed

1. Lay the double plane iron on the frog with the plane iron cap up.

   NOTE: The roller on the lateral adjusting lever should fit into the slot of the plane iron, and the lug on the Y-depth adjusting lever should fit into the slot of the plane iron cap.

2. Place the lever cap over the lever cap screw, slide it down, and clamp the lever cap with the cam, A, figure 8-17.

   NOTE: The clamping pressure of the lever cap on the double plane iron can be varied by turning the lever cap screw, E, figure 8-18. This pressure should be just tight enough to allow the depth and lateral adjustments to be made easily and yet hold these adjustments firmly in place. Too much pressure is likely to break the lever cap cam and too little pressure will not hold the adjustments securely.

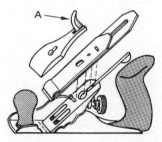

Fig. 8-17 Clamping the lever cap with the cam.

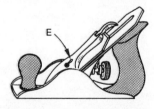

Fig. 8-18 Varying the clamping pressure by turning the lever cap screw.

Adjusting the Plane for Depth of Cut

1. Sight along the bottom of the plane in the direction of a light background.

2. Turn the adjusting nut until the cutting edge projects enough to cut the desired thickness of shaving. See figure 8-19.

   NOTE: The enlarged detail in the figure shows the operation of the adjusting nut; the arrows indicate the direction of the blade movement as related to the direction of the adjusting nut movement.

Fig. 8-19 Sighting for depth of cut.

Adjusting the Plane Iron Laterally

1. Sight along the bottom of the plane.

2. Move the lateral adjusting lever to the right or to the left, figure 8-20, until the cutting edge of the plane iron projects uniformly across the bottom of the plane.

Fig. 8-20 Sighting for lateral adjustment.

Preparing the Jointer, Fore, Jack, and Smooth Planes for Use

If a satisfactory job is to be done, the plane must be tested for sharpness and adjustment.

1. To test the plane, clamp a board into the bench vise so that the edge of the board projects above the top of the bench about 2 inches.

2. Turn the adjusting nut of the plane so that the blade just touches the board when the plane is pushed over the full length of the edge.

3. Make any necessary lateral adjustment.

4. Take several strokes, one right after the other, and gradually adjust the blade to take a lacelike shaving from the full length and width of the edge.

   - If this can be done, the plane is sharp.

   - If this requires great pressure or the plane jumps on the wood, the plane is dull or the cut is too thick.

   - If the cut is rough, it may be because cutting is being done against the grain. Reverse the board and try again.

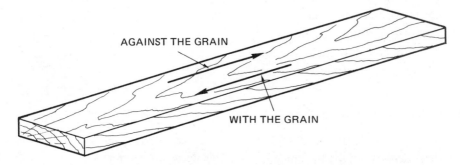

AGAINST THE GRAIN

WITH THE GRAIN

Fig. 8-21 Determining the direction of grain.

5. Adjust the plane to take a very light cut.

   - If it does not take a thin cut, the plane is dull and must be sharpened.

   - The procedure for sharpening a plane iron is given later in this unit.

Planing Faces

1. Clamp the work securely, as shown in figure 8-22, so that both hands can be used to control the plane. Note the direction of the grain. Plane, when possible, in the same

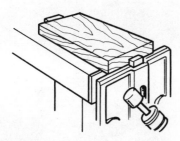

Fig. 8-22 Using a vise and bench stop to hold the work.

Fig. 8-23 Butting the work against a wood strip for planing.

direction. Another method of holding the work for planing a face is to butt it against a strip of wood tacked or clamped to the bench as shown in figure 8-23.

2. Hold the plane with the left hand on the knob and the right hand on the handle.

3. Push down firmly on the knob when beginning the stroke. Push down evenly on both the knob and the handle when in the middle of the stroke. Lighten the pressure on the knob and push down on the handle when finishing the stroke. When learning to plane, keep well over the work so these pressures can be carefully watched. The common fault of dubbing (rounding) the ends of the wood can then be avoided.

4. Plane the entire surface of the board

MAKE DIAGONAL CUTS
WITH JACK PLANE

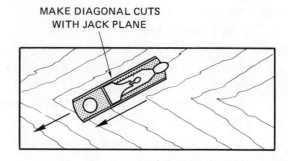

Fig. 8-24 Using a diagonal stroke for smoothing a surface.

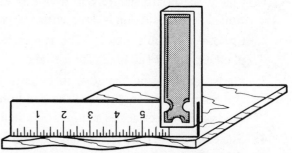

Fig. 8-25 Exaggerated high and low spots.

using strokes diagonally to both corners. See figure 8-24. When the plane cuts the wood surface throughout each of the strokes the surface will be fairly straight. The jointer or fore plane should be used on large surfaces to make the board flat and straight faster.

5. Test the surface for straightness by laying a try or framing square along the surface, figure 8-25. If the edge of the square touches the wood surface at all points when it is placed in several positions, the surface is straight.

6. Test for cup and wind by applying a straightedge across the edge of the board and then diagonally across the board.

7. If there are any high spots, mark them off with a pencil and plane off only the pencil marks. Do not plane where there are no marks. When the marks are planed off, test

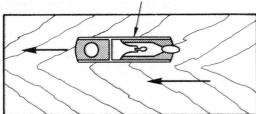

FINISH OFF WITH SMOOTH
PLANE STRAIGHT ACROSS

Fig. 8-26 Using a straight stroke for finishing a surface.

Fig. 8-27 Planing an edge with the board held in a bench vise.

the board surface with the square. When the board is free from high spots, cup, and wind, smooth the surface by lightly planing with the grain. A smooth plane should be used for this and applied in a direction straight along the length of the board as shown in figure 8-26.

NOTE: Before planing a finish, the plane blade should be whetted to a very keen edge to get the best results.

Planing an Edge

1. Clamp the board securely in a vise as shown in figure 8-27. The board should be positioned so that cutting is done with the grain.

2. Choose a suitable plane. The type selected depends on the length of the edge to be planed. Adjust the plane for a trial cut.

3. Place the plane on the edge to be cut. Hold it parallel to and square with the face of the board by bracing it with the hand on the plane knob and placing the fingers against the board face to act as a guide. See figure 8-27.

4. Start the cut with pressure applied on the knob to avoid dubbing the edge. See figure 8-28. Be careful to hold the plane square with the working face of the board for the entire length of the stroke.

APPLY PRESSURE

APPLY PRESSURE

STEP 1

STEP 2

Fig. 8-28 Procedure for planing an edge.

NOTE: If cutting is difficult it is usually because of the following conditions: the cut being taken is too thick, planing is being done against the grain, or the plane blade is dull.

5. At the completion of the stroke, apply pressure at the heel to avoid dubbing the ends.

6. Check the edge with a suitable straightedge. Mark the high spots with a pencil and plane these until removed.

NOTE: When selecting a straightedge for checking the trueness of a planed edge, be sure that it extends the full length of the edge. If this is not possible, sight the edge for trueness.

7. Test the edge for squareness by placing the handle of a try square against the working face, and the blade across the planed edge. Move the try square along the full length of the edge and mark any high spots. See figure 8-29.

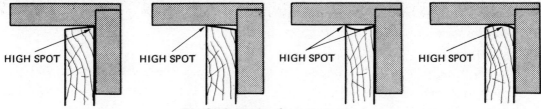

Fig. 8-29 Testing for squareness.

8. Place the plane on the high edge and brace it with the fingers against the board face in such a way as to take only the high section off. Then take a stroke the full length of the board. Test the edge after the stroke to see that the marked low edge is not cut and that a flat surface is started on the high edge as shown in figure 8-30.

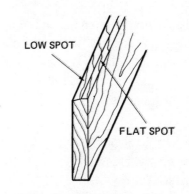

Fig. 8-30 Low edge and high edge of board.

9. Test the flat section to see if it is square with the work face. If it is out of square, take another full stroke on this section, holding and guiding the plane so that the flat section is made square. Keep testing the edge after each stroke until a full width cut is taken over the full length of the board and the edge is square.

Planing an End

1. Choose the proper plane. The width of the board determines which is most suitable. For small widths use a block plane and for larger widths use a smooth or jack plane. Set the blade for a fine cut and make any other necessary adjustments of the plane.

2. Secure the work firmly in a vise or other holding device.

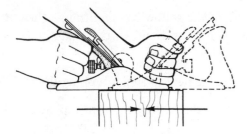

Fig. 8-31 Plane end grain halfway from each edge.

Fig. 8-32 If the plane is pushed all the way, the corners will break.

3. Place the toe of the plane in contact with the surface to be planed. Plane toward the center of the board. Then reverse the plane and start planing from the opposite edge, again toward the center. See figure 8-31. Planing in this manner avoids splintering the edge as shown in figure 8-32.

    NOTE: Two other methods can be used to avoid splintering the board at the corner. These are shown in figures 8-33 and 8-34. In both cases, a full stroke of the plane is used.

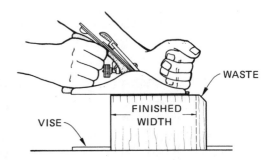

Fig. 8-33 Excess (waste) stock chamfered on corner.

4. Check for squareness and make the necessary strokes with the plane to remove any high spots. Guide the plane as previously described for planing an edge.

Planing a Broad Surface

1. Clamp the material securely to a flat surface.

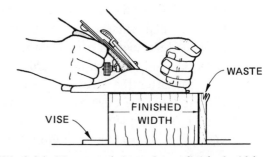

Fig. 8-34 Waste stock butted to a finished width.

2. Select a jointer or fore plane and adjust the blade for a medium-weight cut.

    NOTE: Planing broad surfaces usually involves boards which have been glued together. Often a residue of glue remains on the surfaces at the joints of the boards. This should be scraped off with an old plane iron blade or wood chisel before planing. The first cut should be heavy enough to allow the plane edge to get under any glue remaining on the surface rather than to ride over it. Hardened glue dulls a blade rapidly. This method is also used when planing boards with painted surfaces.

3. Plane straight across the boards, figure 8-35. Apply pressure at the start on the knob and at the heel at the end of the cut as described for other types of planing.

    NOTE: If planing straight across is difficult, plane diagonally across the board. This is sometimes more effective, especially when the surface is irregular.

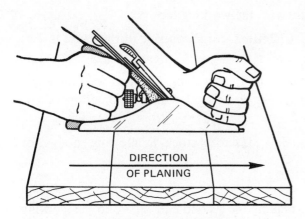

Fig. 8-35 Planing a broad surface.

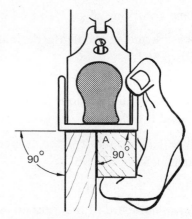

Fig. 8-36 Hold wood strip tightly to the plane sole, as a guide.

4. After the surface is planed straight, plane the surface lengthwise using a fine finish cut.

    NOTE: The plane blade should be very sharp for the finish cut because the glued boards may have their grain running in opposite directions. Therefore, some of the cutting is done against the grain. A sharp blade applied with a light cut lessens the effects of cutting against the grain. However, if a rough cut should result, it may be necessary to use a cabinet scraper to finish the surface.

Planing a Narrow Edge

Use the same procedure that was described for planing an edge. In addition, hold a strip of wood tightly to the plane sole as shown in figure 8-36. This prevents the plane from tilting and acts as a guide to keep it square to the working face of the board.

NOTE: The strip of wood which is held to the sole of the plane should be square at corner A, figure 8-36, if it is to serve as an accurate guide.

Squaring a Board

1. Plane the better of the two faces until it is straight and true. This is now referred to as the working face. See 1, figure 8-37.

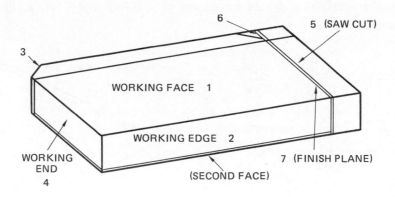

Fig. 8-37 Sequence of cuts for squaring a board.

2. Plane a working edge, 2, so that it is square with the working face.

3. Measure and mark off the desired width. Chamfer a corner outside of the gauge line as shown at 3.

4. Plane a working end, 4, so that it is square to the working face and working edge. Planing should be done at the end which was chamfered with the direction of cut toward the chamfer.

5. Measure and mark off the desired length. Saw off excess stock, 5, allowing enough for finish planing.

6. Chamfer the corner as shown at 6.

7. Plane the board to the finished length, 7, making the second end square to the working face and working edge.

8. Plane the second edge to the finished width of board, 8, making the edge square to the working face and working end.

9. With a marking gauge held against the working face, mark off on all edges the thickness of the board desired, 9.

10. Plane the second face, 9, to the gauge line and check for trueness.

NOTE: Numbers 1 through 9 in figure 8-37 indicate the sequence of cuts.

Planing Chamfers and Bevels

NOTE: A chamfer differs from a bevel in that it does not extend through the full thickness of the stock. See figure 8-38. The chamfer is usually made at an angle of 45 degrees with the edge and surface of the stock. Two types of chamfers are shown in figure 8-39.

1. To plane a through chamfer on an edge, proceed as follows:

a. Mark the width of the chamfer on the face and edge of the stock by pencil gauging, figure 8-40.

NOTE: Do not use a marking gauge for this purpose as the cut will show on the chamfered surface.

b. Secure the work in a vise or by means of a clamp and a vise as shown in figures 8-41 and 8-42.

EDGE CHAMFER   EDGE BEVEL

Fig. 8-38 Comparing a chamfer to a bevel.

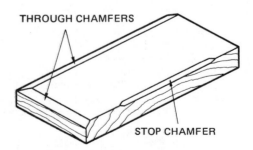

THROUGH CHAMFERS

STOP CHAMFER

Fig. 8-39 Types of chamfers.

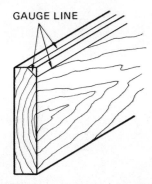

Fig. 8-40 Gauge lines for chamfering.

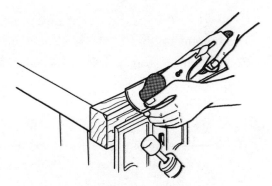

Fig. 8-41 Chamfering an edge in the vise.

c. Plane in a direction parallel with the edge of the board until the finish cut barely removes the pencil marks.

d. Check the angle of the finished chamfer with a sliding T bevel set at the correct angle. See figure 8-43. Also check the straightness as shown in figure 8-44.

2. To plane a through chamfer on an end, proceed as follows:

a. Lay out the pencil gauge lines.

b. Clamp the work in a vise as shown in figure 8-45.

Fig. 8-42 Chamfering an edge with the work held in a clamp.

c. Hold the plane at about a 45-degree angle from the starting edge and plane toward the center. Reverse the plane and stroke from the opposite side toward the center. Cutting in this manner avoids splitting the end grain at the corners.

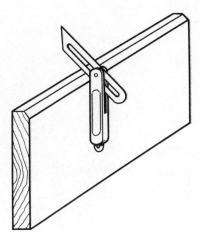

Fig. 8-43 Testing angle

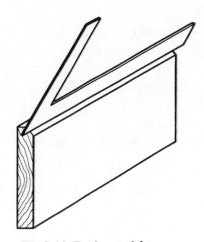

Fig. 8-44 Testing straightness

NOTE: If edge and end chamfers are to be planed, it is best to plane the edge chamfers before the end chamfers.

3. To plane a stop chamfer, proceed as follows:

   a. Lay out the stop chamfer at the location desired.

   b. Work the ends of the chamfer toward its center with a wood chisel to an extent that a smooth or block plane can be used to finish the remaining center portion. Leave enough stock for finishing.

   c. Cut the center portion down to the established depth using a wood chisel.

   d. Place at a 45-degree angle as described for cutting an end chamfer.

   e. Finish the ends of the chamfer by barely removing the pencil lines with a paring action using the wood chisel. Finish the center portion with the plane.

Fig. 8-45 Chamfering an end.

4. To plane a bevel, proceed as follows:

   a. Mark the distance the bevel is to extend in from the edge by gauging with a pencil on the face of the stock.

   b. Plane the edges to be beveled in the same manner as when planing a chamfer.

   c. When planing bevels on the ends of boards, plane from the edges toward the center to prevent the edge fibers from breaking off. The plane should be held at about a 45-degree angle in relation to the edge from which the cut is started. See figure 8-46.

   NOTE: Great care should be used in cutting a bevel because the overall size of the board can be shortened or left unsquare. As

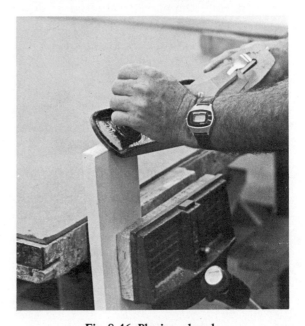

Fig. 8-46 Planing a bevel.

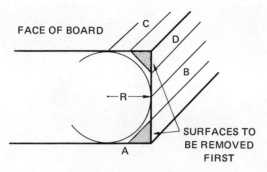

Fig. 8-47 Layout of nosing.

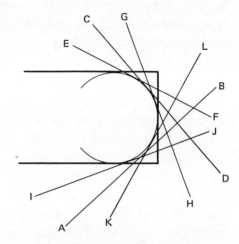

Fig. 8-48 Angles of plane in planing.

indicated for chamfers, the bevel edges should also be planed before planing the ends. The advantage of this practice is that less end grain remains to be cut when end chamfers are made.

d. Check the bevel for correct angle and straightness with a sliding T bevel and straight-edge as described for a chamfer.

e. Mark the high spots with a pencil and plane these until the surface is made true.

NOTE: The bevel should have a perfectly flat finished surface with sharp corners where the edge and end bevels meet. In general, beveled and chamfered surfaces are not sanded because it is difficult to avoid rounding them.

Planing a Nosing

1. To plane a nosing or round on the edge of a board, lay out an arc on the end of the board, the size of the required nosing. See figure 8-47.

2. Lay out the chamfer lines A, B, C, and D as guides to produce surfaces slightly outside the arc of the nosing line.

3. Plane down to the lines A, B, and C, D, figure 8-47, by tilting the plane to 45-degree angles shown by the lines AB and CD in figure 8-48.

4. Plane off corners A, B, C, and D, figure 8-47, by tilting the plane to the angles shown in lines EF, GH, IJ, and KL, figure 8-48.

5. The remaining slight corners can be removed to the nosing outline with coarse sand-paper. Finish the completed rounded nosing with fine sandpaper.

Adjusting a Block Plane

1. To adjust the plane for thickness of shavings (vertical adjustment), hold the plane bottom-side up at eye level with the toe of the plane pointing toward you.

2. Sight along the bottom and turn the adjusting screw (using the right hand) until the plane blade projects slightly above the bottom. The extent of this adjustment should be so that the plane edge produces a thin shaving.

NOTE: A common error that is made is to set the blade too far out, causing the first cut to be too deep and impossible to complete.

3. To adjust the plane to produce an even shaving (lateral adjustment), slightly loosen the lever cap screw or lever cam (depending on the type of plane) and sight along the bottom of the plane. Apply pressure to the upper end (top) of the blade at the corner which is oppostie to the corner of the edge that is low. Move the blade until the cutting edge appears to be parallel with the bottom of the plane.

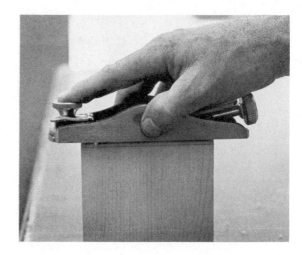

Fig. 8-49 How to hold a block plane.

4. If, after this adjustment, the edge of the blade appears to project more than is desired, gradually pull the blade back by moving it from side to side until it is correctly positioned. Again, make the lateral adjustment.

5. Lock the blade in place and make a test cut.

Using a Block Plane

1. First rest the palm of the hand to be used on the uppermost part of the plane. Then grasp the sides of the plane between the thumb and second finger, with the index finger resting in the hollow of the finger rest at the front of the plane. See figure 8-49.

2. When using the block plane, use only one hand to guide and push it. Pressure should be applied down and forward at the beginning of the stroke. Keep the pressure even throughout the stroke. At the end of the stroke, apply pressure at the heel to avoid dubbing the end as was described for other types of planing.

NOTE: Always plane in the direction of the grain. If the grain is irregular, it may be necessary to change the direction of planing to suit the run of the grain. If cross or curly grain is to be cut, be sure that the plane edge is very sharp and set for a fine cut. Figures 8-50 and 8-51 show two applications of the block plane.

SHARPENING A PLANE IRON

Most of the problems in using planes are due to dull plane irons. Well-sharpened tools are easier to control, more accurate, and safer.

The plane iron is made of carbon tool steel. When hardened and tempered, the steel has a fine grain, is quite hard, and can be sharpened to a keen edge. In some plane irons, an insert or tip of tool steel is welded to the rest of the blade, which is made of mild steel. The blade is made in different sizes to fit various planes. The most common widths are 1 3/8 inches, 1 3/4 inches, 2 inches, and 2 3/8 inches.

Fig. 8-50 Planing end grain.

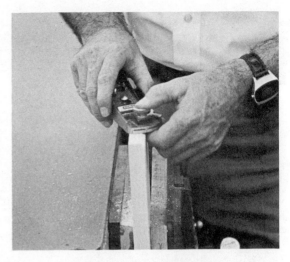

Fig. 8-51 Planing a chamfer.

Sharpening a plane iron is a two-step operation: grinding and whetting. Grinding is not always necessary. Usually the edge can be whetted several times before it needs to be reground.

Plane irons can be ground and whetted according to the kinds of wood on which they are to be used. For planing hardwoods, the angle of the bevel should be from 25 degrees to 30 degrees. When sharpened to this angle, the bevel appears to be slightly longer than twice the thickness of the plane iron. This gives support to the cutting edge. See B, figure 8-52. For planing softer woods, the angle of the bevel should be from 20 degrees to 25 degrees. This produces an edge which enters the wood more easily. See A, figure 8-52.

The cutting edge should be at right angles to the edge of the plane iron. However, if it is not exactly 90 degrees, the lateral adjusting mechanism compensates for the error.

For planing flat surfaces which are to be glued together, the plane iron should be ground and whetted with a straight cutting edge. For less precise work, the plane iron can have a slightly convex edge. See A, figure 8-52. For general purposes, the plane iron should be sharpened so that the cutting edge is straight, the corners are slightly rounded, and the bevel is about 25 degrees (C, figure 8-52).

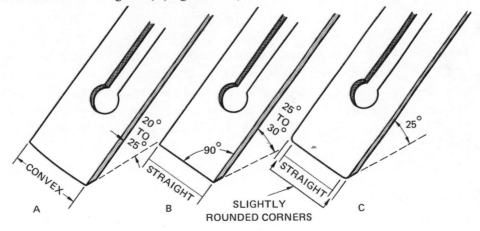

Fig. 8-52 Angles for grinding a plane iron.

Fig. 8-53 Conditions which require grinding of the plane iron.

GRINDING A PLANE IRON

When to Grind a Plane Iron

It is necessary to regrind the plane iron if the cutting edge becomes nicked, or if the bevel has been worn down by careless or excessive whetting, thus not providing enough back clearance.

Grinding Tools and Equipment

A hand or power grinder can be used for grinding a plane iron edge. However, the power grinder is preferred since both hands are free to hold and guide the plane iron. The type of wheel to select, the condition of its face, and the speed at which it rotates are important factors to be considered before starting any grinding.

Grinding wheels of aluminum oxide, #80 grit, are suitable for sharpening most edge tools. The wheels must be dressed (sharpened) true and flat across the face for grinding plane irons. Grinding wheels can be obtained in various diameters, widths, arbor hole, and grit sizes. The speeds at which grinding wheels should rotate for effective grinding are generally specified on the wheel or in literature provided by the manufacturer. Speeds range from 1,500 to 3,300 rpm. In general, the slower the speed at which the wheel rotates, the less danger there is of burning (overheating) the edge of the plane iron. This does not mean that all wheels should be run at a slow speed, but rather that the wheel used should produce a cutting action when revolved at slow speed.

Wet grinders and oilstone grinders are well suited for grinding edge tools since they eliminate the danger of burning the tool and drawing the temper. These types of grinders are found in mills and shops where much grinding is done.

Wheel Dressing

Dressing is the process of restoring the sharpness of the grinding wheel by breaking away the dulled abrasive crystals or by removing the glazed or loaded surface of the wheel. After dressing, the wheel has sharp cutting edges of the abrasive grains. The tools used for dressing are made in a variety of types. One of the most common types is shown in figure 8-54.

> SAFETY NOTE: Safety goggles or safety glass-guards should be used while dressing grinding wheels.

Dressing a Grinding Wheel

1. Support the dresser on the tool rest so that the point of contact between the wheel and the dresser is slightly above the center of the wheel. See figure 8-55.

Fig. 8-54 Grinding wheel dresser (Huntington Dresser).

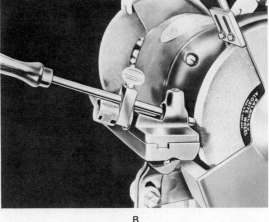

A

2. Pass the dresser back and forth across the face of the wheel while it is in motion.

3. Form the face of the wheel to a straight surface which is square with the sides of the wheel.

4. Stop the grinder and inspect the face of the wheel to be sure that all shiny spots are removed and that the pores of the wheel are clean.

Grinding the Plane Iron

NOTE: A grinder should be used that has an adjustable tool rest which can be set to produce the desired bevel. See figure 8-56.

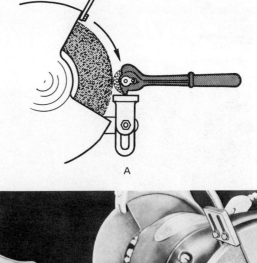

B

Fig. 8-55 Dressing a grinding wheel: (A) with a Huntington dresser (B) with a diamond dresser.

1. Adjust the tool rest so that an included angle of about 25 degrees will be formed on the edge of the plane iron when it contacts the wheel. This adjustment should be made so that the grinding is always done above the center of the wheel. Also, the tool rest should be located as close to the wheel as possible.

2. When the adjustment is completed, tighten the tool rest and adjust the glass guard on the grinder.

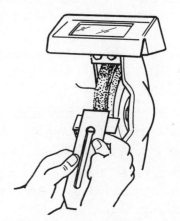

Fig. 8-56 Grinding a plane iron.

SAFETY NOTE: Wear goggles if no guard is provided.

3. Check the squareness of the cutting edge of the plane iron with a try square, figure 8-57. If the edge is not square, mark a pencil line on the side opposite the bevel as close to the edge as possible. Use this as a guide for grinding the edge square.

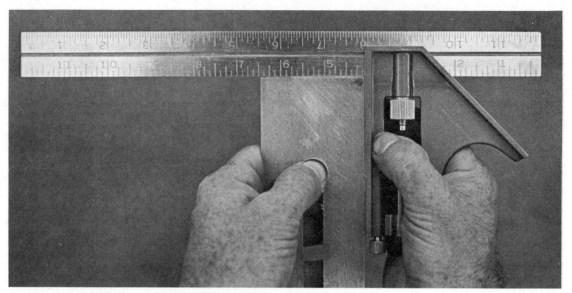

Fig. 8-57 Testing for squareness.

4. Start the grinder and hold the plane iron so that the bevel rests lightly on the face of the wheel. As soon as contact is made with the wheel, move the plane iron from side to side over the full width, evenly across its surface.

    NOTE: The plane iron should lie flat on the tool rest. It is held so that the back of the forefinger of the left hand touches the tool rest. figure 8-56. In this position it acts as a stop and a lateral guide. Do not shift its position on the plane iron (except for slight amounts required to feed it into the grinder) until the grinding is completed. The direction of wheel rotation should be toward you.

5. Cool the plane iron often during the grinding process by dipping it in a can of water. If the wheel has a coolant of lubricant flowing over its surface, cooling by dipping is not necessary. After each cooling, be sure to replace the plane iron on the tool rest in its same position before removal. If the left forefinger is kept in the same position on the plane iron for both cooling and grinding, returning to the same position is not a problem.

    NOTE: The plane iron heats quickly if the wheel is dull. Dress the wheel before any further grinding. A sign that the plane iron has overheated is the discoloration of the edge to a blue-black color.

6. Check the squareness of the edge as it is being ground. Adjust the position of the left forefinger accordingly. Also check the angle of the bevel and make any necessary adjustments of the tool rest.

7. Complete the grinding after making any final adjustments. A feather edge or wire edge usually appears along the full width of the blade which indicates that grinding of the bevel is completed, and that the plane iron is now ready to be whetted.

    NOTE: The back edge of the plane iron should be kept smooth and straight so that when the bevel surface is whetted, the resulting edge is smooth and keen. If the back side of the plane iron is ground, it will be useless for planing.

WHETTING A PLANE IRON

After grinding, the bevel and the straight side of the plane iron are whetted on an oilstone to remove the feather edge and produce the final keen cutting edge. Oilstones used for this purpose are made in coarse, medium, and fine grits. Stones made with one side coarse and the other fine are often preferred for the whetting

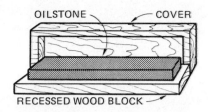

Fig. 8-58 Flat type of oilstone.

operation. The finer the grit size of an oilstone, the smoother the whetted surface will be and the smoother and sharper the edge will be.

A popular size stone is 1 inch by 2 inches by 8 inches. It should be enclosed in a wooden box as in figure 8-58, to prevent damage to its edges. The box can be clamped in a vise (without danger of breaking the stone) so that it can be held steadily when whetting the blade. A cover for the exposed surface of the stone is also desirable since this helps to keep it clean when not in use.

If an oilstone is kept clean and free from dust, grit, and fine metal particles, it works more effectively. Otherwise, foreign particles can clog the pores of the oilstone and prevent the edge of the tool from making proper contact with the stone.

Clean the oilstone with a cloth and thinned oil (a half-and-half mixture of kerosene and oil) before and after using. Also, using plenty of thinned oil while whetting helps keep the stone clean and prevents fine particles from lodging in the pores.

New oilstones have flat surfaces. It is important that the whole surface of the stone be worn down uniformly so the surface remains flat. The whetting of gouges, narrow chisels, and other edge tools only at the center of the stone produces a depression in the stone. This hollow condition of the stone makes it unsuitable for producing flat surfaces on plane irons and wide chisels. Whet over the whole surface of the stone to wear it down evenly and to keep it flat.

Whetting a Plane Iron

1. Choose a combination oilstone. It should be enclosed in a wooden box. Wipe the surfaces of the stone clean, especially the coarse face, since this side of the stone is used first.

2. Clamp the box with the stone (coarse-side face up) in a bench vise and apply a film of thinned oil to the surface of the stone.

3. Hold the plane iron in the right hand with the left hand helping to hold it against the stone. See figure 8-59.

4. Start with the whole bevel in contact with the stone. Then raise the back

Fig. 8-59 Whetting the bevel side.

edge slightly (30 degrees to 35 degrees, as shown in figure 8-60), and move the plane iron back and forth over the stone as indicated by the arrows in figure 8-59. Use an even, medium pressure on the forward stroke and less on the return stroke. The angle between the stone and iron must be kept the same. Try not to rock the iron as it is moved back and forth or the bevel will be rounded.

NOTE: Some carpenters prefer to move the plane iron over the full surface of the stone by using strokes that look like the figure eight. This tends to wear the stone more uniformly and avoids creating any depressions in its surface. However, this technique requires more skill than the method described and should be carefully practiced. A series of small circular strokes applied over the entire surface of the stone is also effective.

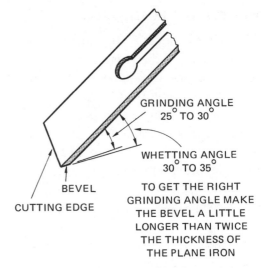

Fig. 8-60 Grinding and whetting angles.

Fig. 8-61 Whetting the straight side.

5. After six to twelve strokes, when the feather edge is formed on the plane iron, turn the stone to the fine side and hold the flat side of the iron in tight contact with the stone. Hold the plane iron firmly in this position and stroke it over the full length of the stone, figure 8-61. Keep the left hand on top of the cutter to avoid lifting it.

6. If the feather edge is not removed after a few strokes, reverse the iron (coarse-side up) and whet the bevel side again. Continue whetting the plane iron using a lighter pressure each time until the feather edge falls away.

7. Wipe all oil and steel particles from the stone.

8. Reverse the stone so that the fine grit side is up. Alternately apply the bevel and the flat side of the iron to the stone for a few strokes. This produces an even keener edge on the plane iron.

NOTE: A sharp plane edge is invisible. An edge that is dull appears as a fine white line. Repeat the whetting process until any nicks or signs of bluntness of the edge are gone.

9. To get a really sharp plane iron, the edge is honed. For this operation, the blade is sharpened on a fine Lily stone in the same way as described for whetting.

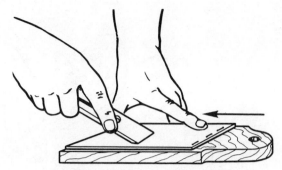

Fig. 8-62 Honing on a leather strop.

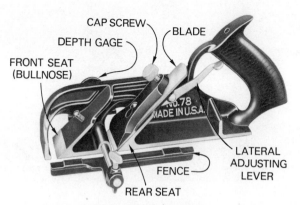

Fig. 8-63 Rabbet plane

10. If a Lily stone is not available, a very good strop can be made from a piece of leather belting about three inches wide and twelve inches long. Glue and clamp it to a board of about three-quarters of an inch by three inches by twelve inches. It can then be used like a whetstone. The stroking of the plane iron over the leather surface must be away from the cutting edge rather than against it. See figure 8-62.

11. Test the plane iron for keenness by lightly touching the edge of the iron to the thumbnail. If the plane iron does not slip over the nail, but seems to stick, the edge is considered sharp. A safer method of testing keenness is to remove a single hair from the head and stroke it against the cutting edge. If the hair is easily cut, the iron is considered sharp. A piece of paper stroked against the cutting edge is another test.

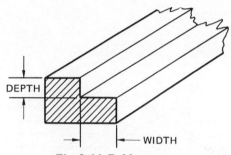

Fig. 8-64 Rabbet cut

Fig. 8-65 Cabinetmaker's planes

SPECIAL PLANES

Special planing tools are designed to make rabbet and dado joints, tongue and groove joints, shapes for moldings, trims, routing, and forming. The special planes that do these jobs are briefly described and illustrated in this unit. They are not

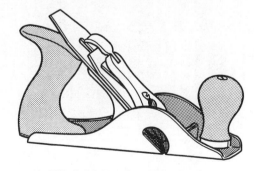

Fig. 8-66 Bench rabbet plane

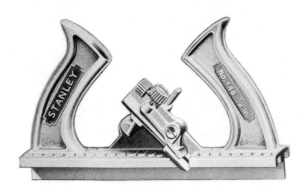

Fig. 8-67 Double end tongue and groove match plane.

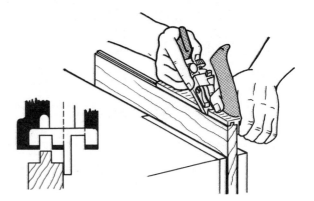

Fig. 8-68 Cutting tongue.

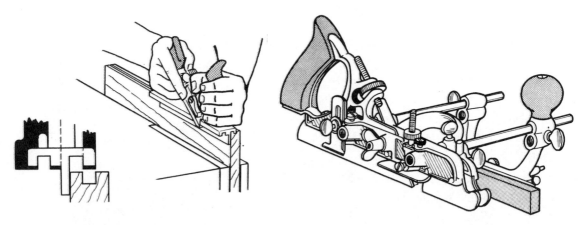

Fig. 8-69 Cutting groove.

Fig. 8-70 Universal plane.

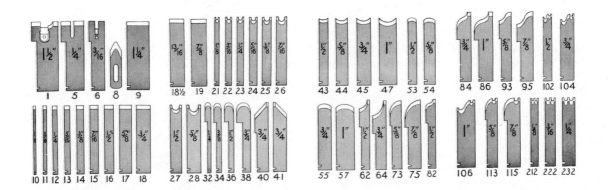

Fig. 8-71 Various blades available for the universal plane.

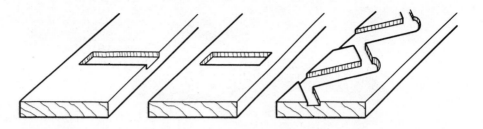

Fig. 8-72 Types of cutouts which may be made with the router plane.

discussed in detail because much of the shaping done by these special planes is now done with an electric router.

- The *rabbet plane* cuts a rectangular recess on the edges or ends of boards. See figures 8-63, 8-64, 8-65 and 8-66.

- The *double end tongue and groove match plane* puts a tongue in the edge of one board and a groove in the edge of another. See figures 8-67, 8-68, and 8-69.

- The *universal (combination) plane,* figure 8-70, is used to make fancy moldings or trim. The illustration of the blades, figure 8-71, shows the variety of shapes this plane can produce.

- The *router plane* is used to remove wood from between sawed or chiseled edges. See figures 8-72 and 8-73.

- The *circular plane,* figure 8-74, is used to plane concave or convex contours on wood.

- The *scrub plane,* figure 8-75, is used to plane off surplus wood when working to irregular lines.

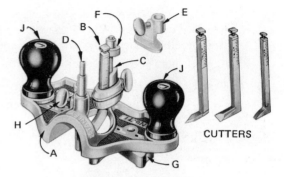

Fig. 8-73 Router plane.

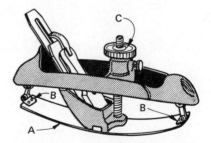

Fig. 8-74 Circular plane.

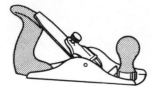

Fig. 8-75 Scrub plane.

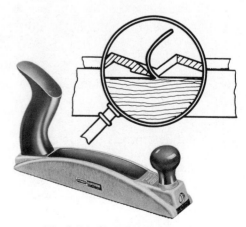

Fig. 8-76 Forming plane.

143

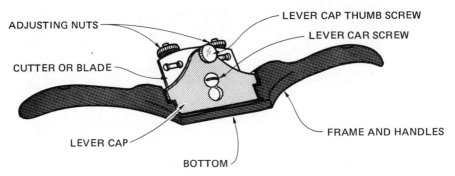

ADJUSTING NUTS

LEVER CAP THUMB SCREW

LEVER CAR SCREW

CUTTER OR BLADE

LEVER CAP

BOTTOM

FRAME AND HANDLES

Fig. 8-77 The spokeshave.

- The *forming plane,* figure 8-76, has a serrated bottom. The serrations act like a series of tiny block planes. The forming plane works well for smoothing end grain or cross grain. It is also good on edges of plywood, composition board, plastics, and soft metals.

- The *spokeshave,* figure 8-77, is a short-bottomed plane. The cutting action is the same as a plane. It can be used to follow convex and concave curves.

REVIEW QUESTIONS

A. Short Answer or Discussion

1. Describe three main differences in the construction of a block plane compared to other bench planes.

2. How can it be determined if a plane iron is sharp?

3. Where should pressure be applied in each case?

    a. when starting a stroke

    b. when finishing a stroke

4. Under what conditions should a board be planed diagonally across its surface?

5. Describe three methods to avoid splintering when planing end grain.

6. What determines the direction of the stroke when jointing?

7. What causes rounding the ends when jointing?

8. When planing end grain, how does the depth of cut differ from other types of planing cuts?

9. Describe a technique for planing an edge narrower than the width of the plane sole.

10. Show by a simple sketch the difference between a bevel and a chamfer.

11. Why use pencil gauging rather than a marking gauge for laying out a chamfer?

12. What tools are used to test the accuracy of a chamfer?

13. What is the difference between a stop chamfer and a through chamfer?

14. Why is it desirable, when cutting end grain, to have a low cutting angle on the plane iron?

15. Describe three conditions which can cause difficult cutting.

16. What is the difference between grinding and whetting?

17. Under what three conditions should a plane iron be ground?

18. What is the process by which the sharpness of a grinding wheel is restored? How often should this process be performed?

19. At what angle should the tool rest be adjusted for grinding a plane iron?

20. What indicates that the blade has been overheated in grinding?

21. Describe three possible motions in passing the plane iron over the oilstone when whetting the blade. How do these methods rate in order of effectiveness?

B. Completion

1. Name the plane preferred for each of the following operations:

    a. to surface a board 1″ x 12″ x 36″ long.

    b. to plane the edge of a door.

    c. to plane the end piece which cannot be fastened in a vise.

    d. to plane a fine finish on a rough-surfaced board.

2. The largest of the bench planes is the _____ which can be as long as _____ inches.

3. The correct angle for grinding a plane iron is _____ degrees and for whetting, the angle is _____ degrees.

4. The distance between the cutting edge of the plane iron and the front edge of the opening is called _____.

5. The throat opening is widened or narrowed by means of the _____.

6. The coarser the cut desired, the _____ the throat opening should be.

7. The double plane iron is adjusted up or down for _____ by means of the _____.

8. The bench plane blade is adjusted right or left by the _____.

9. Whenever possible, planing should be done _____ the grain.

10. The greater the resistance, the _____ should be the angle of bevel of the plane iron.

C. Identification and Interpretation

1. Identify the parts of the plane shown in figure 8-78.

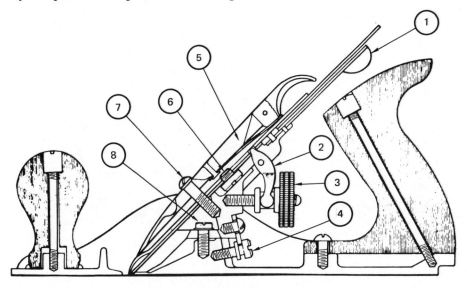

Fig. 8-78

2. Describe the three basic adjustments of the plane and state which parts control these adjustments.

3. Identify each of the planes shown in figure 8-79 and state the adjustments possible for each plane.

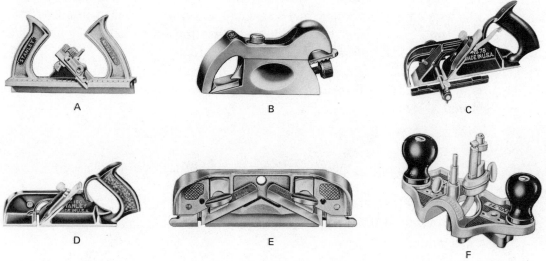

A B C

D E

F

Fig. 8-79

4. Indicate the tool that is preferred for each of the following operations:

    a. Trim the shoulder of a large recess.

    b. Cut a tongue and groove.

    c. Widen the groove of a tongue and groove joint.

    d. Plane a mortise for a drawer lock.

    e. Cut an accurate rabbet on a cabinet door.

    f. Plane the edge of a curved table top.

    g. Size large timber.

    h. Remove paint from a surface.

    i. Perform all the plane operations listed in (a) through (h).

Unit 9 EDGE CUTTING TOOLS

All tools that have a single sharpened cutting edge are known as *edge cutting tools*. The best edge tools are made from the highest quality tool steel. They are hardened and tempered to be very strong and tough, and so that they can be sharpened to a keen edge.

All edge cutting tools should be kept sharp. Sharp tools are more easily controlled, more efficient, and less likely to cause accidents than dull tools.

This unit presents the edge cutting tools (other than planes) most commonly used by the carpenter. These include the hatchet, wood chisel, gouge, marking knife, and several types of solid chisels.

HATCHETS

Hatchets are often used by the woodworker instead of a ripsaw or plane to cut away surplus wood. For rough work, hewing is often faster than ripping or planing.

Hand hatchets are made in many styles, shapes, and weights. Each is suited for a particular type of work. Those most commonly used by carpenters are the claw hatchet, half hatchet, and lathing hatchet.

The Claw Hatchet

The claw hatchet, figure 9-1, is the most practical type to use for all-around carpentry work which requires the use of a hatchet. Its construction features and weight account for its many uses. This type of hatchet has a flat head which can be used for driving, and a claw with a beveled nail slot for removing nails.

The claw hatchet can be purchased with either a single- or double-bevel cutting edge, figure 9-2. A single bevel-edge type is selected for use in trimming wood to a straight line. The bevel falls to the outside of the worker's body. The straight side

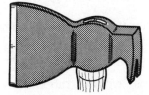

Fig. 9-1 Claw hatchet

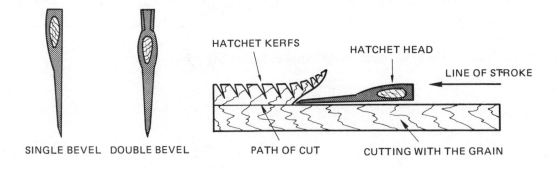

SINGLE BEVEL   DOUBLE BEVEL

HATCHET KERFS

HATCHET HEAD

LINE OF STROKE

PATH OF CUT

CUTTING WITH THE GRAIN

Fig. 9-2 Hewing with a single-bevel blade.

Fig. 9-3 Half hatchet

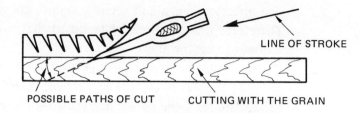

LINE OF STROKE

POSSIBLE PATHS OF CUT   CUTTING WITH THE GRAIN

Fig. 9-4 Hewing with a double-bevel blade.

of the blade is used as a guide to follow the layout line for cutting as shown in figure 9-2. Hatchets with single bevels can be used only by a right-handed worker.

The Half Hatchet

Half hatchets can also be obtained with either a single or double bevel. This type of hatchet is provided with a nail driving head and nail pulling slot, figure 9-3. It weighs less than the claw hatchet and is used mainly for light cutting.

Fig. 9-5 Lathing hatchet

Like the claw hatchet, the single bevel type can be used for hewing to a line, whereas the double bevel is used for general cutting. A double bevel type is not as adaptable for hewing to a straight line because it tends to hog into the wood as shown in figure 9-4.

The Lathing Hatchet

A lathing hatchet, figure 9-5, also referred to as a shingling hatchet, is mainly used for splitting, shaving, and nailing shingles. The blade is long and thin and has a double bevel edge. It includes a nail driving head and a nail pulling slot. Because of its thin blade and lighter weight it should not be used on heavy work.

Using a Hatchet

1. To point a stake, proceed as follows:

   a. Place the end of the stake on a wood surface to protect the cutting edge as the stroke is completed. Tilt it so that a straight chopping stroke will form the desired taper.

   b. With short, uniform chopping strokes, remove the excess material.

   c. If a conical shaped point is desired, rotate the stake with each stroke.

2. To hew to a straight line, proceed as follows:

   a. Lay out a guideline for the amount of stock to be removed.

   b. Place the work in a solid position on a surface that will not damage the edge of the hatchet if it strikes the surface. The first cuts are a series of notching cuts made in a direction across and slightly against the grain. Therefore, first position the board so that cutting is done against the grain.

c. Choose a single bevel-edge hatchet and make a series of deep cuts every inch or two. Strike the surface at an angle of 45 degrees to 60 degrees, as shown in figure 9-6.

d. Reverse the board so that cutting is done with the grain. Apply the straight side of the blade at a very small angle with the surface. Cut off the notched wood down to the depth of the cuts.

e. If more excess stock must be removed before the straight line is reached, make another series of notches. Judge the power of the hatchet strokes so that the cuts are even in depth and do not go beyond the line. Chop these notches off to the bottom of their cuts.

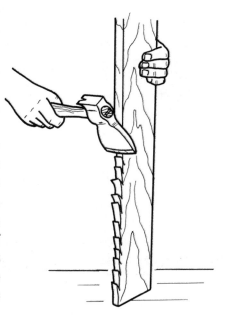

Fig. 9-6 Preliminary cuts for hewing to a straight line.

NOTE: When working close to the line, the bevel side of the blade is sometimes turned to the wood when the grain is irregular or when chopping must be done against the grain. Always chop in the direction of the grain where possible, especially with a single bevel hatchet.

3. To hew rough work, use a hatchet with a double edge and cut with the grain.

NOTE: The double bevel tends to split the wood along the grain if the stroke is heavy and if the direction of the stroke is the same as the grain.

In using either type of blade (single or double), it is better to take light strokes and gradually work off the surplus stock, rather than to take heavy strokes that are not well directed.

4. To nail and drive up tongue and groove flooring tightly, use the backside of the claw hatchet as though it were a hammer. See figure 9-7.

NOTE: When driving the flooring, use a grooved piece of wood to protect the tongue of the flooring.

5. The claw and half hatchets are also used where other types of heavy nailing are required, such as when laying subflooring.

CAUTION: When swinging the hatchet, always be aware of the danger of the sharp cutting edge, particularly on the back stroke.

SHARPENING A HATCHET

Sharpening a hatchet, as with all other edge cutting tools, is a two step operation: grinding and whetting. The edge is ground when the blade is nicked or when the bevel becomes rounded due to wear and too much whetting.

Fig. 9-7 Driving up tongue and groove flooring with a hatchet.

1. Choose a fast cutting, nonglazing type of grinding wheel.

2. Adjust the tool rest to an angle which will result in grinding the correct angle of bevel. See figure 9-8.

3. Hold the handle with the left hand, and the head with the right hand. Grind a uniform bevel with the cutting edge shaped so that it is slightly rounded. This can be done by arcing

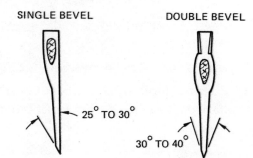

Fig. 9-8 Included angle of hatchet blades.

the edge from side to side across the face of the wheel and keeping it at the correct angle for grinding the bevel. The fingers of the right hand are under the head and in contact with the tool rest. They should act as a guide for forming a uniform bevel. Use light grinding cuts and cool the blade in a can of water.

NOTE: Hatchets with single bevels are ground only on the bevel side. Hatchets with double bevels should be ground so that both bevels are equal.

4. Whet the blade on a bench oilstone or with a handled sharpening stone. Keep the stone well oiled and guide the edge (if a bench oilstone is used) so that it is uniformly whetted. Apply the bevel to the stone at an angle slightly greater than the grinding angle.

THE HATCHET HANDLE

Sometimes it is necessary to replace the handle of a hatchet. When the handle is properly fitted, the annual rings on the end grain should run parallel to the cutting edge.

Most handles are shaped to fit the head of the hatchet in this manner because the greatest strength of the handle should be in the direction of the cutting edge or the hammer end of the blade. If the side of the hatchet is used, there is a danger of breaking the handle because the strain is placed on the weakest part of the wood.

Replacing a Hatchet Handle

1. Saw the handle off near the eye and drive it through the top of the eye with a nail set or chisel. Do not burn the wood from the eye as this destroys the temper of the steel.

2. Shape the·end of the handle so that when the head is fitted it will be square with relation to the handle. See figure 9-9. Shaping can be done with a coarse, flat crosscut file or with the spokeshave.

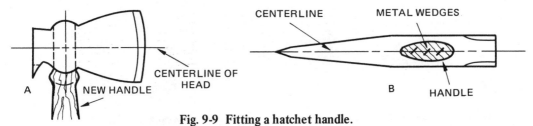

Fig. 9-9 Fitting a hatchet handle.

3. Insert the shaped end into the eye of the head. Fit it loosely enough to keep a center position as shown in figure 9-9.

4. Drive several metal wedges into the head end, A, figure 9-9.

5. Place the head of the hatchet in a can of old machine oil. If allowed to soak overnight, the wood swells and a tighter fit is obtained.

WOOD CHISELS

The carpenter's wood chisel is a steel blade treated along its entire length so that it can be sharpened to hold a keen cutting edge. Two shapes of blades are made, bevel edge and straight edge, figure 9-10. The bevel-edge blade is tapered, whereas the straight type of blade is not tapered. Most carpenters prefer the bevel-edge blade because it can reach into tight places a square-edge blade does not fit.

Blades come in different lengths, widths, and thicknesses. Therefore, some chisels have special qualities which make them better suited for certain kinds of jobs. The following wood chisels have blades of different proportions: paring, butt, firmer, and mortise. These chisels can have either straight or beveled edges.

Fig. 9-10 Wood chisel blade shapes.

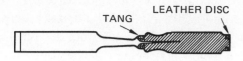

Fig. 9-11 Tang chisel

Fig. 9-12 Socket chisel

Wood chisels are also classified by the way the handle is fastened to the blade. The classifications are: tang, socket, solid, or molded. The solid and molded types are usually referred to as heavy-duty or framing chisels.

The size of a chisel is designated by the width of its blade. Blades are made in sizes from 1/8 inch to 1 inch in increments of 1/8 inch and from 1 inch to 2 inches in increments of 1/4 inch.

When ordering a wood chisel, it could be described as follows: 1/2″, tang, straight-edge, firmer chisel. The specification 1/2″ indicates the width of the blade; tang refers to the method used for fastening the blade to the handle; straightedge refers to the side edges of the blade; and firmer indicates the proportions of the blade.

The Tang Chisel

A tang chisel, figure 9-11, has a tapered end called a tang. The tang is forced into a wood handle or inserted in a molded plastic or composition handle. A metal ferrule on the handle is used to reinforce the area of the handle where the tang enters the handle.

The head end of the handle is often capped with a leather disc to protect it from becoming mushroomed when it is driven with a mallet. However, a chisel with this type of handle should not be driven except with light blows applied by a small wooden or plastic mallet. It is mainly designed for paring and other light work where hand pressure produces the cutting actions.

The Socket Chisel

On a socket chisel, figure 9-12, one end of the blade is formed into a conical shaped socket which fits over the tapered end of a wood or composition handle. The head end of the handle is fitted with a leather or metal disc to withstand the blows of a heavy mallet. Its construction is heavier than the tang chisel and its blade is thicker. Handles can be easily replaced.

The Framing (Heavy-Duty) Chisel

This type of chisel is made so that it can be driven with a steel hammer. It is constructed in one of two different ways. On one type the head of the handle, the shank, ferrule, and

BUTT CHISEL WITH MOLDED PLASTIC HANDLE

WOOD AND STEEL HANDLE CHISEL

Fig. 9-13 Framing (heavy-duty) chisels

blade are all made from one piece of steel with two sections of wood applied to form the handle, A, figure 9-13. On the other, the ferrule end of the blade and a metal head are enclosed within a molded plastic handle, B, figure 9-13. The type made from one piece of steel is preferred because it is designed so that when a blow is struck on the head, the force is carried directly to the cutting edge of the blade.

The Paring Chisel

The word paring refers to the proportions of the blade. A paring blade is lighter and thinner than the blade of other chisels. It can be straight or bevel edged. The straight-edged type is the most common. Since it should be used only for hand chiseling and paring, a tang handle is generally used.

The Firmer Chisel

This chisel differs from the paring chisel, having a longer and thicker blade which can be used for both heavy and light work. A socket type handle arrangement is most often used with this type of blade.

The Butt Chisel

The butt chisel has a shorter blade than any of the other types of chisels. Blade lengths range from 2 3/4 inches to 3 inches. The handle is usually made of plastic, molded to the blade with a metal disc included in the head of the handle. This type of chisel is used for heavy cutting and in places where a long blade does not fit.

MALLETS

Mallets are used for driving wood chisels and gouges. The heads are made from hickory, dogwood, rubber, or plastic and come in several sizes and weights. Complete specifications include the length and diameter of the head, the length of the handle, and the weight in ounces. Wooden chisel and gouge handles, other than the heavy-duty type, are less likely to be split if pounded with a mallet than if pounded with a hammer. See figure 9-14.

Using a mallet is safe when the chisel is cutting across the grain. When cutting with the grain, a mallet is likely to cause the wood to split. The mallet can be used with a chisel to

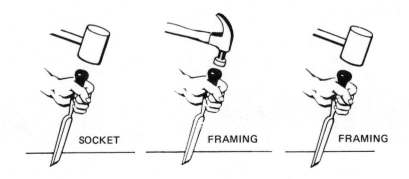

Fig. 9-14 Using force with a chisel.

clean out a mortise, to cut mortise ends when most of the material has been bored out, to cut hardwood, and to remove large amounts of material before reaching the finished size.

SAFETY PRECAUTIONS FOR USING A WOOD CHISEL

Rough cutting (removing large amounts of wood) and finish cutting are done with the wood chisel. The chisel is held with the bevel down for a roughing cut and with the bevel up for a finish cut. However, there are a few exceptions to this rule which will be discussed. When rough cutting, the force is generally applied by tapping the head of the chisel with a mallet or hammer, whereas with finish cutting, hand pressure is used. Cuts made by hand pressure are called paring cuts.

The chisel is responsible for many accidents. The best precautions against injury are to hold the tool correctly and to keep both hands back from the cutting edge at all times. Also, clamp or fasten the work so it can not move while cutting is being done.

> SAFETY NOTE: The cutting edge of the chisel should always move away from the body or any part of the body. Never hold the work in one hand and move the cutting edge of the chisel toward an observer or another operator. Wear safety glasses when making heavy cuts to protect the eyes from flying splinters.

Making a Paring Cut with a Wood Chisel (See figure 9-15).

1. To make a paring cut horizontally with the grain, proceed as follows:

    a. Fasten the work firmly in a bench vise so that cutting is done with the grain.

    b. Position the blade with the bevel side up. The flat side should rest on the surface, tilted only enough to produce a fine shaving.

Fig. 9-15 Making a paring cut.

    c. Grasp the handle of the chisel in the right hand with the thumb extended toward the blade. Hold the blade firmly with the left hand, knuckles up, and the hand well back of the cutting edge.

    d. Use the right hand to force the chisel into the wood. Push it along the surface at a slight diagonal to the direction of the cut, figure 9-16, so that a shearing cut results

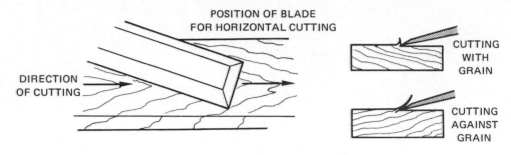

Fig. 9-16 Position of the blade for cutting.

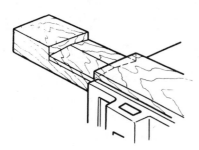

Fig. 9-17 **Roughed out gain**

Fig. 9-18 **Finishing roughed out gain with paring cuts.**

The left hand is pressed downward to control the depth of cut and also act as a guide to control the length of cut.

NOTE: Cutting should always be done with the grain, or splitting can result.

2. To cut a gain horizontally across the grain, proceed as follows: (See figures 9-17, 9-18, and 9-19.)

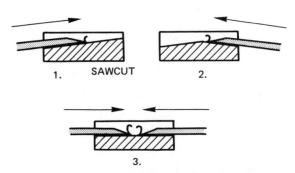

Fig. 9-19 **Sequence of cuts for cutting out a gain.**

a. Cut the shoulder of the gain down to the required distance with a saw. Mark the depth of cut with a straight line on each side of the board.

b. Hold the cutting edge of the chisel a little above the horizontal guideline, bevel face up. Point the chisel at a slight incline between the shoulder cuts so that an upward cut is taken completely across the gain between the shoulder cuts. This should remove the excess stock from the gain in a sloping cut.

c. Make a cut in the same way from the opposite side of the gain. See figure 9-18. The work is now ready to be pared to a finished depth.

d. Make the paring cuts with the flat side of the chisel face down. Use only the pressure of the right hand to drive the chisel and work from each edge toward the center. The forefinger and thumb of the left hand are pressed together to act as a brake for controlling the length of cut.

Using a Wood Chisel to Cut Vertically Across the Grain

1. Clamp the work on a bench block or bench vise. When a vise is used, the cutting is done from both edges toward the center.

2. Hold the chisel with the right hand and guide the blade with the left hand. Use the guide hand as a brake by pressing the forefinger and thumb together on the blade. See figure 9-20.

3. Tilt the chisel slightly to one side to give a shearing action to the cutting edge.

4. Start the cut so that cutting is done with the grain, figure 9-21.

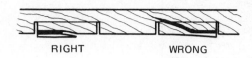

RIGHT   WRONG

Fig. 9-21 Starting a cut.

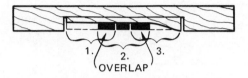

1.   2.   3.
OVERLAP

Fig. 9-22 Sequence of cuts.

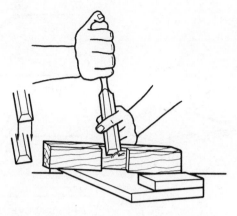

Fig. 9-20 Cutting vertically across grain.

5. If the surface is wider than the chisel, press part of the chisel against the portion just cut, figure 9-22. This helps to guide and keep in line that part of the chisel which is cutting a new portion of the surface.

> SAFETY NOTE: At all times keep both hands back of the cutting edge. Cutting should always be done away from you.

Cutting a Straight Slanting Corner

1. Clamp the work in a vise with the guideline on a horizontal plane.

2. Follow the same technique described for making a paring cut horizontally with the grain. See figure 9-23.

   NOTE: The blade is held to produce a shearing cutting action.

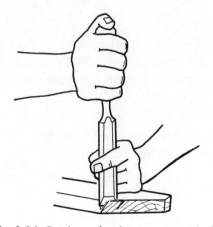

Fig. 9-23 Cutting a straight slanted corner.

Cutting a Slanting Corner, Vertically

1. Lay out a guideline on the face of the board.

2. Use the chisel in the same manner as described for vertical cutting across the grain.

   NOTE: Always work from the edge to be formed toward the end of the board so that the wood will split away from the guideline. Working from the end toward the edge splits and ruins the work, as it is cutting against the grain.

Fig. 9-24 Cutting a slanting corner, vertically.

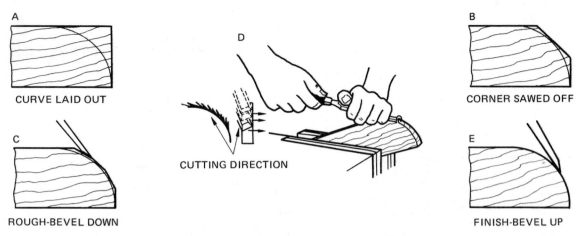

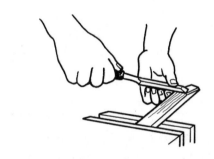

Fig. 9-25 Cutting sequence for forming a round corner.

Cutting a Round Corner

1. Lay out a guideline for the curve to be cut, A, figure 9-25.
2. Saw off the excess stock as shown at B.
3. Rough the curve with the bevel face down, C.
4. Finish with a series of paring cuts close together, each one tangent to the curve, as shown in D and E of figure 9-25. In making these cuts, the chisel is moved sideways across the work (see D) at the same time that it is moved forward, thus producing a shearing action.

Chamfering on End Grain

1. Clamp the board in a bench vise.
2. Hold the chisel bevel side up, figure 9-26.
3. Move the chisel held at a diagonal to the direction of cutting and across the corner of the work to make a shearing horizontal cut.

Cutting a Short Stopped Chamfer with a Wood Chisel

Through and long stopped chamfers are made with the bench plane and finished with a wood chisel. A short stopped chamfer is made entirely with the wood chisel.

Fig. 9-26 Cutting a chamfer on end grain.

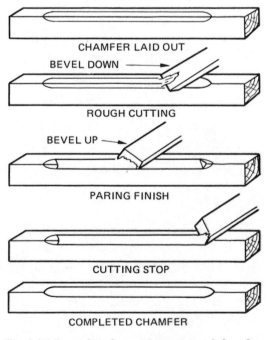

Fig. 9-27 Procedure for cutting a stopped chamfer.

1. Lay out the chamfer, figure 9-27.

2. Hold the face of the chisel parallel to the slope of the chamfer and cut with the grain as in ordinary horizontal paring.

    NOTE: If the ends of the chamfer are to be flat, use the chisel with the bevel up. If the ends are to be curved, work with the bevel face down.

3. Make the cuts from the ends toward the center. Finish the stops of chamfer last.

4. After roughing is completed, use light paring cuts to finish the chamfer to the guidelines.

    NOTE: Until skill in working with the wood chisel is gained, it is better to use a series of light paring cuts to remove all of the stock rather than to take heavy cuts.

Cutting Across a Wide Board
(See figure 9-28)

1. Clamp the work using a bench vise and bench stop.

2. Hold the chisel with the bevel face down, so the handle clears the work and the blade does not dig in too deeply as it is pushed forward.

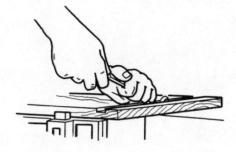

Fig. 9-28 Cutting across a wide board.

Trimming the Corners of a Tenon, Notch, Dado, or Rabbet

1. Grasp the chisel by the blade, near the edge.

2. Raise one corner of the cutting edge by tilting the handle away.

3. Draw the chisel toward you.

> SAFETY NOTE: The work is held with the left hand while the chisel edge is guided by the right hand to act like a knife. The position of the chisel and the way the work is held in figure 9-29 shows that this could be a dangerous situation. Do not rush. Be carefule to keep fingers well away from the cutting line of the chisel.

Fig. 9-29 Trimming with a wood chisel.

Cutting a Concave Curved Corner
(See figure 9-30)

1. Clamp the work in the vise so that cutting will be done with the grain.

2. Hold the bevel side of the chisel against the work with the left hand.

3. With the right hand, press down and back at the same time, giving a sweeping curved direction to the cut.

Cutting Out a Concave Curved Surface
(See figure 9-31)

1. Lay out the span and width of the curve on the surface to be cut.

2. Prepare a templet for checking the curve as it is formed.

3. Apply the chisel bevel face down using a downward and prying motion to form the curve. Work from both ends toward the center.

Cutting a Mortise Opening

Two methods can be used. One is to remove much of the material by drilling a series of overlapping holes and then trimming the remaining material. The other is to remove all of the material with a series of chisel cuts. The first method is preferred because it is easier and results in a better job.

1. When using the drilled hole method, proceed as follows:

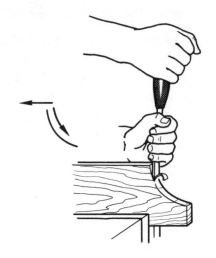

Fig. 9-30 Cutting a concave curved corner.

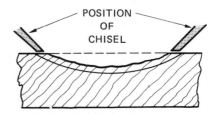

Fig. 9-31 Cutting a concave curved surface.

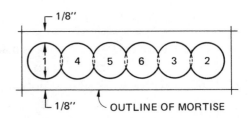

Fig. 9-32 Sequence for drilling holes.

    a. Lay out the mortise on the stock. Cut the outlines of the mortise about 1/8 inch deep with a knife to prevent these edges from splitting. See figure 9-32.

    b. Select an auger bit about 1/4 inch narrower than the width of the mortise. To insure that the depth of each hole is the same, clamp a bit gauge onto the drill at a distance that represents the depth of the mortise. Bore holes marked 1 and 2, figure 9-32, so that the bore comes 1/8 inch from the mortise outline. Now bore the remaining holes, 3, 4, 5, and 6, spacing them so that they overlap.

    c. Choose a narrow mortise or firming chisel. With hand pressure, cut out the sharp points left at the overlapped edges of the bores. Pare these down to the side outlines of the mortise. See figure 9-33.

d. Pare to the end outlines of the mortise. Sometimes this requires more force than hand pressure on the chisel. If so, use a mallet. Be sure to hold the chisel with its straight face toward the end outline of the mortise.

2. When the mortise is cut out completely with a series of chisel cuts, follow the cutting sequence in figures 9-34 and 9-35.

   NOTE: Force is applied with a mallet for the roughing out operation. Use a chisel which is 1/8 inch less in width than the finished mortise width. Finishing to size is done with a series of paring cuts.

SHARPENING A WOOD CHISEL

The method for sharpening a wood chisel is the same as that of sharpening a bench plane iron blade. The edge is first ground to an included angle of 25 degrees to 30 degrees for rough cutting and to 20 degrees for finish cutting (paring). Whetting is done on an oilstone to produce a keen cutting edge.

WOOD GOUGES

A wood gouge is a chisel used for cutting or smoothing hollows and grooves and paring the ends of irregular surfaces which must be matched together. The blade on this type of chisel is curved. Three different blade curvatures are made — a flat sweep, a medium sweep, and a regular sweep, as shown in figure 9-36. The widths of the blades range from 1/8 inch to 2 inches. Handle arrangements are similar to that of the regular flat-faced chisel.

The cutting edge is ground to a bevel on either the inside or the outside of the curved blade. From this, the names inside gouge and outside gouge are applied. See figure 9-37.

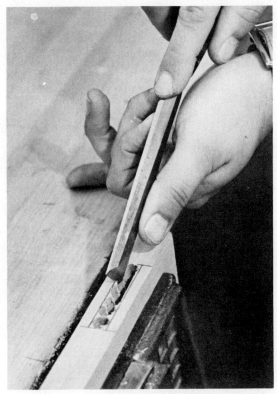

Fig. 9-33 Paring the mortise.

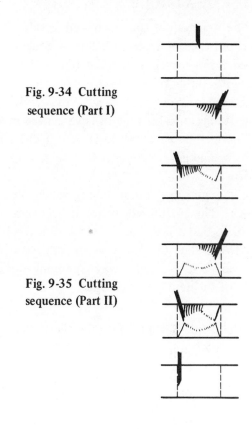

Fig. 9-34 Cutting sequence (Part I)

Fig. 9-35 Cutting sequence (Part II)

FLAT   MIDDLE   REGULAR

Fig. 9-36 Types of blade curvatures.

A   B

Fig. 9-37 (A) Outside ground (B) Inside ground.

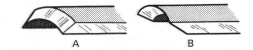

Fig. 9-38 Straight-shank gouge.

The shank of a gouge can be either straight, figure 9-38, or bent, figure 9-39. A bent shank raises the handle clear of the work, allowing it to cut a long groove. The bevel for this type of tool is usually ground on the inside.

In some cases, small chisels, such as carving tools, are used by carpenters for fitting hardware. These tools, as shown in figure 9-40, come in sets made up of various shaped blades with skew and V cutting edges, straight gouges, front-bent gouges, and others. The overall length is about 8 inches. The tools have rounded handles and can be worked easily with one hand.

Fig. 9-39 Bent-shank gouge.

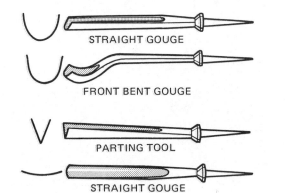

STRAIGHT GOUGE

FRONT BENT GOUGE

PARTING TOOL

STRAIGHT GOUGE

Fig. 9-40 Carving tools.

THE USE OF A GOUGE

The techniques for using an inside- and an outside-bevel gouge differ. A gouge with an inside bevel is handled like a flat chisel with the bevel up, that is, the blade must be held almost parallel with the groove being pared. If it is held tilted too high or out of line, it digs in. This type of edge is used mainly for finishing cuts.

The outside-bevel gouge is used in the same manner as a chisel with the bevel down. It is used for making roughing cuts. The handle is raised when cutting so that it does not interfere with the work.

When gouging, avoid taking heavy cuts; rather take cuts which produce long, thin shavings. The cutting edge should be rotated slightly from side to side as the gouge is pushed forward so that a shearing cutting action results.

Always start the gouge at the edge and work toward the center. In this way, splitting of the edges is avoided. When gouging out a large recess, cut across the grain for better control of the depth of each cut.

Using the Inside-Bevel Gouge (See figure 9-42.)

NOTE: This type of gouge is suitable for cutting short grooves which start from an edge. For long grooves and those which start away from the edge, the bent-shank type or the outside-bevel gouge is used.

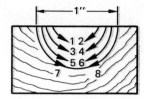

Fig. 9-41 **Sequence of cuts for gouging.**

1. To gouge a one-inch cut of a regular (full) sweep (figure 9-41), proceed as follows:

    a. Select a 1/2-inch or 5/8-inch regular sweep inside gouge.

    NOTE: Do not try to make a con-

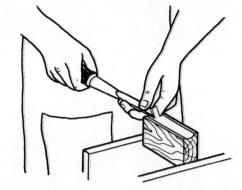

Fig. 9-42 **Cutting a groove with an inside-bevel gouge.**

cave cut into wood by using a gouge the same width as the cut desired.

    b. Hold and work the gouge like a straight chisel with the bevel up.

    c. Start from the edge and on the centerline of the cut and pare to the right and left by first using the right-side cutting edge of the gouge and then the left. Use the sequence of strokes shown in figure 9-41. Work from the edge toward the center.

    NOTE: Do not try to use the full cutting edge of the gouge as it tends to catch into the fibers, making cutting difficult and pulling it out of line.

    d. Take light cuts by rotating the gouge from right to left, for a shearing action. Gradually pare the outlines of the cut as with a straight chisel.

    e. To finish the cut to the outlines, a wider gouge can be used, but never use a gouge so large that both edges of the sweep cut the wood at the same time.

    f. If the outline of the cut is of medium or flat sweep, use a medium- or flat-sweep gouge.

Using the Outside-Bevel Gouge

1. The outside-bevel gouge is used in the same general way as the inside-bevel gouge except that it is held at a greater angle to the surface because the bevel is on the outside.

    NOTE: Once cutting has started, the angle at which the gouge is tilted to produce a cutting action should be maintained constant throughout the cut.

2. When used for cutting a groove stopped at both ends, work from each stop toward the center of the groove.

Sharpening Gouges

NOTE: As with other edge cutting tools, two operations are performed to sharpen a gouge: grinding and whetting.

1. To sharpen an outside-bevel gouge, proceed as follows:

    a. Hold the gouge so that it rests on the tool rest across the wheel as shown in figure 9-43. Rotate the bevel on a vertical plane against the moving grindstone wheel until a feather edge is formed on the straight surface of the gouge.

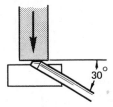

Fig. 9-43 Grinding an outside-bevel gouge.

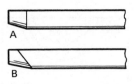

Fig. 9-44 (A) Correctly ground bevel, (B) Incorrectly ground bevel.

NOTE: The completed bevel should appear as in A, figure 9-44. An incorrectly ground bevel is shown in B.

b. Use a slipstone, figure 9-45, to remove the wire edge on the straight side of the gouge. This is done by placing the slipstone within the concave portion of the gouge and rotating it over the entire edge.

c. Apply the bevel to a flat oilstone and move the gouge forward and backward on the stone while using a rocking motion from side to side to remove any of the turned feather edge. See figure 9-46.

d. Alternately whet the bevel and then the straight side until the feather edge is removed and a keen edge is produced.

2. To sharpen an inside-bevel gouge a specially shaped wheel is required. Whetting of the inside bevel is done with a slipstone, and the straight side of the gouge is applied to a flat-faced oilstone.

Fig. 9-45 Types of slipstones.

Fig. 9-46 Whetting an outside-bevel gouge.

Fig. 9-47 Marking knife (Sloyd knife).

THE MARKING KNIFE

The marking knife, figure 9-47, often referred to as a Sloyd knife, has a blade sharpened with a double bevel. The marking knife is used for accurate marking across the grain of the wood. The mark made with this tool has two purposes: to produce a guideline for cutting and to score the grain to prevent splitting when a cut is made to the mark. In order that the mark can be easily seen, a sharp pencil is drawn along the scored mark.

The marking knife is also used for whittling and light paring. When used for this purpose, direct the stroke away from the body to avoid injury. The pocket jacknife can be used in place of the marking knife to fulfill the same functions. In many cases, the jackknife is preferred as a marking tool because of its thinner blade and gently tapering bevels.

Using a Marking Knife

1. When marking a guideline across grain, proceed as follows:
   a. Measure off the distance to locate the point or points at which scored marks are to be made.
   b. Hold the knife along a straightedge tilted at about 60 degrees in the direction of cutting and, starting at the far side, pull the knife toward you. Use enough pressure to produce a fine scored mark. Go over this mark with a sharp pencil to make it visible.
   c. If cutting is to be done to the mark, go over the mark several times to make it deeper. Then, tilt the blade slightly to the side and cut away the fibers so that the blade has clearance on the waste side as shown in figure 9-48.

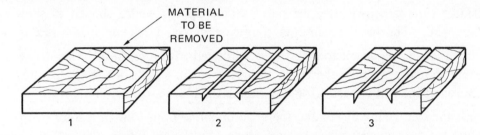

Fig. 9-48 Sequence for marking with a knife.

2. Figure 9-49 illustrates other uses of the knife. Notice that in each case the actual part to be fitted is used as the straightedge. If a board is used as a straightedge, as in B, great care must be taken to keep the cutting edge from cutting the board used as a guide.

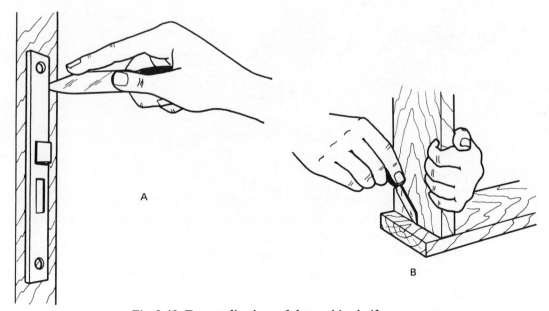

Fig. 9-49 Two applications of the marking knife.

Sharpening a Marking Knife

> NOTE: Generally this type of edge does not need grinding. The blade is fine enough so that it can be sharpened by applying it to a rough oilstone to remove any knicks and then to a fine oilstone for final sharpening.

Fig. 9-50 Two types of bevels.

1. If grinding is necessary, use the bevel on the blade as a guide for the correct angle of application to the wheel. The sides of the grinding wheel are generally used for this type of grinding.

2. Apply the knife to the wheel with the edge up and use very light pressure to produce the grinding action. Grind the opposite bevel on the other side of the wheel and alternately grind each side until a feather edge appears. Guide the blade so that grinding is done evenly with an equal amount done on both sides of the blade.

   NOTE: For carpentry use, the bevel should appear wedge shaped as shown in A, figure 9-50. The bevel commonly found on newly purchased blades is shown in B.

3. Whet the blade on an oilstone until the feathered edge is removed. Use strokes against the cutting edge, moving the blade along the entire length of the stone. Reverse the direction at the end of each stroke by rolling the blade as shown in figure 9-51.

4. Finish the sharpening by honing the edge on a fine Lily stone or leather strop. Stroke against the cutting edge when using a stone. Stroke away from the cutting edge when using a leather strop.

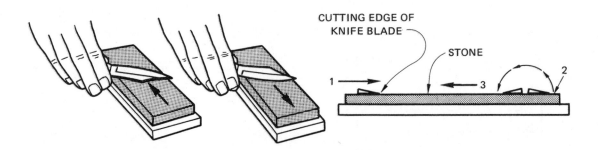

Fig. 9-51 Whetting a knife.

OTHER TYPES OF CHISELS

Other types of chisels, figure 9-52, are used by the carpenter to perform operations that are not possible with the common wood chisel. These tools are designed to cut nails, concrete, and other hard materials.

The cold chisel is mainly used to do metal cutting such as shearing a bolt or cutting heavy wire mesh. A long-bladed cold chisel (sometimes called a floor and clapboard chisel) is used for cutting through floors, lath, etc. where there is danger of hitting nails. The wide-bladed cold chisel (electrician's cutting chisel) is designed to cut off the tongue on floorboards

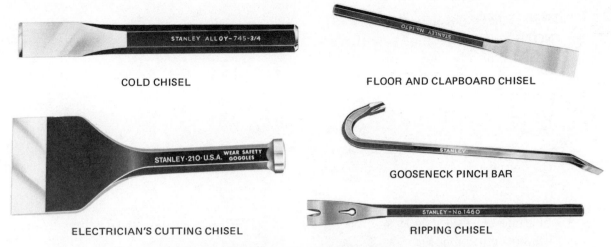

COLD CHISEL   FLOOR AND CLAPBOARD CHISEL

GOOSENECK PINCH BAR

ELECTRICIAN'S CUTTING CHISEL   RIPPING CHISEL

Fig. 9-52 Miscellaneous types of chisels used by carpenters.

and for use where a lot of cutting is needed which can also involve cutting into metal. The pinch bar and ripping chisel are used for ripping up flooring and siding and for other heavy dismantling operations. Slots are provided in these tools for pulling nails.

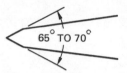

Fig. 9-53 Included angle.

These tools are made so that a hammer or sledge can be used on them to start the cutting or ripping action. Heads which become mushroomed should be renewed to their original shape by grinding.

These tools are sharpened by grinding. The bevels on cold chisels are ground to an included angle of 65 degrees to 70 degrees, figure 9-53. It is good practice to grind the tool to its original bevel.

REVIEW QUESTIONS

A. Short Answer or Discussion

1. Why is hewing to a line more difficult with a double bevel-edge hatchet than with one having a single bevel edge?

2. Describe two safety precautions to observe in using hatchets.

3. When using a hatchet to drive up tongue and groove flooring, how is the tongue of the flooring protected from damage?

4. Why is a hatchet handle likely to break if the side of the hatchet is used for striking a hammer blow?

5. How is the size of a chisel designated?

6. Which chisels are designed to be used with a mallet and which are designed for hand pressure alone?

7. In general, where should the bevel of the chisel face for (a) roughing cuts, and (b) finishing cuts?

8. In using the drilled hole method for cutting a mortise, what layout technique helps prevent splitting of the mortise edges?

9. State two precautions to observe when using chisels and gouges.

10. How does the wood gouge blade differ from the wood chisel blade?

11. What is the advantage of a bent-shank wood gouge?

12. What do the terms "inside" and "outside" refer to in distinguishing these two types of wood gouges?

13. How do the techniques for using an inside- and an outside-bevel gouge differ?

14. Describe two situations where a marking knife rather than a pencil is desired for laying out a guideline.

B. Completion

1. In hewing to a straight line with a hatchet, the first series of cuts should be _____ the grain.

2. The chisel handle which can be driven with a steel hammer is the _____ type.

3. When finish cutting with a wood chisel, pressure is applied by _____.

4. The curve of a wood gouge is called _____.

5. When cutting short grooves which start from an edge, the _____ gouge should be used.

6. When making a concave cut with a gouge, the gouge size should be _____ the width of the cut.

7. The weakest of the three handle arrangements used on chisels is the _____ type.

8. The chisel with the thinnest blade, and thus the weakest, is the _____ chisel.

9. To avoid splitting the grain, chisel cuts should be made from the _____ toward the _____.

10. The technique for sharpening a wood chisel is the same as that for sharpening _____.

C. Identification

Explain what, if anything, is wrong in A, B, C, and D, figure 9-54.

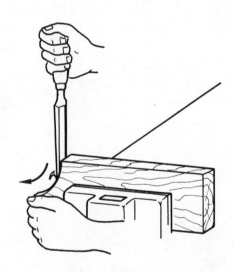

A. TRIMMING A CONCAVE EDGE

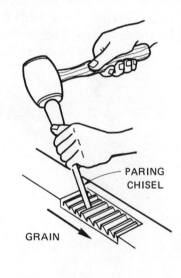

B. CHISELING A HINGE GAIN

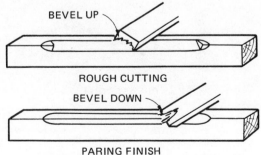

C. CUTTING A STOPPED CHAMFER

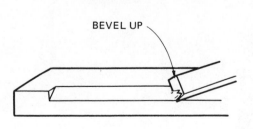

D. CUTTING A STOPPED CHAMFER WITH FLAT ENDS

Fig. 9-54

Unit 10 BORING TOOLS

Boring tools used by the carpenter include the bit brace, corner brace, hand drill, breast drill, and the automatic drill, figure 10-1. Cutters (drills and bits) inserted into these tools are used to bore holes for bolts, screws, and pipe, to provide a starting point for inside sawing and to aid in making various types of wood joints.

BITS AND DRILLS

The bits and drills used for boring tools are the auger bit, straight-shank twist drill, brace drills (twist drill and bit stock drill), Forstner bit, expansive bit, and fluted drill (automatic drill bit), figure 10-2. The material, size, location, and purpose of the hole to be drilled or bored determine the type of bit used.

Drills or bits which have a tapered square tang on the end of the shank are used with the bit brace. Bits with flats ground on the shank are used with a brace, breast drill, or power drill. Straight-shank twist drills are used with the hand and breast drill, and fluted drills with the automatic drill.

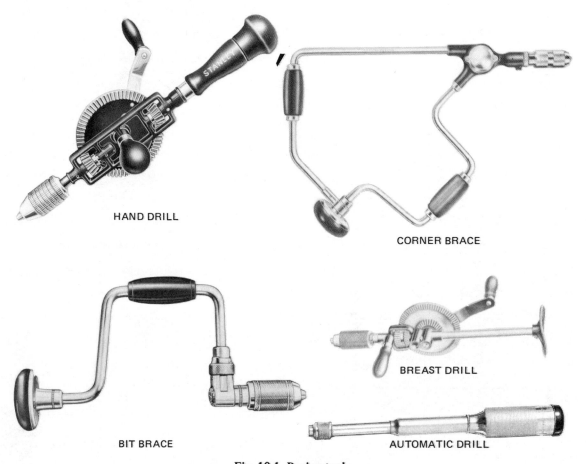

HAND DRILL

CORNER BRACE

BIT BRACE

BREAST DRILL

AUTOMATIC DRILL

Fig. 10-1 Boring tools

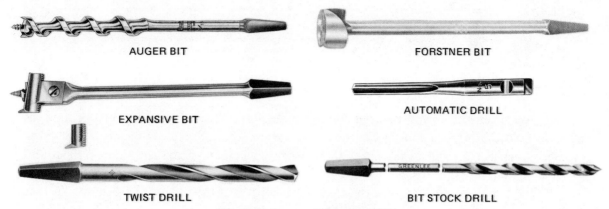

AUGER BIT

FORSTNER BIT

EXPANSIVE BIT

AUTOMATIC DRILL

TWIST DRILL

BIT STOCK DRILL

Fig. 10-2 Types of bits and drills.

Other tools which can be used with the various braces and hand drills include the screwdriver bit; countersink; combination wood drill and countersink; and combination wood drill, countersink and counterbore, figure 10-3. A detailed explanation of each is presented later in this unit.

THE AUGER BIT

The auger bit is used in a brace for drilling holes in wood and other soft materials. It cannot be used for drilling metal.

In general, auger bits are made in three lengths. The dowel (short) bit is about 5 inches long, the medium length about 8 inches long, and the ship (long) bit is between 18 inches and 24 inches long. Other lengths (special purpose bits) are also made. Manufacturers of bits often use their own terms for their bits. Therefore, refer to the manufacturer's catalog when ordering auger bits.

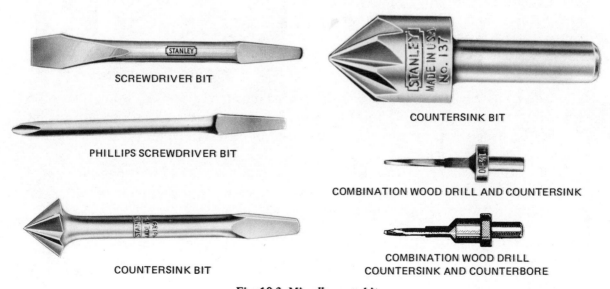

SCREWDRIVER BIT

COUNTERSINK BIT

PHILLIPS SCREWDRIVER BIT

COMBINATION WOOD DRILL AND COUNTERSINK

COUNTERSINK BIT

COMBINATION WOOD DRILL
COUNTERSINK AND COUNTERBORE

Fig. 10-3 Miscellaneous bits.

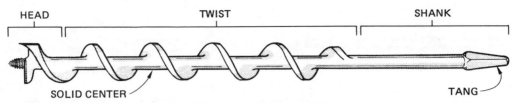

SOLID CENTER   TANG

Fig. 10-4 Parts of an auger bit.

Short auger bits should be used whenever possible. When a long bit must be used, be sure to hold the bit at a constant angle to the surface being bored. If the angle is changed while boring, the bit will bend. For general work the carpenter uses the medium length bit with a medium thread feedscrew.

All types of auger bits have the same parts with slight differences, figure 10-4. Like parts serve the same purpose for all bits.

The Twist

There are three styles of auger bits. The difference is in the twist and the center core. The styles are straight-core or solid-center auger bits, single twist (spiral center), and double twist, as shown in figure 10-5.

Carpenters prefer the single-twist, solid-center bit. These bits are stronger and clear themselves of chips quickly.

A single-twist bit has less tendency to bind in certain materials than the solid-center bit.

The double-twist bit bores more slowly than the others but cuts more smoothly and accurately. This type of bit is often used to bore holes required for doweled joints.

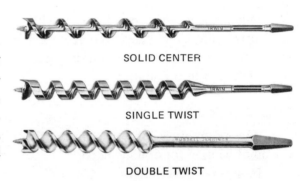

SOLID CENTER

SINGLE TWIST

DOUBLE TWIST

Fig. 10-5 Types of bits.

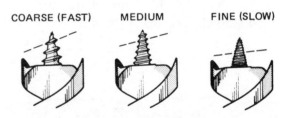

COARSE (FAST)   MEDIUM   FINE (SLOW)

Fig. 10-6 Types of screws.

The Screw

Auger bits come with coarse-, medium-, and fine-thread screws, figure 10-6. The screw centers and pulls the bit into the material. The cut made on each turn of the bit depends on the pitch of the threads of the screw. In other words, the pitch of the screw determines the feed of the bit.

The medium-screw type bit is used for general carpentry work. Fine-screw bits are used where a fine feed is needed to produce a smooth surface. Coarse-screw bits are used where rapid cutting is necessary, such as rough boring by electricians.

The Spurs

The spurs, as shown in figure 10-7, touch the wood immediately after the screw. The spurs score the outer edge of the chip ahead of the cutter. A short spur does not cut the

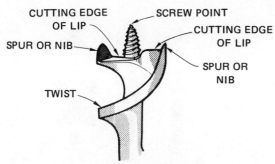

Fig. 10-7 Parts of the head.

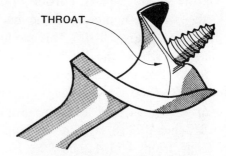

Fig. 10-8 Location of the throat.

edge of the chip completely and makes boring difficult. An ideal spur is one whose length is suited to the feed of the bit, with enough metal back of the cutting edge for strength. If this area is too thick the spur will act as a wedge and drag in the wood.

The Cutting Lips

The cutting lips follow the spurs and cut the chips starting them up the throat to the twist. It is important that the edges of the two opposite cutters be on the same level and that they are beveled to the proper angle for clearance. If the lips are not in line, one lip does more than half the work. As chips leave the cutter, they flow through the throat of the bit.

The Throat (Clearance) (See figure 10-8.)

When choosing a bit, pick one with enough room in the throat for the chips to leave the cutting lips. The twist receives the chips from the throat and conveys them to the mouth of the hole. Ample room in the twist keeps the chips moving freely. The outside diameter of the twist of a bit should be slightly less than the diameter of the head. This difference allows the twist to follow the head into the hole without friction.

The Shank

The shank, figure 10-9, is the part of the bit that fits into the chuck of the brace. Its end has four tapered sides (square-shaped tang). All four sides must have exactly the same bevel, or the bit tends to swing off center.

Some auger bits are made so that they can be used in an electric hand drill or in a brace. These bits come with a square, tapered shank, and six equally spaced flats are ground on the shank just below the tang. When used with a power drill, the square, tapered portion must be sawed off to fit the drill chuck. Since there are three jaws in the chuck of the power drill, they clamp on every other flat ground on the shank. The bit can still be used in a hand brace by clamping any two opposite corners of the flats in the grooves of the chuck.

Fig. 10-9 Auger bit with an adapter shank.

On the square, tapered portion of the shank the size (a number) of the bit is stamped. See figure 10-10. This number represents the size of the drill in sixteenths of an inch. For example, a bit with the number 7 stamped on the tang indicates a size of 7/16 inch, and a number 8 indicates a 1/2-inch drill (8/16 inch = 1/2 inch). Sizes range from 4 (1/4 inch), to 16 (1 inch), in increments of 1/16 inch.

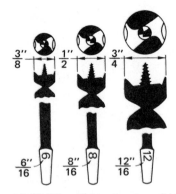

Fig. 10-10 Identifying the size of a bit.

For holes under 1/4 inch and over 1 inch, other types of drills are used. Holes less than 1/4 inch in diameter are made with a straight-shank twist drill or double-fluted drill. Sizes larger than 1 inch in diameter are bored with an expansive or Forstner bit. In all cases, the size of the drill or bit is stamped on the shank. However, different methods are used to indicate the size. An explanation of this is given as each drill is described in detail later in this unit.

Fig. 10-11 Marking with a scratch awl.

Starting an Auger Bit

1. Locate the position of the hole with two intersecting lines (figure 10-11).

2. With a scratch awl, make an impression in the board deep enough so that the point of the feedscrew easily seats itself and will not wander as the brace is turned.

CARING FOR AUGER BITS

Things to consider in the care of a bit are preventing it from rusting, storing it properly, and keeping it sharp. Moisture from the hand, or sap from green timber can cause rust spots. This can be prevented by wiping off the bit with an oily rag after each use if the bit gets wet.

Bits should be stored in special containers rather than mixed in with other tools. Wood chests or plastic bags with seats or pockets for each bit are made for this purpose. Cutting edges can also be protected by fastening a cork or block of wood on the feedscrew.

When the spurs and cutters on a bit become dull, they are sharpened by filing. In general, bits are filed more than is necessary. It is not possible to file away much metal from the head of the bit without reducing its boring quality. Look at the bit carefully before filing it. The screw should not be touched with a file.

Resharpening a Spur on an Auger Bit

1. Select an auger bit file, figure 10-12.

2. Rest the bit on a board with the screw pointing up. File the inside of the spurs with the flat side of the file, using only forward strokes to produce the filing action. See figure 10-13.

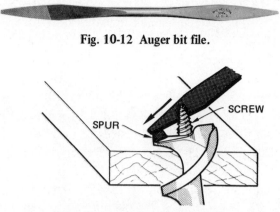

Fig. 10-12 Auger bit file.

3. Continue to file until the leading edge of the spur has a knifelike edge. NOTE: Filing must be done so that there is enough clearance toward the back of the spur. Therefore, filing should be done across the complete inside face of the spur rather than just on the leading edge.

Fig. 10-13 Sharpening the spur.

4. Do not file the outside of the spur unless the bit is damaged so much that it enlarges the outside diameter of the bit. If this is the case, carefully lay the flat side of the file flat against the outside of the spur. Rotate the file around the spur surface until the curled metal is brought in line with the outside of the lip. Then, file the inside edge of the spur to a sharp edge.

NOTE: Unnecessary filing of the spur on the outside removes some of the clearance of the bit which causes binding when cutting. Another method for bringing a bent spur in line is to place the inside of the spur on the edge of an anvil and then to tap the bent portion with a hammer.

Sharpening the Cutters on an Auger Bit

1. Choose an auger bit file. A good second cut, half-round or three-cornered file can also be used, providing its size fits the surfaces to be filed.

2. Rest the bit on a board with the screw down. Tilt the bit so that the cutter can be sharpened. See figure 10-14.

3. Apply the flat, serrated side of the file to the underside of the lips, the side toward the shank. Never file the side toward the screw. Use forward strokes to produce the filing action. File far back into the throat. Do not leave the edge too blunt; the desirable result is a gradual taper from a keen edge.

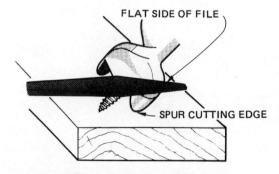

Fig. 10-14 Sharpening a cutting lip.

4. Reposition the bit, and file the opposite cutting edge in a like manner. Both edges should be filed to the same level to produce chips of equal thickness.

Restraightening an Auger Bit

1. Roll the bit on a level wood surface until the bend is located.

2. Tap it on the high side with light blows of a hammer.

3. Check it for final trueness by rolling it on a flat metal surface.

THE STRAIGHT-SHANK TWIST DRILL

The straight-shank twist drill, figure 10-15, is used in the hand drill or breast drill for drilling holes in wood or metal.

Fig. 10-15 Straight-shank twist drill.

The size of a straight-shank twist drill is given in one of three ways: by a fraction (in increments of 1/64 inch); by a number; or by a letter which is stamped on the shank.

The fraction designation is the actual diameter of the drill. The number or letter only identifies the drill. The sizes of number and letter sized drills can be found on a chart or drill gauge. These sizes are given in decimals of an inch. For example, a drill with the letter W stamped on its shank is 0.386 inch in diameter, and a number 10 drill is 0.166 inch in diameter. Numbered drills range from 1 (0.338 inch) through 80 (0.0135 inch). Lettered sizes range from A (0.234 inch) through Z (0.413 inch). Note that the numbered drills are the smaller sizes and the letter sizes start where the numbered sizes end.

Starting a Twist Drill

1. Lay out intersecting lines to locate where the hole is to be drilled.
2. Use a center punch and hammer to make an impression in the surface. A scratch awl can be used for this purpose if wood is to be drilled.
3. Fit the point of the drill in the impression and start drilling.

Sharpening a Straight-Shank Twist Drill

NOTE: Sharpening this type of drill must be done on a grinder.

1. With the tool rest adjusted on a horizontal plane, scribe 59-degree lines on its face as shown in A, figure 10-16. In this case the tool rest serves only as a reference point for sighting the angle at which to hold the drill and not as a support.

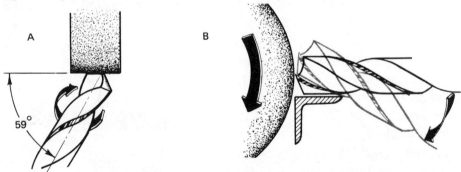

Fig. 10-16 Sharpening a straight-shank twist drill.

2. Place one cutting edge (lip) against the face of the wheel at a 59-degree angle (A, figure 10-16). As soon as the edge touches the grinder, raise the cutting edge and at the same time lower the shank end of the drill rotating it very slightly (B, figure 10-16). This movement should produce the correct drill angles. See figure 10-17.

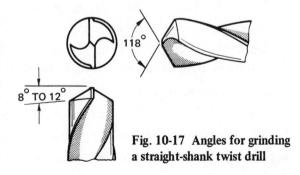

Fig. 10-17 Angles for grinding a straight-shank twist drill

NOTE: Keep the cutting edge on a horizontal plane throughout the grinding operation. Cool the drill often by dipping it in a can of water to avoid burning the cutting edges.

3. Grind the opposite cutting edge in the same way. The same amount of grinding should be done on each cutting edge so that the point of the drill will be centered.

4. Check the size (span) of each cutting edge with a steel scale graduated in sixty-fourths of an inch. Grind the longest edge until both edges are equal.

BRACE DRILLS

Two types of brace drills are used by the carpenter: the wood-boring twist drill, used to drill holes in hardwood; and the bit stock drill, also called an iron drill, used to drill metal. Both types include a square, tapered tang on the end of the shank, as shown in figure 10-18.

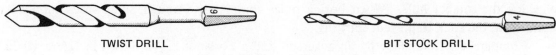

TWIST DRILL   BIT STOCK DRILL

Fig. 10-18 Types of brace drills.

The wood-boring twist drills range in size from 1/8 inch to 1/2 inch in increments of thirty-seconds of an inch. See figure 10-19. The number of thirty-seconds is marked on the tang. This drill has the point ground to an included angle of 60 degrees so that it can enter the wood easily, whereas the bit stock drill has the point ground to an included angle of 118 degrees. The bit stock drills range in size from 1/16 inch to 5/8 inch in increments of sixty-fourths of an inch, and are used on metal, and sometimes wood.

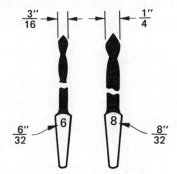

Fig. 10-19 Twist drill sizes.

Sharpening Brace Drills

Follow the same procedure described for sharpening a straight-shank twist drill. However, when grinding the wood-boring type, grind the point to an included angle of 60 degrees with a clearance angle of from 10 degrees to 12 degrees. See figure 10-20.

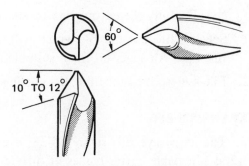

Fig. 10-20 Point angles for grinding twist drills.

FORSTNER BIT

The Forstner bit, figure 10-21, is a different type of bit. It has no screw, spurs, or twist. Cutting is done by two lips and a

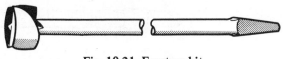

Fig. 10-21 Forstner bit.

circular steel rim. Sizes of these bits range from 1/4 inch to 2 inches in diameter. They are numbered on the tang in the same way as an auger bit. For example, a number 6 Forstner bit is 6/16 inch or 3/8 inch in diameter. This bit is used to bore holes not possible with auger bits. Where a hole must be bored partway through the stock, the auger bit screw or spur can pierce through the stock. The Forstner bit, which

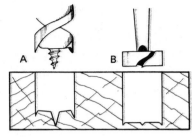

Fig. 10-22 Holes made by (A) auger bit and (B) Forstner bit.

has no screw or spur, prevents this from happening. This bit can also be used on end grain, thin wood, or near an end where an auger bit would split the work. Because it has no screw, it can be used to bore a larger hole where a smaller hole has already been bored without first plugging the smaller hole. When boring holes completely through, scrap stock should be clamped to the back to prevent splitting.

Compare the hole made by an auger bit and a Forstner bit as shown in figure 10-22.

NOTE: The Forstner bit provides a smooth bottom to the bore, while the auger bit leaves the impression of the feedscrew and spurs. Since this type of bit has no screw, centering it is more difficult.

Starting a Forstner Bit

1. Lay out intersecting lines to locate the hole.

2. Scribe a circle the size of the hole using dividers. Go over the circle several times so that the dividers score the wood rather deeply.

3. Press the rim of the Forstner bit into the scribed circle.

4. Start to bore as with an auger bit.

Sharpening a Forstner Bit

NOTE: Only the cutting lips are sharpened on this type of bit.

1. Select a fine-cut flat file which will fit into the openings forming the bevels of the cutting lips. An auger bit file is suitable for this purpose.

2. File as described for filing the cutting lips of an auger bit.

EXPANSIVE BIT

The expansive bit, figure 10-23, is used to bore holes larger than 1 inch in diameter. Several adjustable cutter blades of different sizes are supplied with this bit. The bit can be

Fig. 10-23 Expansive bit

adjusted to a range of sizes up to 4 inches. Each cutter can be adjusted for a range of sizes within its own limits of span by an integral screw type device on the head of the bit.

The expansive bit is made in several styles. One style uses a micro-dial in the head of the bit for making size adjustments. Another style uses a simple screw arrangement. For the screw arrangement, one complete turn of the cutter adjusting screw enlarges or reduces the hole 1/8 inch; one-half turn, 1/16 inch.

After the cutter is set, it is locked in place with a setscrew. Size adjustments are checked by measuring from the tip of the feedscrew to the outside edge of the spur, and by making trial cuts in scrap wood. These should be made only after the cutter is locked in place.

When using this bit, bore until the lead screw appears on one side. Then turn the work over and finish boring from the opposite side. The spur and cutting lip on the cutter are sharpened while held in the head of the bit in the same way as described for sharpening an auger bit. The bit and cutters should be kept in a protective case so that the cutting edges are not damaged.

THE AUTOMATIC DRILL BIT (FLUTED)

This type of bit, shown in figure 10-24, is made especially for use with the automatic drill. However, it can be used in a hand drill. The application of this bit is mainly for boring small holes in wood. It cannot be used to drill metal. Sizes are stamped on the shank and range from 1/16 inch to 11/64 inch in increments of sixty-fourths of an inch.

SCREWDRIVER BITS

The straight screwdriver bit, A, figure 10-25, and a Phillips point, B, are made for use with the brace. Both types are manufactured in a variety of sizes. Regular screwdriver bits have tips which range in size from 3/16 inch to 1/2 inch. The Phillips type is made in three point sizes, numbers 1, 2, and 3. The Phillips bits are capable of driving Phillips screws and bolts, numbers 4 to 16 and smaller.

Driving screws with the brace takes less effort and it can be done quickly. A disadvantage is the danger of twisting off a screw because of the great amount of leverage possible. When selecting a screwdriver bit for use, it is very important that it fits the head of the screw properly.

COUNTERSINKS

Countersinks are used to seat the head of a flathead screw flush with the surface that is countersunk. These are made for both the bit brace and the hand drill. Observe that

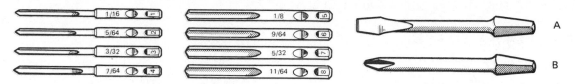

Fig. 10-24 Automatic drill bits.   Fig. 10-25 Screwdriver bits.

Fig. 10-26 Types of countersinks.

there are two distinct types which can be used with the hand drill (B and C, figure 10-26). Type C is preferred for use when a smoothly finished countersunk hole is desired. Type B cuts more rapidly, but produces a rough surface.

Countersinking is usually done after the hole has been drilled. A countersunk hole can be checked for size by holding the screw head up against the hole.

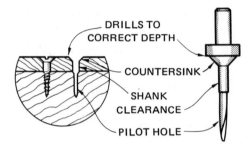

Fig. 10-27 Combination wood drill and countersink

THE COMBINATION WOOD DRILL AND COUNTERSINK

This type of drill, shown in figure 10-27, makes the pilot hole, shank clearance, and countersink to correct depth for woodscrews in one operation. It is suitable for use in a hand, breast, or power drill.

A variety of sizes are made (ranging from 1/2 x No. 5 to 2 x No. 12) capable

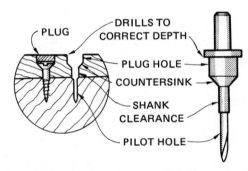

Fig. 10-28 Combination wood drill, countersink and counterbore

of drilling the holes necessary for driving the common sizes of screws used by carpenters. The size of the drill determines the size of the screw for which it is suited. For example, a 1/2 x No. 5 drill is used for a flathead woodscrew 1/2 inch long having a number 5 (about 1/8 inch) body size. A size 2 x No. 12 indicates that it is used for a screw 2 inches long having a number 12 (about 7/32 inch) body size.

THE COMBINATION WOOD DRILL, COUNTERSINK, AND COUNTERBORE

This type of drill, shown in figure 10-28, performs all the operations done by the combination wood drill and countersink, plus drilling holes for wood plugs (counterboring). It is made in a number of sizes ranging from 1 x No. 8 to 2 x No. 18. The significance of its size is similar to that of the combination wood drill and countersink.

THE BIT BRACE

A bit brace, figure 10-29, is used to hold, turn, and guide bits, drills, and countersinks which have a square tang or have flats ground on the shank. A universal type of chuck which holds all sizes of square-shank bits is most commonly used.

Bit braces are made with or without a ratchet device. The ratchet type is useful because it functions well in confined spaces where there is not enough room to make a complete sweep (turn) of the handle. The ratchet can be locked or made to operate in either direction (clockwise or counterclockwise).

A brace's size is determined by the sweep of its handle, that is, the diameter made by revolving the handle. Where the leverage is needed, a brace with a small 8-inch sweep is used. Larger-sweep braces are used for turning expansive bits or for boring large holes in hardwood. A 10-inch sweep brace is an average size for general carpentry work.

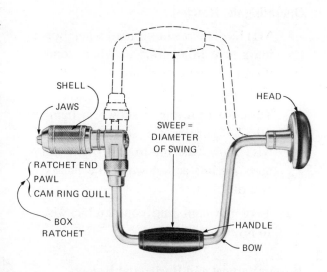

Fig. 10-29 Parts of a bit brace.

The better quality braces have ball bearing heads and are nickel-plated to resist rust. Oil holes are usually provided at the working parts. Oiling should be done from time to time so the brace works smoothly.

Inserting a Bit in a Brace

1. To open the chuck for inserting a bit, grasp the chuck with the left hand. With the right hand, turn the handle to the left to unscrew the chuck body from the shell (A, figure 10-30). A few turns will open up the jaws so that the bit tang and shank can be inserted into the socket (B, figure 10-30).

2. When the bit is in place, grasp the handle with the right hand and the chuck with the left hand. Turn the handle to the right until the bit is held firmly in the jaws.

Figure 10-31 shows the working details of a common bit brace chuck. Note that each jaw has a v-shaped groove. Two opposite corners of the taper shank of the bit should be carefully seated in these v grooves, or else the drill revolves off center.

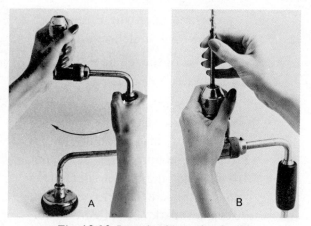

Fig. 10-30 Inserting bit in the chuck.

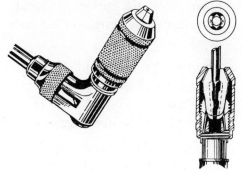

Fig. 10-31 Details of bit brace chuck.

Operating the Ratchet

NOTE: The ratchet is used when boring a hole in a corner or where some object prevents making a full turn with the handle.

1. Turn the cam ring as shown in figure 10-32. Turning the cam ring clockwise allows the bit to turn right and gives ratchet action when the handle is turned left.

2. Turn the cam ring counterclockwise to reverse the action.

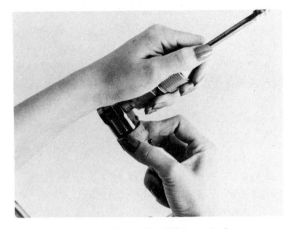

Fig. 10-32 Setting the ratchet.

Boring Vertical and Horizontal Holes

1. To bore a vertical hole, proceed as follows:

    a. Be sure the stock to be bored is in a fixed position so that it does not move when being bored.

    b. Lay out and mark the location of the hole with a scratch awl.

    c. Insert a bit of the required size into the bit brace.

    d. Place the point of the bit on the center mark. Hold the brace so that the bit is at right angles to the surface to be bored. See A, figure 10-33. Test the bit for squareness with a try square from two positions 90 degrees apart. See B, figure 10-33.

    NOTE: One clue that the bit is square with the surface is if both spurs scribe the surface at the same depth.

    e. Revolve the sweep of the brace slowly clockwise, and at the same time bear down on the knob of the brace so that the bit screw enters the wood. Try to keep the knob in a steady position and keep an even pressure.

Fig. 10-33 Boring a vertical hole.

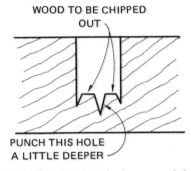

WOOD TO BE CHIPPED OUT

PUNCH THIS HOLE A LITTLE DEEPER

Fig. 10-34 Chipping out the bottom of the bore.

NOTE: If the pressure used is not enough, the threads of the feedscrew fill up with broken off wood chips, making boring difficult. To correct this condition, remove the bit from the bore and chip out the bottom of the bore with a chisel, figure 10-34.

With a nail set or nail, make the impression of the feedscrew a little deeper. Also clean out the threads on the feedscrew. Be careful not to damage the threads.

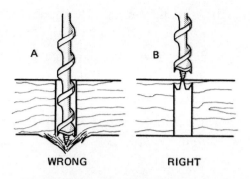

f. Continue boring. If the hole is to be through the entire thickness of the board, stop boring as soon as the feedscrew shows on the opposite side of the board.

NOTE: If the bit enters the wood with difficulty, back it out occasionally to clean the chips from the hole. This reduces friction and heating which can cause the bit to bend.

Fig. 10-35 Wrong and right methods of boring.

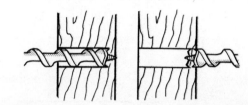

g. Withdraw the bit from the hole by turning the handle in the opposite direction (counterclockwise).

h. Finish boring the hole from the opposite side of the board, using the feedscrew hole as a center. Use a light pressure and guard against breaking through to the starting side. See A, figure 10-35.

NOTE: Another method of boring a hole completely through without splintering is to back up the board with a piece of scrap.

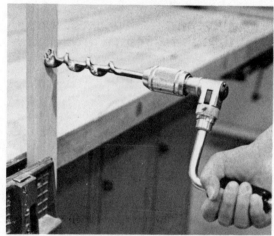

Fig. 10-36 Horizontal boring.

2. To bore a horizontal hole, proceed as follows:

a. Locate, insert, and start the bit as described for vertical boring.

b. Sight the drill for squareness on a horizontal and vertical plane as the handle is slowly revolved. Bore slowly to control the bit and maintain it in its correct position.

c. Complete the boring as described for vertical boring.

NOTE: If drilling is to be done near an end such as in figure 10-36, the board can split due to the wedging action of the feedscrew. To avoid this, first drill a pilot hole about 3/16 inch in diameter through the board before boring.

Boring a Hole at an Angle

1. When a hole is to be bored at a slight angle, proceed as follows:

a. Lay out the angle on a thin piece of cardboard or plywood. This can be used as a guide in the same manner as the try square. A sliding T bevel set at the correct angle can be used in the same way.

b. Align the bit with the guides. Check the angles from two reference points. The bit should be tilted toward the operator in line with the length of the hole.

c. Bore slowly and continue to bore until the feedscrew shows on the opposite side.

d. Finish boring from the opposite side, keeping the bit in line with the part of the hole already bored.

2. When a hole is to be bored at a sharp angle, proceed as follows:

NOTE: For this type of boring, a wood guide is necessary.

a. Prepare a guide as follows.

1. Bore a vertical hole through a block of wood using the same size auger bit that will be used in making the finished hole. See A, figure 10-37.

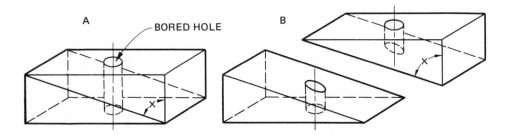

Fig. 10-37 Guide for boring.

2. Lay out angle X (A, figure 10-37), which is the guide angle of the hole, and saw off the bottom of the block.

b. With a compass or dividers, scribe the circumference of the hole to be bored on the surface of the board.

c. Line up the guide hole circumference with the scribed circumference and fasten the block to the board by nailing or clamping. See figure 10-38.

d. Insert the bit in the guide hole and start to bore slowly. When boring a through hole, clamp a scrap piece to the back of the board and complete the boring by cutting into the scrap piece.

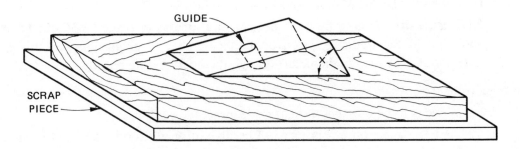

Fig. 10-38 Guide in position for boring.

Enlarging a Hole with an Auger Bit

1. Plug the hole already bored with a dowel rod flush with both surfaces.

2. Lay out and mark the center of the larger hole to be bored.

3. Place the feedscrew on the center mark and proceed to bore.

    NOTE: This method is often used to rebore holes which have been bored off center or out of line.

Boring a Hole to a Depth

NOTE: When drilling or boring a hole to a certain depth, one of several types of bit gauges is used. Bit gauges are made to clamp or fit to an auger bit or countersink. Several types are shown in figure 10-39.

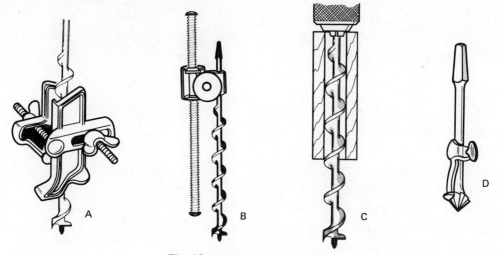

Fig. 10-39 Types of bit gauges.

A piece of a block of wood bored and cut to a given length is shown at C. This is slipped over the bit, with the length of the bit beyond the block equal to the depth of the hole to be drilled. The block is forced against the chuck of the brace and acts as a stop. At D is shown a depth gauge for the countersink.

1. Select the type of bit gauge to be used. If type A, figure 10-40, is used, open it to permit fitting the bit by releasing the wingnuts.

2. Slide the bit gauge down over the screw of the bit from the tang end. This way the gauge does not hit and possibly damage the feedscrew, cutting lips, or the spurs.

3. Set the gauge close to the depth of cut desired and tighten the wing nuts.

4. With a rule, measure the setting from the cutting lip to the bottom of the bit gauge. Make any necessary adjustment by loosening the wing nuts only enough to allow moving the stop to the correct setting.

5. Tighten the bit gauge in place and make a final check of the depth setting.

    NOTE: Care should be taken not to draw up the wing nut too tightly. If too much pressure is used, the cast iron gauge can break.

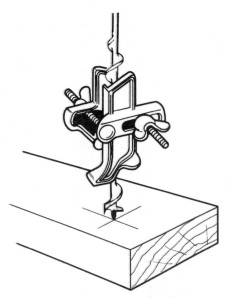

Fig. 10-40 Boring a hole to depth with a bit gauge.

6. Refer to figure 10-40. Insert the bit with the attached bit gauge in a brace and bore as described for vertical boring.

7. As the bottom of the bit gauge approaches the surface of the board, reduce the boring speed. Continue to bore until the bit stop contacts the surface. After contacting the surface, revolve the bit about one complete turn (using no pressure) to clean out the bottom of the hole.

8. Remove the bit from the hole, using a counterclockwise motion.

9. Use the other types of gauges in a like manner. For type B, figure 10-39, the stop is fastened to the shank.

Fig. 10-41 Doweling jig.

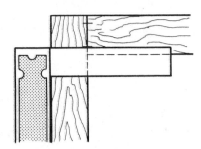

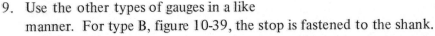

Fig. 10-42 Laying out holes.

NOTE: For all types of bit stops, when the stop touches the surface being bored, release the pressure and make one full turn with the brace. This keeps the surface from being scratched by the stop. This also cleans out the bottom of the hole.

THE DOWELING JIG

A doweling jig, figure 10-41, is a device used to guide an auger bit for boring dowel holes in the end, edge, or surface of wood with ease and accuracy. It is also used as a guide for boring out holes for a mortise. The clamping device on the doweling jig can be used on material up to three inches thick.

The doweling jig is useful for drilling holes at right angles and in line with one another. It reduces the amount of layout work. Holes can be drilled a certain distance from the edge. This distance can be duplicated on another edge easily.

Guides into which the bit is inserted range in size from 3/16 inch to 3/4 inch. A depth gauge (bit stop) is also made which is to be used with the doweling jig.

Using a Doweling Jig

NOTE: The procedure described applies to making a corner dowel joint.

1. Mark on the face side of the two parts a centerline for any number of dowels desired.

2. Choose the proper size bit guide and set it, bevel end up, in the slide with the bottom of the guide flush with the underside. See figure 10-43.

   NOTE: The size of the bit guide selected is the size of the dowel rod to be used.

3. Adjust the slide, aligning the index line for the guide chosen. This determines the distance the hole will be drilled from the top face side of the material.

   NOTE: An index line, figure 10-44, is given for each guide or bit size. To use and set a No. 6 guide, use the No. 6 index on the slide for a graduation. The graduation represents the distance from the center of a 1-inch piece of wood. Adjust the slide to the 1/2-inch graduation mark and fasten it securely with the thumbscrew.

4. Place the jig on one of the pieces of stock with the fence next to the face side of the board. Bring the centerline, A, of the jig in alignment with one of the center marks on the board.

   NOTE: Clamp the jig securely.

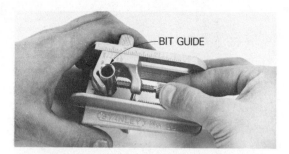

Fig. 10-43 Locking bit guide in place.

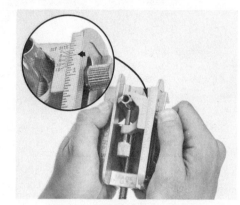

Fig. 10-44 Aligning index line.

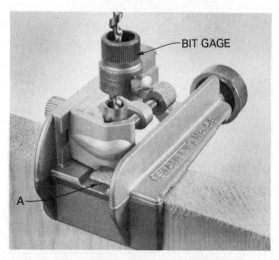

Fig. 10-45 Attaching and aligning the doweling jig.

Fig. 10-46 Boring with a doweling jig.

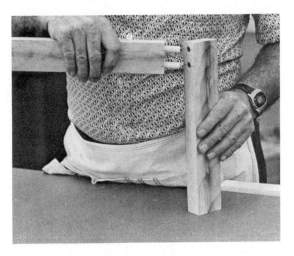

Fig. 10-47 Assembling a dowel joint.

5. Slide the bit gauge over the shank of the bit and tighten it lightly near the top of the twist. Insert and fasten the drill in the brace.

    NOTE: The wider opening of the bit gauge is placed face down. When not used with a doweling jig it is reversed. See figure 10-45.

6. Measure the vertical distance from the tip of the twist to the cutting lip. It is about 1/4 inch.

7. Refer to figure 10-46. Place the bit into the guide using care not to strike the cutting edges of the bit against the guide. Rest the tip of the feedscrew lightly on the side of the board.

8. Adjust the bit gauge for depth of bore taking into consideration the vertical distance (1/4 inch) of the feedscrew. If a 1-inch depth is desired, the gap between the guide and bit gauge should be 1 inch plus 1/4 inch (the vertical distance from the tip of the feedscrew to the cutting lip).

9. Proceed to bore until the bit gauge contacts the guide.

10. Reposition the jig and bore the remaining holes using the same method of setting up for each.

11. Refer to figure 10-47. Place the dowels in the holes and complete the joint.

THE CORNER BIT BRACE

There are several types of corner braces. They are used for boring holes located in corners. The type shown in figure 10-48 is short so that it can be used under shelving. A ratchet device permits boring without making a full sweep of the handle.

Fig. 10-48 Corner bit brace.

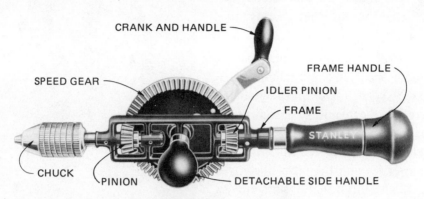

CRANK AND HANDLE

FRAME HANDLE

SPEED GEAR

IDLER PINION

FRAME

CHUCK

PINION

DETACHABLE SIDE HANDLE

Fig. 10-49 Parts of a hand drill.

THE HAND DRILL

Hand drills, figure 10-49, are for drilling holes 1/4 inch or less in either wood or metal. Straight-shank twist drills are most often used with this tool, however, automatic drill bits are also used. The largest size chuck for this type of drill is 1/4 inch. For larger size drills, the breast drill is used.

Many manufacturers of this drill make a hollow handle with a screw top for storing drills. Drills ranging in sizes from 1/16 inch to 11/64 inch in diameter are included.

Inserting and Removing Bits from the Chuck of the Hand Drill

1. Open the chuck larger than the diameter of the bit and insert the bit. Tighten the chuck by pushing forward on the crank with the right hand, while holding the chuck shell with the left hand, figure 10-50.

2. To remove the bit, hold the chuck shell with the left hand and turn the crank backward with the right hand as shown by the arrow in figure 10-51.

Drilling Holes with a Hand Drill

1. Locate the holes to be drilled with intersecting lines. If holes are to be drilled in wood, make an impression in the wood with a scratch awl for starting the drill. When drilling into metal, make a mark with a center punch.

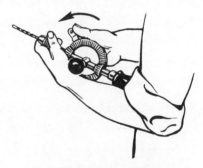

Fig. 10-50 Inserting a bit.

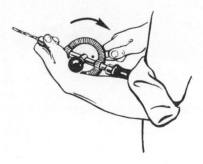

Fig. 10-51 Removing a bit.

2. Insert the bit in the chuck as previously described. Be sure that it is fastened tightly, and that it bottoms in the chuck.

3. Rest the drill point on the impression and rotate the crank and handle at a moderate speed. Use only enough pressure on the handle to produce a cutting action. Do not wobble the drill while turning, or the hole will be drilled oversize and the bit is likely to break. Sight the drill for squareness of drilling.

4. As the drill nears the end, reduce the speed of drilling and the pressure applied.

   NOTE: This is done when drilling holes through wood. The reduced speed and pressure prevent the end of the hole from splintering. When drilling metal, it must be done to avoid breaking the bit. Do not drill beyond the length of the twist on the bit because the chips will not be able to be cleared from the hole.

Fig. 10-52 Drilling a vertical hole.

5. When drilling horizontal holes, use the drill as shown in A, figure 10-53. Again, sight the drill for squareness of drilling.

   NOTE: The gear to which the crank handle is attached is held on a vertical plane and falls to the right. The hand drill is best controlled in this position.

   Sometimes it helps to hold the drill by the side handle and press the body against the frame handle like a breast drill. See B, figure 10-53.

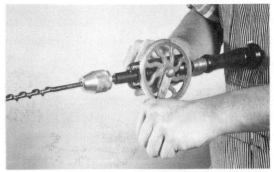

A   B

Fig. 10-53 Drilling a horizontal hole.

Drilling Holes to a Uniform Depth

NOTE: To drill holes of uniform depth it is necessary that a depth gauge be made.

1. Cut a piece of wood or dowel to a length which allows the drill to project the desired depth.

2. Drill the dowel completely through with the hole perpendicular to the bottom of the dowel.

3. Slip the dowel over the bit as shown in figure 10-54. Check the amount that the bit projects with a rule. Slight adjustments can be made by sliding the shank of the bit in or out of the chuck.

4. Proceed to drill the hole until the dowel meets the surface of the wood.

5. Remove the drill by continuing to turn it in the same direction (clockwise) and at the same time withdrawing the drill. This technique keeps the bit from becoming loose in the chuck and getting stuck as the hand drill is withdrawn.

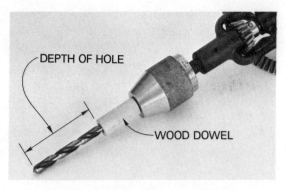

DEPTH OF HOLE

WOOD DOWEL

Fig. 10-54 Dowel used as a depth gauge.

HAND DRILL   BREAST DRILL

Fig. 10-55 A comparison of the hand drill and the breast drill.

THE BREAST DRILL

A breast drill is a larger and stronger version of the hand drill. A comparison of its size with the hand drill is shown in figure 10-55.

This type of drill usually has a chuck that can hold drills up to 1/2 inch diameter. As with the hand drill, straight-shank drills must be used in the chuck.

The breast drill is fitted with a plate, C, figure 10-55, instead of a handle. For feeding the drill, pressure is applied to the plate by the chest or stomach of the operator. Most breast drills have two speeds.

A speed change is made by engaging the driving wheel spindle in either of two driving gears, A or B, figure 10-55. When engaged in the larger gear, B, a high-speed spindle revolution is produced. This higher speed is used with small size drills. It is better to use the regular hand drill for drilling holes less than 1/4 inch in diameter. The smaller driving gear, A, transmits greater power but less speed to the spindle and is preferred for drilling large holes or drilling in hard materials.

Using a Breast Drill

1. Insert the bit in the chuck as described for the hand drill.

2. Locate and mark the hole (for wood, with a scratch awl; for metal, with a center punch).

3. Locate the drill point in the mark. With the chest resting on the plate, proceed to drill by turning the crank and handle in a clockwise direction. See figure 10-56. Only a minimum of pressure should be applied to the plate.

NOTE: Follow the same precautions as described for using the hand drill.

THE AUTOMATIC DRILL

The automatic drill, figure 10-57 (often referred to as the automatic push drill), is used for rapidly drilling small holes (from 1/16 inch to 11/64 inch) in wood. It is useful to make pilot holes for woodscrews.

Only straight fluted drills with special shanks can be used in the chuck of this type of drill. Storage of the drills is provided for in the handle.

This tool differs from others in the rotation of the drill. A forward (clockwise) and backward (counterclockwise) rotating motion is given to the drill by alternately pushing down on the handle and at the end of the stroke releasing the pressure. The return spring action reverses the rotation of the drill point clearing the chips from the hole.

Fig. 10-56 Using a breast drill.

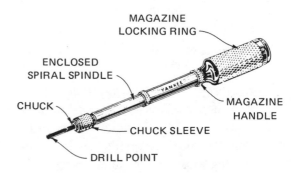

Fig. 10-57 Automatic drill.

Using the Automatic Drill

1. Determine the drill size to use. For screw holes, refer to table 10-1 describing drill points to use in an automatic drill for wood screws.

Number Of Screw	0	1	2	3	4	5	6	7	8
Body Diameter Of Screw	1/16"	5/64"	3/32"	3/32"	7/64"	1/8"	9/64"	5/32"	11/64"
Drill To Use For First Hole For The Smooth Shank Of Screw	1/16"	5/64"	3/32"	7/64"	1/8"	1/8"	9/64"	5/32"	11/64"
Drill To Use For Pilot Hole For Threaded End Of Screw	X	X	1/16"	5/64"	5/64"	3/32"	7/64"	1/8"	1/8"

Table 10-1 Drill points to use in automatic drill for wood screws.

2. Choose the drill point from the magazine. To open the magazine handle, turn the lock ring to the left, A, figure 10-58. Draw the magazine handle down and turn it to select the desired drill size, B, figure 10-58. After selecting the drill, slide the magazine handle back in place and lock it.

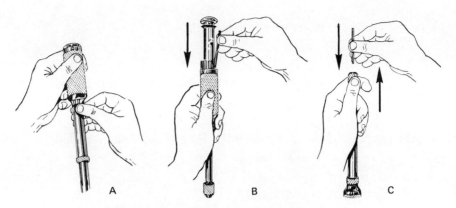

Fig. 10-58 Selecting and inserting drill point.

3. Push the chuck sleeve forward. Insert the drill point and turn it until
   seated. See C, figure 10-58. Release
   the chuck sleeve. Drilling can now
   be done.

4. Place the drill point on the mark for
   locating the hole and begin drilling as
   shown in figure 10-59. Apply pressure to the handle in line with the drill
   point, or else the point can bend or
   break.

5. Remove the drill by pulling it directly
   back from the hole.

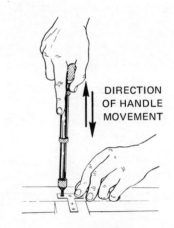

DIRECTION
OF HANDLE
MOVEMENT

Fig. 10-59 Drilling.

REVIEW QUESTIONS

A. Short Answer or Discussion

1. Describe the uses of each of the parts of the head and twist of an auger bit.

2. What type of twist is most commonly used? Why?

3. What is the purpose of the adaptor shank provided on some types of auger bits?

4. By what three methods are the sizes of straight-shank twist drills designated?

5. What is signified by the number 8 on the tang of a wood-boring twist drill? If this
   same number appears on the tang of a bit stock (iron) drill, what is signified? What is
   the difference in size increments between these two types of brace bits?

6. What are the unique features of a Forstner bit?

7. Describe the advantages of the Forstner bit. What disadvantage does it have?

8. What is the purpose of the expansive bit? How is the size expanded?

9. What is the purpose of a countersink?

10. What is signified by a 3/4 x No. 12 combination wood drill and countersink?

11. What types of tools can use a combination wood drill, countersink, and counterbore?

12. What types of tangs does the bit brace require?

13. If the auger bit feedscrew tends to fill up with broken off wood chips when boring with the bit brace, how can this be corrected?

14. Describe two ways of avoiding splintering when boring a through hole.

15. How can splitting the wood be avoided when boring near the end of a board?

16. Describe the technique for making a guide to bore holes accurately at an angle.

17. What technique is used with an auger bit to bore a larger hole than one already bored, or to correct a hole bored off center or out of line?

18. Describe how to improvise a simple bit gauge.

19. What are the main differences between a hand drill and a breast drill?

B. Completion

1. The three lengths of auger bits are the _____ bit, about 5 inches long, the _____ bit, about _____ long, and the _____ bit, from 18 inches to 24 inches long.

2. Twist drills are sized in _____ of an inch.

3. The less the pitch of the auger bit screw, the _____ the feed of the bit.

4. The size of a bit brace is determined by its _____.

5. The auger bit _____ score the wood ahead of the cutting lips.

6. Wood-boring twist drills are sized in _____ of an inch.

7. The outside diameter of the twist of a bit should be _____ than the diameter of the head.

8. Auger bits are sized in _____ of an inch; therefore, the number 9 on the _____ indicates a _____ bit.

9. Bit stock (iron) drills are sized in _____ of an inch.

10. Holes under 1/4 inch in diameter are made with _____ or _____ bits.

11. Forstner bits are sized in _____ of an inch.

12. The device used to govern the depth of drilled or bored holes is the _____.

13. Holes over 1 inch in diameter are bored with _____ or _____ bits.

14. Wood-boring twist drills are sharpened to an included angle of _____ while bit stock (iron) drills are sharpened to a _____ included angle.

15. Automatic or fluted drill bits are sized in _____ of an inch.

16. Drills sized in sixty-fourths of an inch are suitable for drilling _____.

C. Identification and Interpretation

1. On the sketch in figure 10-60, a vertical hole has been bored before making an angle gauge. Show how to lay out the saw cut to make a gauge to bore holes at a 60-degree angle with the surface of the wood.

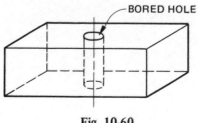

Fig. 10-60

2. Identify each bit or drill shown in figure 10-61. State the range of sizes, size increments, and the tools in which each can be used.

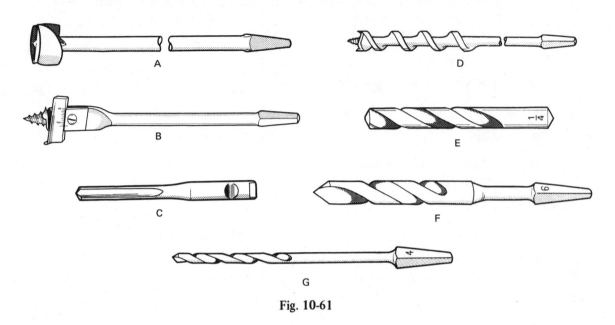

Fig. 10-61

Unit 11 FASTENERS – NAILS

This unit concerns nails and corrugated fasteners used by the carpenter in building construction. The unit also explains how fasteners and tools for these fasteners are used.

THE HOLDING POWER OF NAILS

The holding power of a nail depends on its size, shape, and surface treatment. The pressure of the wood fibers in contact with the surface of the nail also affects the holding power. Wood fibers are compressed and displaced from their original location when the nail is driven. The tendency of these fibers to spring back to their original location builds a pressure against the surface of the nail. It also increases the holding power even on smooth surface nails. Hardwood fibers give greater pressure than softwood fibers.

To increase their holding power, nails are barbed, grooved or coated, or are made with shanks of different shapes, figure 11-1. Nails can be barbed either their full length or partially, near the head. Fully barbed nails are desirable in shorter lengths since less nail is being used to provide holding power. Grooved nails are grooved for their full length, either with longitudinal or spiral-type grooves. As the nail is driven into the wood, fibers are compressed into the grooves holding the nail more firmly. Coated nails give more holding power by the adhesive action of the coating between the nail and the wood fibers. The coating also prevents rust.

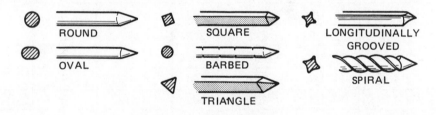

Fig. 11-1 Types of shanks.

The point of the nail, figure 11-2, also contributes to its holding power. In general, nails having long points have greater holding capacity. Points which are blunt have less tendency to split the work.

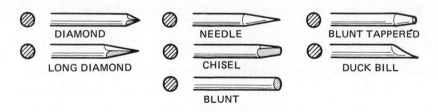

Fig. 11-2 Types of nail points.

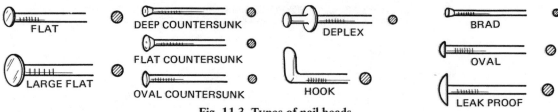

Fig. 11-3 Types of nail heads.

Nails are prepared with various shaped heads, figure 11-3, to suit specific job needs. Generally, nails with broad heads have greater holding power.

NAIL SIZES

Most nails are sized by the penny system of measure. Originally, this system indicated price per hundred. It still uses the abbreviation "d" for *denarius,* an ancient Roman coin and the penny of Biblical days. Today, however, the system indicates the length of the nail. The length and diameter (given as a gauge number) are standard for each type and weight of nail, and are given in table 11-1. Note that a 2d nail is one inch in length. For each additional penny, 1/4 inch is added up to 3 inches. After 3 inches, this rule does not apply.

Size	Length (inches)	Gauge #	Approx. No. to lb.	Size	Length (inches)	Gauge #	Approx. No. to lb.
2d	1	15	876	10d	3	9	69
3d	1 1/4	14	568	12d	3 1/4	9	63
4d	1 1/2	12 1/2	316	16d	3 1/2	8	49
5d	1 3/4	12 1/2	271	20d	4	6	31
6d	2	11 1/2	181	30d	4 1/2	5	24
7d	2 1/4	11 1/2	161	40d	5	4	18
8d	2 1/2	10 1/4	106	50d	5 1/2	3	14
9d	2 3/4	10 1/4	96	60d	6	2	11

Table 11-1 Common wire nails.

Nails larger than 20d are called *spikes* and are generally sized by inches, such as 4 1/2 inches, 5 inches, etc. Those smaller than 2d are also sized by inch measure in fractions. Certain types of nails are designated by the inch system of measure for their full range of sizes. These include brads, roofing nails, hinge nails, and drywall nails.

CONVENTIONAL FORMS OF NAILS

Conventional forms of nails include the common wire nail, box nail, finishing nail, casing nail, flooring brad, cut nail, clinch nail, and special purpose nails. Each type, except for the cut nail, is a piece of wire of suitable length with one end flattened to form a head. Cut nails are made from flat metal sheets.

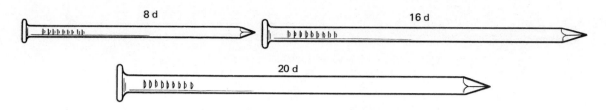

Fig. 11-4 Common nails (actual size).

Common Wire Nails

Common wire nails, figure 11-4, are used by the carpenter for joining together all framing members and for securing sheathing, subflooring and roofing boards to the framework. A size commonly used in fastening framing materials together is the 16d (16 penny) nail which is 3 1/2 inches long and is made from 8-gauge wire. An 8-gauge wire is about 5/32 inch in diameter.

The 8d nail, which is 2 1/2 inches long, is made from 10 1/4-gauge wire, which is slightly over 1/8 inch in diameter. This size is used a great deal in fastening subflooring, wall sheathing, and roofing boards to the framework.

Spikes (nails over 20d size) are often used in fastening headers and trimmers in floors, sidewalls, and roof framing. The 16d or 20d nails are used in building up plates, girders, corner posts, and in fastening studding and rafters in place.

Box Nail

A box nail, figure 11-5, is similar to a common nail except that it is more slender; thus it has less tendency to cause splitting. It is used in fastening wall insulating boards

6 d

Fig. 11-5 Box nail

and outside surface coverings such as bevel siding. The shank of this nail is often barbed and rosin coated to prevent corrosion and increase holding power. The length and diameter (gauge number) for smooth and barbed box nails are given in table 11-2.

Size	Length (inches)	Gauge #	Approx. No. to lb.	Size	Length (inches)	Gauge #	Approx. No. to lb.
2d	1	15 1/2	1010	9d	2 3/4	11 1/2	132
3d	1 1/4	14 1/2	635	10d	3	10 1/2	94
4d	1 1/2	14	473	12d	3 1/4	10 1/2	88
5d	1 3/4	14	406	16d	3 1/2	10	71
6d	2	12 1/2	236	20d	4	9	52
7d	2 1/4	12 1/2	210	30d	4 1/2	9	46
8d	2 1/2	11 1/2	145	40d	5	8	35

Table 11-2 Smoothed and barbed nails.

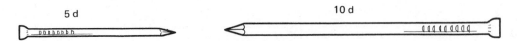

Fig. 11-6 Finishing nails (actual size).

Finishing Nails

Finishing nails, figure 11-6, are of a lighter gauge than the common nail. The heads are tulip-shaped, and they can be easily set below the wood surface and covered with putty to conceal their location. These nails are used on interior finish trimwork. Finishing nails sizes are given in table 11-3.

Size	Length (inches)	Gauge #	Approx. No. to lb.	Size	Length (inches)	Gauge #	Approx. No. to lb.
2d	1	16 1/2	1351	8d	2 1/2	12 1/2	189
3d	1 1/4	15 1/2	807	9d	2 3/4	12 1/2	172
4d	1 1/2	15	584	10d	3	11 1/2	121
5d	1 3/4	15	500	12d	3 1/4	11 1/2	113
6d	2	13	309	16d	3 1/2	11	90
7d	2 1/4	13	238	20d	4	10	62

Table 11-3 Finishing nails.

Wire Brads

Wire brads are similar to finishing nails but are made in a number of combinations of lengths and wire sizes. For example, wire brads 2 inches long come in number 12, 13, 14, or 15 wire sizes, while a 2 inch or 6d finishing nail is made only in number 13 wire size. Brads can be considered as special finishing nails.

Flathead Wire Nails

Flathead wire nails, like wire brads, can be purchased in various combinations of lengths and wire sizes. Thus 2 5/8-inch flathead wire nail can be secured in number 20, 19, 18, or 17 wire sizes.

Casing Nails

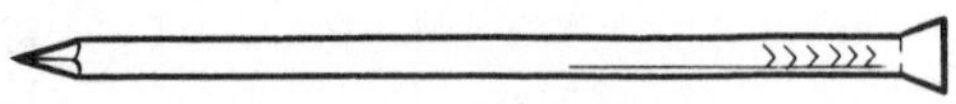

The casing nail, figure 11-7, is like the finishing nail except that the head is larger and tapered on the bottom. The gauge is also larger. Like finishing nails, the head

Fig. 11-7 Casing nail.

can be set with a nail set leaving only a small hole to be puttied. The sizes and gauge numbers for this type of nail are identical to those for the box nail. The 8d and 10d sizes are used for fastening exterior trim such as casings, corner boards, and fascias. Sizes smaller than 8d and larger than 10d are seldom used in light-frame construction.

Flooring Brads

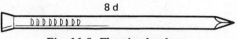

Fig. 11-8 Flooring brads.

Flooring brads or nails, figure 11-8, are similar to casing nails, but are tapered to a larger head. They range in size from 6 penny to 20 penny and are mainly used for interior trim work. They can also be used on exterior trim where the nails are to be set and puttied.

Cut Nails

Cut nails are made from iron or steel with a tapered rectangular shaped shank. The head and point are also rectangular in shape. The blunt point punches out a hole to get the nail started. It does not tend to wedge the wood fibers apart and cause splitting as would a pointed wire nail.

Cut nails have good holding power and are often specified as a fastening for flooring. They come in lengths similar to those of the common wire nails.

To avoid splitting the wood when driving a cut nail, the straight sides should be placed in the wood parallel with the grain so that the tapered edges of the nail act as a wedge in the direction which is less likely to cause splitting. See figure 11-9.

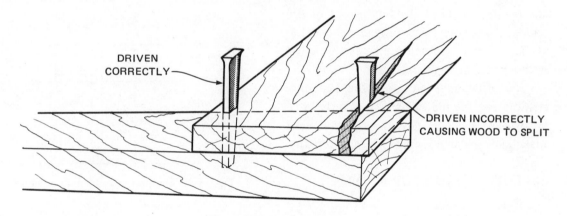

Fig. 11-9 Driving cut nails.

Clinch (Wrought) Nails

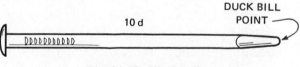

Fig. 11-10 Clinch nail.

Clinch nails, figure 11-10, are made of wrought iron. These nails are soft and tough. They are used where clinching is desired, such as in crates, planking, and on small boats and other places where there is a great strain on the members that are fastened together. The head of this nail is slightly crowned. The point has a duck bill shape, or can be formed with a long, sharp taper.

Special Purpose Nails

A variety of special purpose nails are shown in figure 11-11. Only the duplex head and roofing nails will be described.

Duplex head nails are used for temporary construction work, such as scaffolding, staging, or bracing. This nail has a double head. The lower head can be driven into the wood to

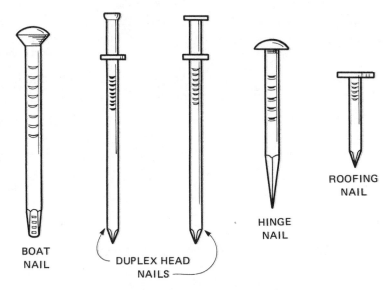

Fig. 11-11 Special purpose nails.

secure the maximum holding power of the nail. The upper head projects above the surface so that the nail can be easily pulled with a hammer or pinch bar.

Roofing nails are used for fastening flexible roofing materials. They have large heads, are usually galvanized to prevent rust, and are made in different lengths.

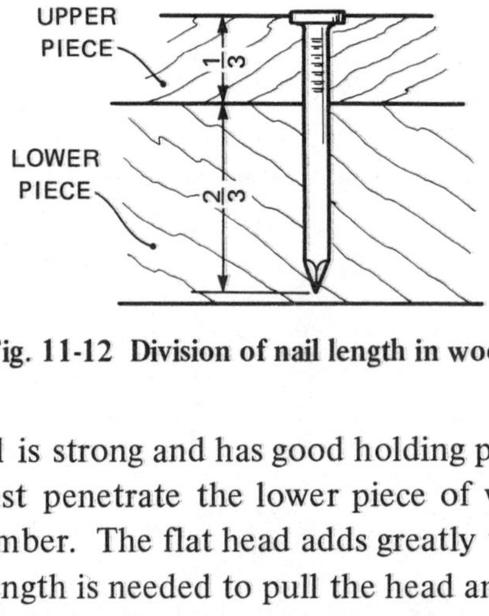

SELECTING NAILS FOR A JOB

Fig. 11-12 Division of nail length in wood.

Nails used for framing a building must have strength and holding power. The common nail is strong and has good holding power.

Two-thirds of the length of the nail body must penetrate the lower piece of wood. The upper third of the nail should be in the top member. The flat head adds greatly to the holding power of the top third of the nail. More strength is needed to pull the head and the one-third length of the nail through the top piece of the lumber than to pull the two-thirds of nail length through the bottom piece. See figure 11-12.

When selecting nails for a job, these points should be considered.

- The type of material which is to be nailed.

- The strain to which the nailing will be subjected.

- The conditions, weather and otherwise, to which the nail will be exposed.

- The appearance of the finished job.

When all of these factors have been considered, the length, gauge, and type of nail to select is then determined. When nailing special-type materials, refer to the manufacturer's literature for recommended fastening devices and techniques.

IMPROVED NAILS

Today in construction many improved forms of the wire nail are used. Changes in nail forms have come about with the development of new types of building materials. Some new materials require special fastening devices.

Warping and shrinking are two things that affected the holding power of nails in the past. However, laminates, composition boards, and various types of synthetics have reduced the occurrence of warping and shrinking. Elimination of such problems also created new problems which have made it necessary for improved nail forms.

Improved nails, sometimes referred to as thread nails, are basically the same as the conventional form nail. They differ in that a portion of the nail shank is threaded with annular or helical threads, and in some instances, is heat treated (hardened or tempered).

The deep, full annular or helical threads along the nail shank provide dents into which the wood fibers can penetrate. Thus, both frictional and shear resistance are provided to nail withdrawal.

An improved nail can be compared in shape to a common wood screw. As with the wood screw, a section just beneath the head is left unthreaded to provide clearance for the shank. Because of this, it can rotate in the top wood member and thus draw the wood members together.

SELECTING IMPROVED NAILS FOR A JOB

The improved nail, figure 11-13, has greater holding power, and thus can be used to obtain the same holding power that the larger common nail provides. It can be driven more easily and used in places where the larger nail can split the wood.

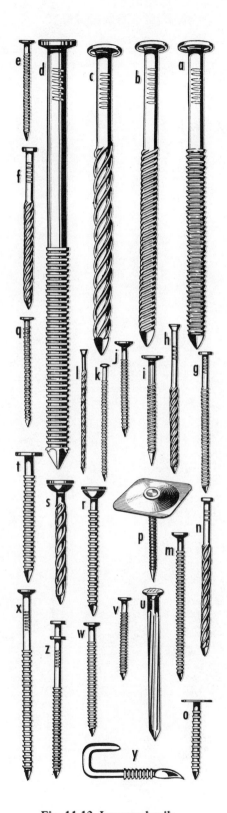

Fig. 11-13 Improved nails.

THREADED NAIL WORKSHOP REFERENCE CHART

The nails referred to in this article are STRONGHOLD® Annular Thread, SCREW-TITE® Spiral Thread and STRONGHOLD® Screw Thread Nails, made exclusively by Independent Nail & Packing Company, Bridgewater, Mass.

Type	Specific Application	Penny	Length and Diameter	Number Per Lb.	Metal	Finish	Thread	Head Type	Point Type	Point Size
			Bright / Hardened	Bright / Hardened						
Framing	Framing	6	2 x .113 / 2 x .105	167 / 190						
		8	2½ x .135 / 2½ x .120	101 / 117						
		10	3 x .148 / 3 x .135	66 / 82		Bright				
a	(For Trussed Rafters the	12	3¼ x .148 / 3¼ x .135	61 / 73		or				
	same range applies for	16	3½ x .162 / 3½ x .148	47 / 57	Steel	Hardened	Annular*	Flat	Diamond	M
b	nails with helical	20	4 x .192 / 4 x .177	29 / 35		as				
	threads)	30	4½ x .207 / 4½ x .177	22 / 31		indicated				
c		40	5 x .225 / 5 x .177	17 / 28						
		50	5½ x .244 / 5½ x .177	13 / 23						
		60	6 x .262 / 6 x .177	10 / 21						
Spikes	Rafter Anchor	—	Bright / Hardened	Bright / Hardened						
			7 x .312 / 7 x .203	6 / 15						
d			8 x .375 / 8 x .203	4 / 13	Steel	Bright	Annular	Flat	Diamond	M
			9 x .375 / 9 x .207	3½ / 11½						
			10 x .375	3						
			11 x .375	2¾						
			12 x .375	2½						
Sheathing	Asbestos—e	3	1¼ x .083	432		Hard. & Galv.	Annular*	Flat & Csk.	Diamond	B
	"	4	1½ x .083	416		"	"	"	"	"
	Plywood	5	1¾ x .120	165		Bright	"	Flat	"	M
	Insulation	5	1¾ x .120	156	Steel	"	"	"	"	"
	Gypsum	5	1¾ x .120	156		"	"	"	"	B
	Masonite—f	6	2 x .115	162		Hard. & Galv.	Helical	Flat & Csk.	Needle	M
	Wood	6	2 x .120	147		Bright	Annular*	Flat	Diamond	"
Siding	Asbestos (see Roofing)									
	Shingle to Plywood		1⅛ x .102	1193	Aluminum	Bright	Annular*	Flat	Diamond	L
	Insul. Brick, Wood Shing.—g		1¾ x .095	252	Steel	Galvanized	"	"	"	M
	Wood Shing. to Ins. Sheath		1¾-2 x .083	308-282	"	Galv. & Enam.	"	Finishing	"	B
	"		1¾-2 x .105	725-585	Aluminum	Bright	"	"	"	"
	Wood, Plywood h		1¾ x .105	180	Sil. Bronze	"	Helical	Csk.	"	"
	"		1⅞ x .109	613	Aluminum	"	"	"	Needle	M
Drywall	Gypsum Board—i	—	1⅜ x .101	327	Steel	Bright or Blued	Annular*	Flat	Diamond	L
Plasterboard	Gypsum Lath—j	3	1¼ x .101	355	Steel	Bright or Blued	Annular*	Flat	Diamond	L
Finishing	Paneling & Trim	2	1 x .065	1030	Stainless	Bright	Annular	Casing	Diamond	M
		2	1 x .072	827-2440	Steel or Alum.	"	Hel. or Ann.	"	"	"
		2-3	1-1¼ x .054	1520-1200	Steel	Hard. & Enam.	Annular	Finishing	"	L
		3½	1⅜ x .083	500	"	Bright & Enam.	"	Flat & Csk.	"	M
	k	4	1½ x .072	510	Monel	Bright	"	Oval	"	"
		4	1½ x .076	510	Stainless	"	Helical	Oval	"	"
		4	1½ x .083	416	Steel	"	"	Casing	"	"
	l	5	1¾ x .083	356	"	"	"	"	"	"
		8	2½ x .105	155	"	"	"	"	"	"
Subflooring and Underlayment	To sleepers and joists, etc. m	—	1 x .083	642	Steel	Bright	Annular	Flat	Diamond	M
			1¼ x .083	500	"	Bright or Hard.	"	"	"	"
			1⅜ x .098	314	"	Bright	"	"	"	"
			2⅛ x .115	182	"	"	"	"	"	"
Flooring	To subflooring	2½	1⅛ x .072	742	Steel	Hardened	Annular	Flat, Csk.	Diamond	B
	n	6	2 x .115	173	"	"	Helical	"	"	"
		7	2¼ x .115	151	"	"	"	"	"	"
		8	2½ x .115	142	"	"	"	"	"	"
Roofing	Asphalt Shingle—o	—	1 x .120	830	Aluminum	Bright	Annular	Flat	Diamond	B
	Roll-Roofing —p		1⅛ x .105	94	Steel	Galvanized	"	Square	"	M
	Asbestos Shingle		1½-1¾ x .076	457-434	Stainless	Bright	Annular* (or file)	Flat	"	"
	" " q		1½-1¾ x .083	387-326	Bronze	"	"	"	"	"
	" "		1½-1¾ x .105	840-725	Aluminum	"	"	"	"	"
	Sheet Metal (with		1½ x .135	135	Steel	Galvanized	Annular	"	"	L
	" Neoprene r		1½ x .145	351	Aluminum	Bright	Helical	"	"	"
	" washer) s		1¾ x .135	111	Steel	Galvanized	Annular	"	"	"
	"		1¾ x .145	303	Aluminum	Bright	Helical	"	"	"
	Wood Shingle—t		1¾-2 x .105	725-585	"	"	Annular	"	"	B
Masonry	For anchoring to concrete and masonry u	—	1½ x .148	129	Steel	Hardened	Fluted Helical	Flat	Diamond	L
			2½ x .148	76	"	"	"	Checkered	"	"
			2¾ x .148	52	"	"	"	"	"	"
			3¼ x .250	28½	"	"	"	"	Needle	M
Copper	Flashing—v	—	1⅛ x .110	271	Copper	Bright	Annular	Flat	Diamond	M
	Gutter Strap—w		1½ x .120	162	"	"	"	"	"	B
	Downspout—x		2½ x .135	90	"	"	"	"	"	M
	Gutter Spikes		7-8 x .187	15-14	"	"	"	"	"	"
L-Staple	Fence Wire	—	1½ x .148	103	Steel	Bright or Hard.	Annular	Wire	Shear	M
	Electrical Conduit y		1¾ x .162	33	"	Electro-Plated	"	"	Needle	"
Duplex-Head	Falsework and Scaffolding, etc. z	6	2 x .113	142	Steel	Bright or Hard.	Annular*	Flat	Diamond	M
		8	2½ x .135	88	"	"	"	"	"	"
		10	3 x .148	62	"	"	"	"	"	"

* or with small lead angle B = Blunt; L = Long; M = Medium

Table 11-4 Reference chart for nails.

Another advantage of the improved nail is that fewer nails need to be used. Even though fewer nails are used, the holding power is the same. The result is a savings in cost and labor.

Problems found with regular-type nails can be solved with improved nails. For example, the conventional 1 5/8-inch cement-coated plain-shank nail used to be recommended for fastening gypsum board. This nail tended to pop out. When replaced by a threaded nail 1 3/8 inches long with a flat head, the nails remained fixed.

Figure 11-13 shows some of the types of improved nails. The letters next to each nail identify the nail on the reference chart, table 11-4.

The chart gives information about the uses of the various types of nails, penny size, length and diameter, number per pound, type of metal, finish, thread type, head type, point type, and point size.

A careful study of the chart should be made to understand the various nail types and their uses. This knowledge helps the carpenter cope with many of the nailing problems which arise.

TOOLS FOR DRIVING AND PULLING NAILS

The tools commonly used by the carpenter for the application and removal of nails are nail hammers, nail sets, and the gooseneck pinchbar. Techniques of how to hold and use these tools should be learned before trying to put them to use.

HAMMERS

Hammers are made in a variety of qualities. Those made with a tough alloy drop-forged steel head are the best. When tempered and heat treated properly, they are stronger than ordinary steel. Hammers made with cast heads are brittle and are not suitable for carpentry work. The parts of a hammer are shown in figure 11-14.

Two shapes of hammer heads are made, the curved-claw hammer and the ripping-(straight) claw hammer. The ripping-claw hammer is preferred to the curved claw for

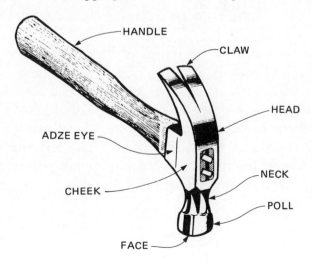

Fig. 11-14 Parts of a hammer.

prying woodwork apart. The shape of the claw permits wedging like a chisel to loosen fastened members. Curved-claw hammers are more suitable for pulling nails.

Claw hammers can be bell faced or plain faced. Bell-faced hammers have a slightly convex face, whereas a plain-faced hammer has a flat face.

A bell-faced hammer is more difficult to use because of its curved face. However, it is preferred because a nail can be driven flush or even slightly below the surface of the wood without leaving marks. The plain-faced hammer tends to leave hammer marks when used to drive nails flush. Therefore, it is mainly used for rough framing and similar rough work.

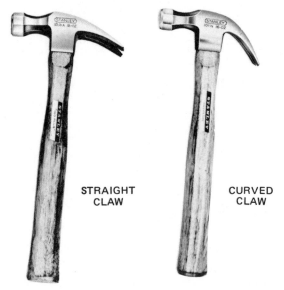

STRAIGHT CLAW   CURVED CLAW

Fig. 11-15 Types of hammer heads.

Smooth or cross-checkered faces are made for the various types of hammers. See B, figure 11-16. The cross-checkered face reduces the tendency of the hammer to slip off the surface being hammered. Its disadvantage is that cross marks are impressed in the wood when a nail is hammered flush.

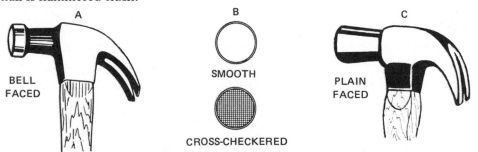

A   BELL FACED   B   SMOOTH   CROSS-CHECKERED   C   PLAIN FACED

Fig. 11-16 Types of hammer faces.

Nailing hammers are sized by the weight of their heads. The most common sizes are 7 ounces, 16 ounces (1 pound), and 20 ounces (1 1/4 pounds). The 16-ounce size is used for general carpentry work. Twenty-ounce hammers are preferred for heavy nailing. The hammer weight selected should suit the size and type of nail.

Hammer handles can be wood (usually hickory), metal with a leather overlay at the end for holding, and fiberglass. All types of handles have certain advantages. Many carpenters prefer wood handles because of their balance. Others prefer the metal type because the handles never need replacement. Some prefer fiberglass for its combination of balance and shock absorbing qualities.

Replacing a Hammer Handle

1. Saw off the broken or splintered handle near the eye.

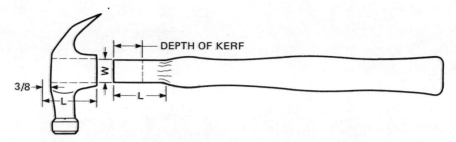

Fig. 11-17 Fitting hammer handle.

2. Drive out the remaining portion with a chisel or punch. Drive towards the outside of the head of the hammer because the eye is tapered in that direction. If the wedges are un-damaged, save them for the new handle.

Fig. 11-18 Saw kerf for wooden wedge.

3. With a spokeshave and wood file, shape the end of the handle to fit inside the small end of the eye. Hold the handle in a wood vise when shaping it.

4. Shape the end to a slight taper so that it can be worked into the head about 3/8 inch beyond the width of the head. See figure 11-17. The end should be shaped so that it is aligned with the rest of the handle.

5. Before inserting the handle into the eye, make a saw kerf in the end as shown in figure 11-18. Use a backsaw for small handles and a handsaw for making the kerf on larger handles. Make the kerf to a depth about three-fourths the distance through the eye.

6. Insert the handle in the eye and drive it so that it projects about 3/8 inch through the eye. Driving is done by first holding the handle in a vertical position with the head at the top, and then bringing the back end of the handle down on a solid wood surface with a series of firm taps until it is properly seated.

7. See figure 11-19. Prepare a thin wedge equal in width to the eye and about 1 1/4 inches long. Drive it into the kerf to its maximum tightness.

8. Saw off the excess projecting portion of the handle to about 1/8 inch out-side of the hammer head.

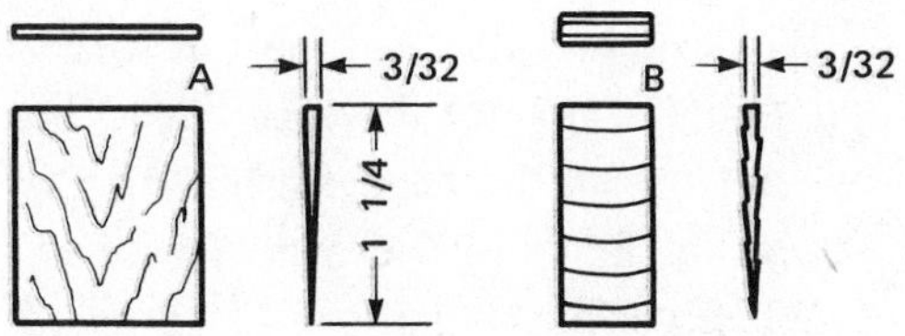

Fig. 11-19 Sizes of wood and metal wedges.

9. Form starting grooves for the metal wedges with a cold chisel. Two grooves should be made across the end at a slight diagonal. See the location of the wedges on figure 11-20.

10. Drive the wedges as deep as possible with the flat side of a ball peen hammer.

11. With a hacksaw, cut off the remaining excess portion of the handles and wedges.

12. Finish the end with a coarse, double-cut file. Avoid filing the hammer head. The completed job should appear as shown in figure 11-20.

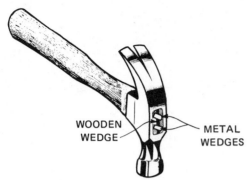

Fig. 11-20 Location of wedges.

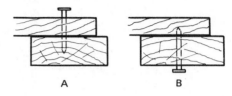

Fig. 11-21 (A) Correct method of nailing. (B) Incorrect method of nailing.

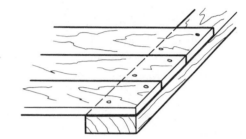

Fig. 11-22 Nails correctly spaced and staggered.

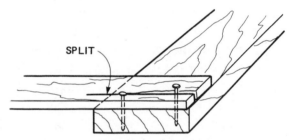

Fig. 11-23 Nails driven in line causing splitting.

NAILING

Always nail from a thin piece into a thick piece (A, figure 11-21) as this results in greater nail holding power. Wherever possible, drive nails across grain rather than into end grain. Nails driven into end grain have less holding power.

When locating nails, do not drive them too close together or in line with one another. Stagger them as in figure 11-22. The result of driving nails in line with one another is shown in figure 11-23. Space out the nails so that the holding power is distributed over a wide area. Do not nail close to an edge.

Where there is danger of splitting a board, use nails of a smaller gauge, or drill holes about three-fourths of the diameter of the nail partially through the board before driving. To prevent splitting in thin boards, cut the nail points off with nippers or pliers. The points thus prepared are less likely to cause splitting.

When driving flathead nails in soft texture materials, such as composition sheathing and wood shingles, do not drive the head below the surface. Finish driving the nail with a light blow that brings the head flush with the surface. To make nailing easier in hardwood, dip the point of the nail in beeswax or soap.

When driving aluminum nails, use the same procedure as in driving common nails, but be careful not to strike the nails with heavy blows as the nails bend easily. It is sometimes better to drill holes for this type of nail, especially where the wood is hard. Aluminum and coated nails are more expensive than steel nails and therefore particular care should be exercised when using them.

Facenailing

1. Choose a suitable weight hammer. Nails up to 4 penny should be driven with a 7-ounce hammer. Nails from 6 to 20 penny are generally driven with a 16-ounce hammer.

Fig. 11-24 Correct method of holding a hammer.

2. Rub the face of the hammer with a piece of sandpaper to clean grease or dirt off the face. Grease and dirt can cause the hammer to slip off the nail-head when the nail is being driven.

3. Grasp the handle firmly near the end as shown in figure 11-24.

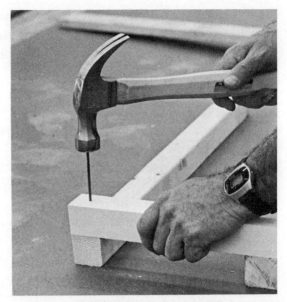

Fig. 11-25 Starting a nail.

4. Hold the nail between the thumb and forefinger. Place it in location and point it in the direction in which it is to be driven. See figure 11-25.

5. Tap the nail squarely and lightly with the hammer. Support the nail until it has entered the wood far enough to support itself in a straight and rigid position. Then take the fingers off the nail.

6. To drive the nail home, figure 11-26, swing the hammer by bending the elbow and giving a well-directed blow that hits the nail squarely on the head. If the handle is kept at an angle of 90 degrees to the line of the nail, the face of the hammer generally hits the nail squarely. Try to strike the nail with the center of the hammer head.

Fig. 11-26 Driving a nail.

NOTE: Blows are delivered through the wrist, the elbow, and the shoulder. One or all are used depending on the force of the blow desired. For light driving, use a wrist and slight elbow motion; for moderate hammering, use a wrist and greater elbow action; and for heavy hammering, use wrist, elbow, and shoulder action.

7. To complete driving the nail, gauge the force of the blows so that the next to last blow brings the nail about 1/16 inch above the wood surface. Then, with the last blow, bring the nail flush with the surface.

NOTE: If a nail bends, draw it out and start a new one in its place. If this one also bends, it is probably because it is striking a knot, a hidden nail, or other metal. Withdraw it and start a new one in another place, or drill a hole past the obstruction and try again.

8. When driving casing and finishing nails, govern the driving blows so that the last blow leaves the head of the nail slightly above the surface of the wood. This avoids marring the surface with the hammer head. Then, set the nail with a nail set.

Setting a Nail

NOTE: Generally, nails are set in finished surfaces and covered with putty, plastic wood, or sawdust mixed with glue to avoid marring the appearance of the surface. Finishing nails (those with small heads) are most commonly used for this type of nailing. However, flathead nails can also be set, as when nailing clapboard siding.

1. Drive the nail in the usual manner until it is almost, but not quite, flush with the surface.

2. Choose a suitable size nail set, figure 11-27. Use a size which does not enlarge the hole made by the head of the nail and yet is large enough to transmit the force of the blow effectively.

Fig. 11-27 Nail set.

NOTE: Sets are made in several sizes. The most common sizes are 1/32 inch, 2/32 inch, and 4/32 inch. The size refers to the diameter of the small end of the tapered portion. The point of the set is hollowed to prevent it from slipping as the blow is struck.

3. Refer to figure 11-28. Hold the set between the thumb and forefinger and apply the point so that it is centered on the head of the nail. Rest the little finger on the work to steady the hand as setting is being done.

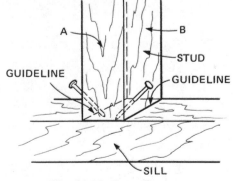

Fig. 11-28 Using the nail set.

4. With the nail set held in line, set the head with a light tap of the hammer about 1/16 inch below the surface. Try to set the nail below the surface with one hammer blow.

Toenailing

NOTE: The purpose of toenailing is to fasten a wood member to another which it butts against. See figure 11-29.

Fig. 11-29 Toenailing.

Toenailing is done on the faces of members. Do not nail through the edges, A and B, as splitting will probably result.

1. Position the vertical member in place.

2. Mark lines along each side of the stud on the face of the plate. This locates the stud.

3. Place the point of the nail so that one-third the length of the nail goes through the stud, figure 11-29, and two-thirds of the length enters the sill.

4. Start the nail as in facenailing. After the nail has entered the wood at right angles, tip it to the angle in which it is to toe. This allows the nail to get a good start in the wood. If the nail is started on a slant, it might slip down the wood.

5. Drive the nails home on the first side. When driving the nail, put pressure on the opposite side with a foot or pull against the direction of nailing, to keep the board in its proper position. Even with this support, the board will move off the guidelines in the direction of nailing. Disregard this because the error can be corrected when nails are driven in from the opposite side.

6. Start the nails on the opposite side so that they do not line up with those just driven.

7. Drive the nails home. Support the board from the opposite side as the board becomes correctly positioned. Continue striking the nails until the board is centered between the guidelines.

Nailing Flooring or Sheathing

1. Start the nail at about a 50-degree angle in the top of the tongue joint. See figure 11-30.
   NOTE: Driving nails at an angle draws the board up tight to the surface it is butted against.

2. Drive the nail until the nail head approaches the surface of the flooring using blows in the direction indicated by arrows 1 and 2 in figure 11-30. Avoid striking the finished edge of the flooring.

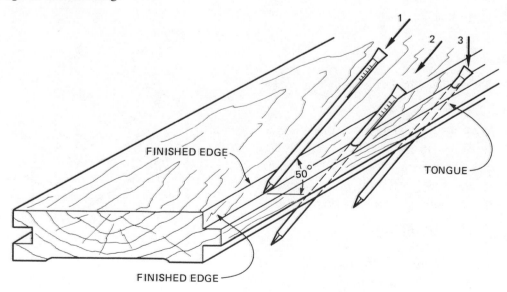

Fig. 11-30 Correct method of toenailing flooring.

3. At point 3, the nail is shown as the head enters the tongue of the joint. Direct the blow at this point as indicated by the arrow. This avoids hitting the finish edge.

4. If the tongue is damaged by the hammer, be sure to remove the damaged area and any splinters which will interfere with bringing up the next board tight.

Clinching a Nail

NOTE: This method of nailing is used mainly in rough work when two thin pieces of material are being nailed together. For this, long nails are bent over or clinched to secure the required holding power.

1. Drive the nail as described for facenailing until the head is seated on the uppermost member.

2. Turn the two members over and strike the point from the side to bend it down.

3. Place the head on a flat metal surface. Strike the bent end with a firm, direct blow so that the bent portion becomes seated in the grain of the wood.

NOTE: Clinching with the grain gives a smooth surface. However, clinching across the grain makes a stronger and tighter joint. See figure 11-31.

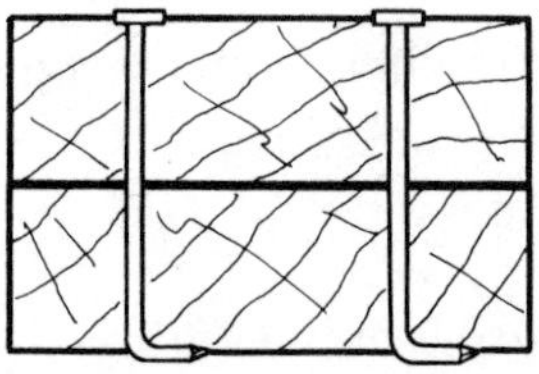

The direction of clinching is determined by the direction of force against the nail. If the force tends to move the top board to the left, then the points of the nails should be bent in an opposite direction (to the right).

Fig. 11-31 Clinching.

4. Another method for clinching is to place the two boards on a metal block. As the point is driven through the wood, contact with the metal turns the point to clinch the nail. The disadvantage of this method is that the direction of bending cannot be controlled.

Nailing into End Grain

1. Determine where the nails are to be located.

2. Drive the nails at angles to one another as shown in figure 11-32. By doing this, the nails also enter the end grain at an angle, resulting in a clinching effect and greater holding power.

NOTE: Do not nail too close to the end as splitting can result. Drilling holes slightly less than the diameter of the nail through the top member helps to avoid this.

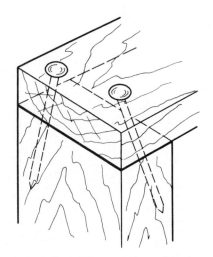

Fig. 11-32 Nailing into an end grain.

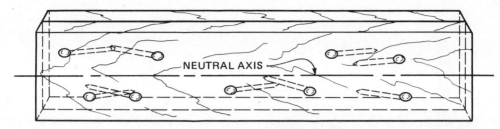

Fig. 11-33 Nailing two boards together.

Nailing Bearing Members Together

1. Locate the nails or spikes so that they are staggered and at the top or bottom side of the beam. See figure 11-33.

   NOTE: Avoid nailing along the center of the neutral axle.

2. Drive the nails so that they slant toward each other. Stagger them along the face of the board.

Using the Hammer to Withdraw a Nail

1. If the head is above the surface, slip the claw of the hammer under the head of the nail and pull the handle to an almost vertical position, A and B, figure 11-34.

2. If the head is below the surface, place the claw against the nail head as in A, figure 11-34, and strike the face of the hammer with a soft-face hammer. This will force the claw down below and around the nail head.

   NOTE: The face of the hammer is made of hardened steel. Do not strike the face with another hammer; to do so can chip the hardened face.

3. When the hammer has pulled the nail to the position shown at B, figure 11-34, release the hammer and place a piece of scrap wood so that the claw can again be placed on the nail and on top of the scrap wood as shown at C. Then withdraw the nail by pulling the hammer handle to the position shown at B.

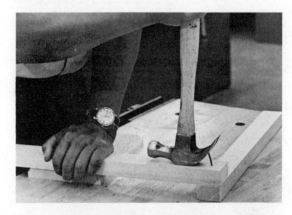

Fig. 11-34 Using a hammer to withdraw a nail.

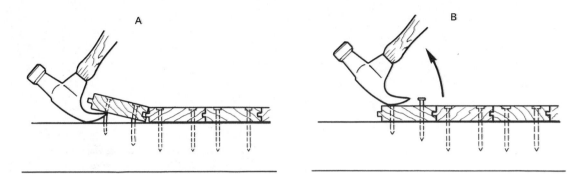

Fig. 11-35 Alternate method of withdrawing a nail.

4. Sometimes it is possible to pry the nailed board loose with the claw hammer as shown in figure 11-35. Then strike the board back to the nailed position with a sharp blow of the hammer. This causes the nail to project through the face of the board, B. The nail can then be withdrawn.

5. To withdraw a nail which has a broken head, drive the claw on the body of the nail, if possible. Twist the hammer around to the right or left about one-quarter turn. This forms a cut in the nail and it can be withdrawn in the usual manner.

6. If it is impossible to get the claw on the nail, drive the nail through the board with a nail set, then clinch the hammer claw on the pointed end of the nail. This method should be used to protect the face of the board. The same method is used if the nail head is set below the surface of the wood. Generally, when a nail that has been set is backed out, the surface wood fibers will split.

7. If it is impossible to get at the pointed end of the nail, first raise the board by prying. Then slip a hacksaw blade between the nailed boards and cut the nail.

Withdrawing Spikes

1. To withdraw spikes, use a gooseneck pinchbar, figure 11-36. If the spike head is below the surface, set the claw of the bar against the spike head. Drive the claw under the spike head by striking the bar with a hammer at A, figure 11-36. Then withdraw the spike by pulling on the bar handle as shown by the arrow.

2. An alternate method for withdrawing nails with the pinchbar is shown in

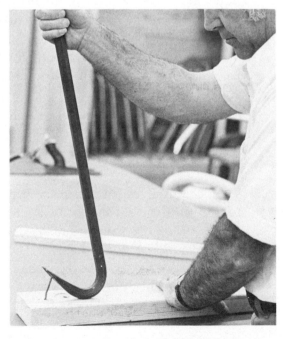

Fig. 11-36 Removing a nail with a pinchbar.

figure 11-37. The board is first raised by wedging the claw and raising the board slightly as shown at board A. The face of the board is then struck a blow near the nails and driven back into position. As a result, the nail heads are raised enough to be withdrawn as shown in B, figure 11-37.

CORRUGATED FASTENERS

Corrugated fasteners, figure 11-38, are used to assemble wood joints which are flush, such as the butt and miter. Two types are made, one for use in hardwood and the other for softwood. Both types

Fig. 11-37 Alternate method of drawing out nails.

are made so that the corrugations are toed toward the center. As a result, when driven, the members of a joint are pulled together. These fasteners come in depths of 1/4 inch to 1 inch and in various lengths.

In fastening joints with corrugated fasteners, the fastener is located away from edges and diagonally to the grain to avoid splitting the wood. It should be driven with light hammer blows evenly distributed across the edge of the fastener.

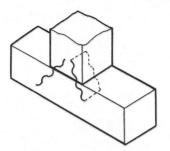

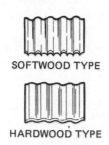

SOFTWOOD TYPE

HARDWOOD TYPE

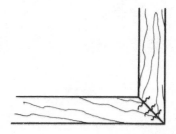

Fig. 11-38 Types of corrugated fasteners.

REVIEW QUESTIONS

A. Short Answer or Discussion

1. How does the type of wood used affect the holding power of a nail?

2. What features of the nail affect its holding power?

3. Explain the different surface treatments used to increase holding power.

4. How does the penny system signify nail sizes?

5. Which of the conventional nails is not made from wire?

6. How long should a nail be for secure fastening?

7. What is an essential characteristic of improved nails?

8. Describe three advantages of improved nails over conventional nails.

9. To prevent splitting in thin woods, how can nails be adapted on the job?

10. Describe the two usual types of hammer heads and the preferred use of each.

11. What are the advantages and disadvantages of each type of hammer face?

12. At what angle should nails be driven for tongue and groove flooring?

13. Why is a block placed under the hammer claw to withdraw nails?

14. Describe a method for withdrawing nails when it is not possible to get the claw on the nail head.

15. Why should nailing into end grain be avoided if possible?

B. Completion

1. For the best holding power in joining two pieces of wood, nailing should be done from the _____ piece into the _____ piece.

2. A blunt nail has _____ tendency to split the wood than a sharp-pointed nail.

3. To distribute holding power over a wider area, nails should be _____.

4. Driving nails into hardwood can be made easier by applying a _____ to the shank.

5. A _____ is used to drive the nail head below the wood surface.

6. Toenailing should be done on the _____, not on the _____, of the members being joined.

7. Corrugated fasteners should be applied in a direction _____ to the grain.

8. Nails which are not sized by the penny system include _____, _____, _____, and _____.

9. Those nails described in question 8 are sized by _____.

10. The identifying characteristic of a duplex head nail is its _____.

11. The higher the penny number of the nail, the _____ its size.

12. In drilling a hole for driving a nail, the drill size should be about _____ the diameter of the nail.

C. Identification and Interpretation

1. Identify each type of nail shown in figure 11-39.

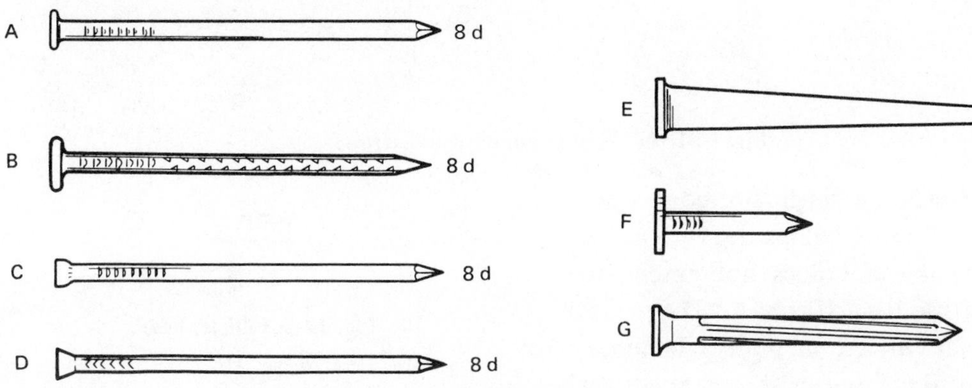

Fig. 11-39

2. Match the nails shown in figure 11-39 with the uses described.

If no nail is shown for a listed use, state the nail to use.

a. To nail sleepers to a concrete floor.
b. To blind-nail tongue and groove flooring.
c. To frame sidewall studs.
d. To lay shiplap subflooring.
e. To apply felt roofing paper.
f. To make a built-up girder of three 2 x 10's.
g. To nail baseboard trim.
h. To nail the fascia to the ends of rafters.
i. To assemble a shipping case.

Unit 12 FASTENERS – SCREWS AND OTHERS

Aside from nails, the wood screw is the most common fastening device used by carpenters. This type of fastening device has greater holding power than a nail and can be taken apart and put together with ease and without danger of damage. However, screws are not used as often as nails because of their cost and the time it takes to drive them.

WOOD SCREW SPECIFICATIONS

Wood screws are specified by the shape of their head, the type of slot on the head, the gauge (body diameter), length, material of the screw, type of finish, and special screws. Figure 12-1 shows the three shapes of heads most commonly found on wood screws – flat, round, and oval. Another type sometimes used is the fillister head shown in figure 12-2.

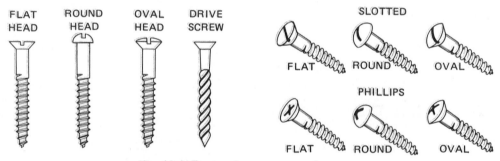

Fig. 12-1 Types of common wood screws.

Screwheads are single slotted or have recessed cross slots (Phillips head). On the drive screw, the slot does not extend to the sides of the head (figure 12-3) because it is partially driven in with a hammer, and then driven home with a screwdriver that fits the slot. If the slot went to the sides of the screw, the head might easily be broken off with the blows of a hammer.

The size of a screw is designated by a gauge number and by its length. The gauge number is the outside diameter of the shank. The American Screwmakers' gauge is used to determine the gauge number. The length refers to the distance from the point of the screw to the point where the base of the head begins. See figure 12-4.

Fig. 12-2 Fillister head.

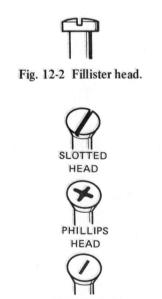

Fig. 12-3 Three types of screw heads.

Length	1/4″	3/8″	1/2″	5/8″	3/4″	7/8″	1″	1 1/4″	1 3/4″
Gauge	0-4	0-8	1-10	2-12	2-14	3-14	3-16	4-18	6-20
Length	2″	2 1/4″	2 1/2″	2 3/4″	3″	3 1/2″	4″	4 1/2″	5″
Gauge	6-20	6-20	6-20	8-20	8-24	10-24	12-24	14-24	14-24

Table 12-1 Length of screws for each gauge.

Table 12-1 shows the various lengths and gauge sizes of screws. A screw 1/4 inch long ranges in gauges from zero to four (American Screwmakers' gauge). A 5-inch screw is made in gauges from 14 to 24.

The actual size of the head for gauge sizes from one through fourteen is shown in figure 12-5. The gauge numbers in inch measure can be obtained from a table or by

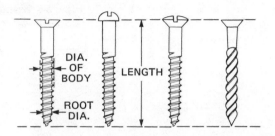

Fig. 12-4 Finding the size of a screw.

measuring the *shank* (unthreaded portion of the body) with outside calipers.

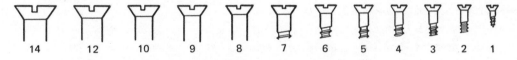

Fig. 12-5 Actual size of head and gauge numbers.

Screws are made of soft steel, copper alloys (brass, bronze), and aluminum. The soft steel screw is commonly called an iron screw. The steel screw can be plated with nickel, brass, cadmium, or zinc (galvanized) to retard corrosion. Screws are also plated to match the finish of hardware for which the screws can be used. Flathead screws most often used have a bright (uncoated) finish, and the roundhead type is blued or nickeled.

Screws are packed one hundred in a box. The box is labeled with the type of head, gauge number, length, finish, and type of material from which the screws are made.

SELECTING SCREWS FOR A JOB

A screw has a greater surface area than a nail. Because the threads are spread out beyond the root diameter of the screw, the screw grips wood better than a nail. Bright metal screws give the greatest holding power of any member of the screw family because the edges of the screw threads are sharp. The coating on screws decreases their holding power because the screw is coated after the threads are cut, and the coating tends to round the sharp edges of the threads. Sometimes they are overcoated. These should not be used if the slots and threads are filled. To get the greatest holding power, 2/3 of the length of the screw should enter the lower board.

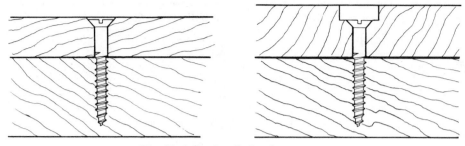

Fig. 12-6 Setting flathead screws.

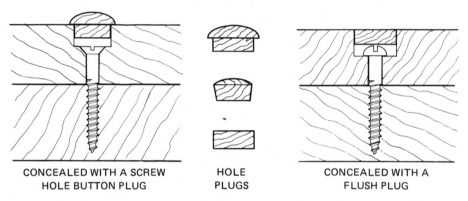

CONCEALED WITH A SCREW
HOLE BUTTON PLUG

HOLE
PLUGS

CONCEALED WITH A
FLUSH PLUG

Fig. 12-7 Methods of concealing a screw hole.

Screws are chosen according to the job. For ordinary work where speed is needed and the screws are not exposed to moisture, the bright screw can be used. For high-grade work and where the screws can come in contact with moisture, brass, bronze, coated, or plated screws should be used.

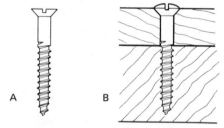

Fig. 12-8 (A) Flathead screw, (B) Ovalhead screw.

Flathead screws are used where the head of the screw must be flush with or below the surface of the wood. The shoulders of the hole must be countersunk or counterbored to fit the outside diameter of the head. See figure 12-6.

Roundhead screws are used when the surface does not have to appear flat. Sometimes they are used in an ornamental pattern. At other times the roundhead is preferred to the flathead because the flathead acts as a wedge and can split the work. Both flathead and roundhead wood screws can be hidden by counterboring and then plugging the hole, figure 12-7.

Ovalhead screws have uses where the slightly raised portion of the head lends itself to produce an ornamental effect. It is also sometimes preferred over the flathead type because of the greater strength of its head. This is apparent from a study of figure 12-8. This type of screw is used for fastening exposed door hinges. Countersinking is required for seating the head, and is done to a depth so that only the curved portion of the head is above the surface. See B, figure 12-8.

Phillips head screws are best suited for production work. The special slots, together with a special type of screwdriver, permit these screws to be driven quickly and with less chance of the screwdriver slipping from the slot.

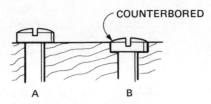

Fig. 12-9 Fillister head screws.

Fig. 12-10 Drive head.

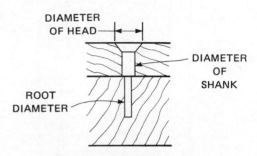

Fig. 12-11 Screw diameters.

Screws with fillister heads are used for the same reasons as ovalhead screws. However, in some instances, they are preferred to the ovalhead type because the flat underside of the head does not produce a wedging action which can cause splitting. This type of screw can be used with the entire head above the surface (A, figure 12-9) or it can be seated by counterboring so that only the oval part of the head protrudes, as in B.

The drive screw is used where speed and economy are important factors. It is especially good where holding power is needed and when appearance is not stressed. This type of screw is most suitable for use in softwood. When used in softwood, countersinking is not necessary. The head, figure 12-10, seats itself by compressing the wood fibers.

PREPARATION FOR DRIVING WOOD SCREWS

When driving flathead and ovalhead wood screws to fasten two boards, first drill a clearance hole (diameter of shank) through the top board. See figure 12-11. Then drill a pilot into the bottom piece the size of the core or root diameter of the screw threads. For hardwoods the pilot hole should be drilled to slightly more than the full depth to which the screw will be driven. For softwoods, the pilot hole can be drilled to one-half this depth. Finally, the top piece is countersunk to receive the head of the screw. The selection of drills for clearance and pilot holes can be found on table 12-2 prepared for this purpose.

The preparation of screw holes, other than for flathead and ovalhead screws, is done in a similar manner except that countersinking is not done. In some cases counterboring is a part of the preparation for driving a screw. Counterboring can be done for recessing all types of screw heads. Table 12-2 includes counterbore drill sizes for various size screw heads.

When a screw hole is to be prepared with a counterbore, the counterbore must be bored first if a bit is used. This is not necessary when a drill is used. However, a counterbored hole drilled after the body and pilot hole have been drilled usually does not have as clean cut an edge at the surface as it would if it were drilled first.

TOOLS FOR DRIVING SCREWS

The tools used for driving screws include the conventional type of screwdriver, square-shank screwdriver, ratchet screwdriver, spiral-ratchet screwdriver, Phillips screwdriver, and the brace and screwdriver bit.

No. of Screw	BIT or DRILL SIZES									No. of AUGER BIT
	FOR SHANK CLEARANCE HOLES		FOR PILOT HOLES*							
			HARD WOODS			SOFT WOODS				
	TWIST BIT	DRILL	TWIST BIT	DRILL		TWIST BIT	DRILL			
	(Nearest size in fractions of an inch) Slotted & Phillips	Gauge No. or Letter *To be used for maximum holding power* Slotted & Phillips	*(Nearest size in fractions of an inch)* Slotted Phillips	Gauge No. *To be used for maximum holding power* Slotted	Phillips	*(Nearest size in fractions of an inch)* Slotted Phillips	Gauge No. *To be used for maximum holding power* Slotted	Phillips		to counter-bore for sinking head (by 16ths) Slotted & Phillips
2	3/32	42	3/64 1/32	56	70	1/32 1/64	65	75		3
3	7/64	37	1/16 1/32	54	66	3/64 1/32	58	71		4
4	7/64	32	1/16 3/64	52	56	3/64 1/32	55	65		4
5	1/8	30	5/64 1/16	49	54	1/16 3/64	53	58		4
6	9/64	27	5/64 1/16	47	52	1/16 3/64	52	55		5
7	5/32	22	3/32 5/64	44	49	1/16 3/64	51	53		5
8	11/64	18	3/32 5/64	40	47	5/64 1/16	48	52		6
9	3/16	14	7/64 3/32	37	44	5/64 1/16	45	51		6
10	3/16	10	7/64 3/32	33	40	3/32 5/64	43	48		6
12	7/32	2	1/8 7/64	30	33	7/64 3/32	38	43		7
14	1/4	D	9/64 1/8	25	31	7/64 3/32	32	40		8
16	17/64	I	5/32 1/8	18	30	9/64 7/64	29	38		9
18	19/64	N	3/16 9/64	13	25	9/64 7/64	26	32		10

Table 12-2 The selection of drills for clearance and pilot holes.

The main purpose of these tools is to tighten or loosen screws. Each type has a design feature which makes it more suitable for certain types of work than for others. The following materials describes each tool and its particular use.

THE CONVENTIONAL SCREWDRIVER

Many sizes and styles of this type of screwdriver are made. The size determined by the length of its blade. For example, an 8-inch screwdriver has a blade 8 inches long, figure 12-12.

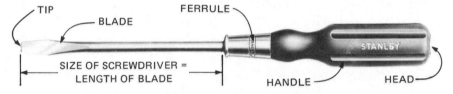

Fig. 12-12 Parts of a screwdriver.

Screwdrivers with long blades require less effort for driving screws than short ones. However, they are not suitable for driving small screws because of danger of twisting and breaking the screw.

Screwsdrivers with small tips are intended for use on small screws. Those having wide tips are for large screws. A range of tip widths is necessary for properly driving various size screws.

The conventional type of screwdriver is used for general purpose work. Its range of sizes makes it useful for heavy- or light-duty work in restricted or unrestricted areas. It is not practical for use when many screws are to be driven, or when speed is important.

THE SQUARE-SHANK SCREWDRIVER

The square-shank screwdriver (A, figure 12-13) differs from the conventional type only in the shape of the shank portion of the blade. As shown in B, the shank is made square so that a wrench can be applied to give added leverage in driving or drawing screws.

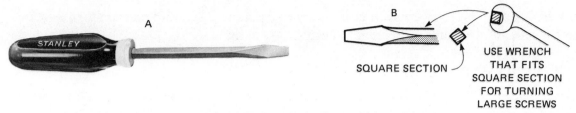

Fig. 12-13 Square-shank screwdriver.

RATCHET SCREWDRIVERS

The simple ratchet screwdriver, figure 12-14, includes a ratchet device on the ferrule portion of the handle which operates in the same manner as the ratchet found on a ratchet bit brace. The ratchet makes it possible to drive screws at a faster rate and with greater ease. It also can be disengaged so that the screwdriver can be used as a conventional screwdriver.

Spiral-ratchet screwdrivers, figure 12-15, can be compared to automatic drills. The turning motion of the screwdriver bit is produced by pushing down on the handle causing the spiral-groove spindle to revolve. They are made with various length spiral-groove spindles. Those with short spindles are better suited for driving short screws.

An assortment of screwdriver bit sizes is usually provided. The bits are easily interchangeable by simply sliding the chuck sleeve.

The spiral-ratchet screwdriver is most useful for rapid driving and drawing of screws. It is very practical for repeated production work. It can be used with or without the ratchet in operation.

THE PHILLIPS SCREWDRIVER

The Phillips screwdriver, figure 12-16, is very similar to the conventional type of screwdriver. However the blade is shaped like a cross so that it fits into the slots on Phillips head screws.

As with the conventional type of screwdriver, the length of the blade signifies the size of the screwdriver. In addition, a size is also given to the tip.

Tip sizes range from #1 through #4. Each tip size fits a particular range of screw sizes. Refer to table 12-3 to find the appropriate size tip to use for various size Phillips screws.

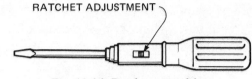

Fig. 12-14 Ratchet screwdriver.

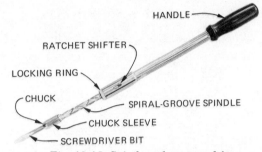

Fig. 12-15 Spiral-ratchet screwdriver.

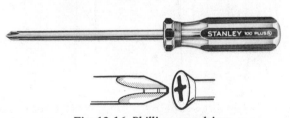

Fig. 12-16 Phillips screwdriver.

Phillips Bit No.	Screw Gauge Size
Bit No. 1	Number 4 and smaller
Bit No. 2	Number 5 to 9 inclusive
Bit No. 3	Number 10 to 16 inclusive
Bit No. 4	Number 18 and larger

Table 12-3 Tip sizes.

In driving with this screwdriver, it is necessary to use more downward pressure than used for other types of screwdrivers, in order to keep the tip in the slots.

THE BRACE AND SCREWDRIVER BIT

Screwdriver bits with square tangs are used with the bit brace to drive and withdraw slotted and Phillips head screws. The bits for slotted screws are sized by the width of their tips (3/16 inch to 3/4 inch), and those for Phillips head screws are sized similarly to the Phillips screwdriver (#1 through #4). This type of driving device is preferred for driving and withdrawing large screws because of the greater leverage possible.

A ratchet device on the brace permits its use in a limited space. Its disadvantage is the danger of twisting off the screw head. This leverage makes it hard to sense the amount of force that is being applied.

THE SELECTION OF A SCREWDRIVER

When selecting a screwdriver, check that the tip is in good condition, and that it properly fits the screw slot. If the tip is rounded, it should be ground to a correct shape. See figure 12-17. Since the tip is hardened and tempered, care must be used not to burn (overheat) the tip. Do not try to file the tip to shape because in most cases it is too hard for filing.

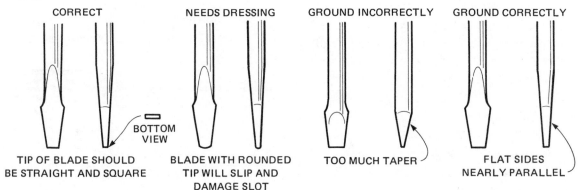

Fig. 12-17 Checking the tip of the screwdriver.

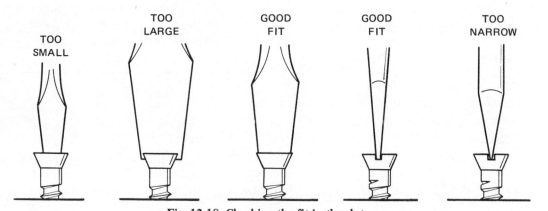

Fig. 12-18 Checking the fit in the slot.

The tip selected should fit the slot snugly and extend the full length of the slot. See figure 12-18. If the tip is wider than the slot, the work surface will be marred around the head as the tip is seated. A blade that is too narrow in width and thickness causes burring of the screw head and often results in damage to the tip itself. See figure 12-18.

Driving a Screw

1. Prepare the screw holes (clearance hole, pilot hole, and if required, countersink or counterbore.

2. Select the proper type and size of screwdriver.

   NOTE: Steps 3 through 6 apply to driving a screw with the conventional type of screwdriver.

3. Place the screw in the clearance hole and tap or press it to start it in the pilot hole.

4. Center the tip of the screwdriver in the slot and hold it in line with the direction of the hole as shown in figure 12-19.

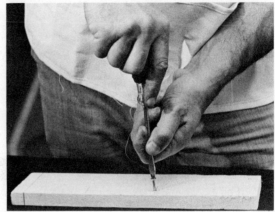

Fig. 12-19 Proper position of hands for driving a screw.

5. Turn the screw slowly in a clockwise direction, applying enough pressure to drive the screw squarely into the pilot hole.

   NOTE: Keep the fingers near the blade tip away from the underside of the screw head to avoid injury in the event the screwdriver slips out of the slot.

6. Continue driving the screw with a series of turns by taking a fresh grip on the handle with each turn. Relax the grip on the blade as the handle is turned and tighten it as the grip on the handle is renewed.

   NOTE: Take care not to drive the screw beyond seating it firmly, or the threads formed in the wood can be stripped.

7. If the screws are large or are to be driven in hardwood, use the bit brace and screwdriver bit. See figure 12-20.

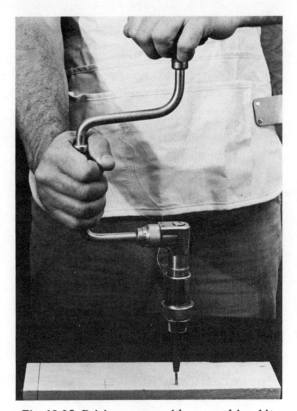

Fig. 12-20 Driving a screw with a screwdriver bit.

Use great care to prevent twisting them off. In cases where the screws drive hard, coat them with soap, beeswax, graphite, or oil before driving them. These substances act as lubricants and also help to prevent rusting. Screws treated with these substances are easier to withdraw if necessary.

8. If the screws are the Phillips head type, use the same technique described in steps 1 through 7.

   However, in addition, use greater pressure when driving to avoid having the tip slip out of the slots.

9. When driving soft metal screws (brass, aluminum, etc.) in hardwood, there is a greater danger of twisting off the head or shank. This can be avoided by applying soap to the threads, or first driving an iron screw to form the threads, and then replacing it with the softer screw.

Withdrawing a Screw

1. Clean the slot on the screw head so that the tip of the screwdriver seats itself fully.

2. The screwdriver is used in the same way described for driving a screw except that the direction of rotation is counterclockwise.

3. If the screw is very tight, and it cannot be withdrawn on the first attempt, try turning it clockwise slightly to loosen it, and then turn it counterclockwise.

4. If a screw should tend to bind as it is withdrawn, work it both ways, gradually working it out of the hole.

5. If the screw slot becomes damaged, grasp the head with a pair of pliers after it is partly out and complete the withdrawal with the pliers.

6. Tight screws can also be removed with a brace and screwdriver bit. The leverage possible with this tool makes it ideal for this purpose.

SPECIAL SHAPE WOOD SCREWS

Screws and screw hooks, figure 12-21, are used by the carpenter to hang or attach articles. These types of screws do not serve as fasteners in the same sense as a nail or the common wood screw. The threaded portion of the shank is anchored in wood so that the curved or bent head can be used as a point of attachment.

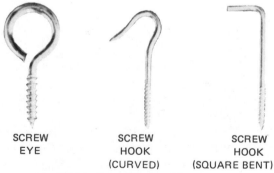

SCREW EYE   SCREW HOOK (CURVED)   SCREW HOOK (SQUARE BENT)

Fig. 12-21 Screw hooks and screw eye.

The method for sizing these screws varies. In some instances they are measured by length, or by the size of the formed portion, and in others by a gauge or catalog number. It is suggested that reference be made to manufacturers' literature when purchasing these items.

Driving Screw Eyes and Screw Hooks

1. Prepare a pilot hole equal in size to the root diameter of the thread (similar to that for the conventional type of wood screw).

   NOTE: No clearance hole is prepared. These types of screws are driven only to the extent of the threaded portion and the remainder protrudes.

2. Start the screw in the pilot hole by grasping the head portion with the thumb and forefinger and turning it clockwise until the point is seated.

3. Fit an open-end adjustable wrench across the head and drive the screw as though turning a nut.

4. An alternate method for driving the screw eye and screw hook is to insert the round shank of a screwdriver within the head and then revolve it. For the square, bent hook, a short length of small pipe can be fitted over the bent portion and used as a handle to drive it.

LAG SCREWS AND HANGER BOLTS

Lag screws, figure 12-22, are like large, ordinary wood screws except that the head is square and unslotted. A wrench instead of a screwdriver must be used to drive or withdraw this type of screw.

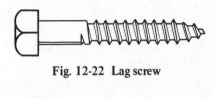

Fig. 12-22 Lag screw

Lag screws are sized by diameter and length. Common diameter sizes are 1/4 inch, 5/16 inch, 3/8 inch, 1/2 inch, and 5/8 inch. Lengths range from 1 inch to 6 inches in 1/2-inch steps, and from 6 inches to 12 inches in 1-inch steps. They are made in black iron, galvanized iron, and bronze.

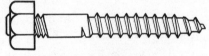

Fig. 12-23 Hanger bolt

This screw is used where great holding power is needed in rough work. Its uses include fastening heavy parts (wood or metal)

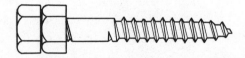

Fig. 12-24 Preparing hanger bolt for driving.

to wooden surfaces and masonry surfaces into which expansion shields have been placed. As with the ordinary wood screw, pilot and clearance holes are prepared if two parts are to be held together. A metal washer should be placed under the head so that it does not cut into the wood surface as it is driven home.

Hanger bolts, figure 12-23, have both ends threaded. The head end has a standard machine screw thread to which a square or hexagon nut is applied. Like the lag screw, the hanger bolt is sized by diameter and length.

Hanger bolts are used the same way as lag screws. They work better than lag screws where parts must be unfastened for repairs or replacement. Since only the nut which forms the head is unscrewed, the wood screw portion is never removed.

In driving this type of screw, two nuts are first locked together short of the shoulder of the thread. See figure 12-24. A wrench is then applied to the top nut for driving. On

Lag Screw Size (dia. in inches)	1/4	5/16	3/8	1/2	5/8	3/4
Outside Dia. of Expansion Shield	1/2	1/2	5/8	3/4	7/8	1
Short Lengths Available (Shield)	1	1 1/4	1 3/4	2	2	2
Long Lengths Available (Shield)	1 1/2	1 3/4	2 1/2	3	3 1/2	3 1/2

Table 12-4 Expansion shield sizes.

completion of the driving, the extra nut is removed. This technique prevents jamming of the nut on the shoulder of the thread, which would cause the entire bolt to come loose.

THE LAG SCREW EXPANSION SHIELD

A lag screw expansion shield is a malleable iron split casting with internal threads. The shield is an anchoring device for lag screws which are to be driven in masonry walls.

Expansion shields are also made for use with machine bolts. The threads within this type of shield are different. Be sure the proper shield is selected for the job.

Lag screw expansion shields are made in sizes for use with 1/4-inch, 5/16-inch, 3/8-inch, 7/16-inch, 1/2-inch, 5/8-inch, and 3/4-inch lag screws. Two lengths are available, short and long. The outside diameter of the shield is a standard fractional size so that the selection of drills for preparing a hole for the shield is not a problem. For example, a shield for a 1/4-inch lag screw has an outside diameter of 1/2 inch and is made in 1 inch and 1 1/2 inch lengths. See table 12-4. Similar information for other types of shields can be obtained from manufacturers of shields.

To use this device, a hole equal to the outside diameter of the shield is first drilled into the masonry. The depth of the hole should be equal to, or slightly greater than the length of the shield. The shield is then inserted in the hole as in figure 12-25. The proper size lag screw driven into the threads causes the shield to expand (more at end B, figure 12-25 than at end A) and put pressure on the sides of the hole, thus providing a secure anchor in the masonry.

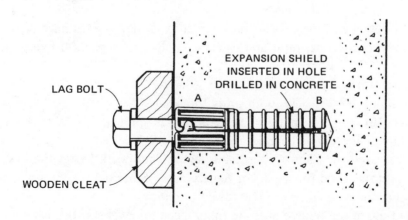

Fig. 12-25 Lag screw expansion shield fitted in masonry wall.

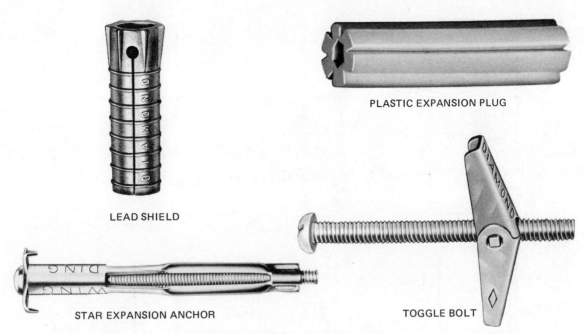

LEAD SHIELD

PLASTIC EXPANSION PLUG

STAR EXPANSION ANCHOR

TOGGLE BOLT

Fig. 12-26 Other anchoring devices.

OTHER ANCHORING DEVICES

Several other devices used for anchoring screws in masonry walls are lead shields, plastic and fiber expansion (rawl) plugs, star expansion anchors, and toggle bolts. See figure 12-26.

Lead shields and expansion plugs have an unthreaded hole. The threads of the screw cut into the soft material of the plug causing it to expand to anchor the screw. See figure 12-27. The outside diameter of these anchors range from 5/32 inch to 3/4 inch. Each diameter size can be obtained in various lengths.

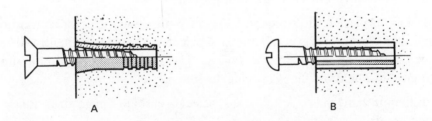

A

B

Fig. 12-27 (A) Application of a lead shield (B) Application of a plastic expansion plug

Star expansion anchors, figure 12-26, are used to fasten fixtures to plastered walls and composition wallboard. To apply this device (see figure 12-28), a hole is drilled in the wall for the unit. Prongs on the shield are forced into the surface of the wall to prevent the shield from turning while the anchor screw is driven. About ten turns of the screwdriver completes spreading of the shield within the hole. This anchors the shield to the wall. The screw is then removed from the shield, inserted through the fixture to be attached, and then redriven.

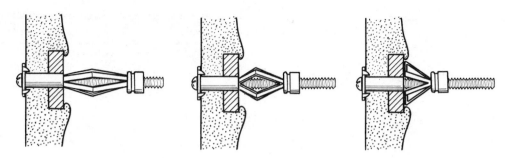

Fig. 12-28 Locking a star expansion anchor into place.

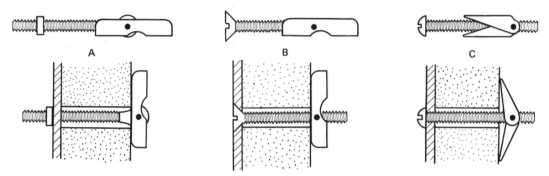

Fig. 12-29 Types of toggle bolts and their method of application.

Toggle bolts, figure 12-29, are used to fasten woodwork to hollow tile walls. The section which expands folds down so that it can be inserted in a hole drilled through the tile surface. After the bolt is inserted the expanding portion pivots or spreads out so it cannot be withdrawn. The screw (A and B, figure 12-29) or nut (C, figure 12-29) can then be tightened to fasten the object to the wall.

Drilling Holes in Masonry Walls for Anchoring Devices

1. For drilling in plaster and other soft masonry materials, select a conventional type of straight-shank drill. In general, the size selected should be equal in diameter to the outside diameter of the anchoring device. The size of the drilled hole should be such that it gives a snug fit of the anchoring device.

2. For drilling in hard masonry materials, select a carbide-tipped drill, figure 12-30, and proceed to drill as with an ordinary drill. Water used as a cutting lubricant speeds the cutting.

    CAUTION: Water as a lubricant should not be used if drilling is done with a portable electric drill.

Fig. 12-30 Carbide-tipped drill

3. Drilling masonry can also be done with a star drill, figure 12-31. This tool is like the cold chisel except that the

Fig. 12-31 Star drill

point is star shaped. These drills are generally made in 8-inch and 12-inch lengths. The point sizes for the 8-inch lengths range from 1/4 inch through 3/4 inch and for the 12-inch lengths from 1/4 inch through 1 1/4 inches. Like a conventional chisel, it is driven with a hammer. When using the star drill, tap it lightly and keep revolving it, or else it binds or breaks out the inside of the masonry (if a hollow type).

> CAUTION: Goggles should be worn for eye protection when doing this type of drilling.

BOLTS AND NUTS USED IN CARPENTRY

Various types of bolts are used to fasten wooden members together. Those most often used by the carpenter are shown in figure 12-32.

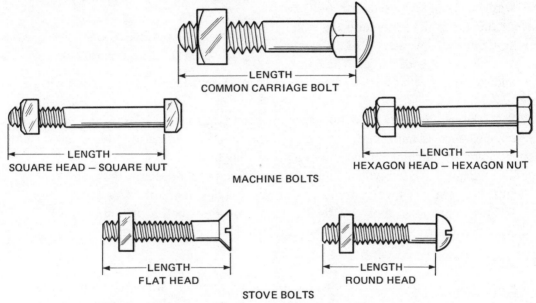

Fig. 12-32 Machine bolts and stove bolts

Bolts differ from wood screws in that they are not threaded into the wood. Holes must be drilled through the wood or metal members so that the bolt passes through. A nut is then threaded to the end to hold the members together.

Bolt sizes are specified by the diameter of the thread or body and by length. The length is measured from the bottom of the head to the end except for the flathead stove bolt which is measured from the top of the head to the end.

Compared to other bolts, stove bolts are rather small, ranging in lengths from 3/8 inch to 4 inches and in body diameter from 1/8 inch to 3/8 inch. Carriage and machine bolts range from 3/4 inch to 20 inches long and from 3/16 inch to 3/4 inch in diameter.

Refer to figure 12-33. The carriage bolt has a square section below the head which is embedded in the wood as the nut is drawn up, thus preventing the bolt from turning as the nut is tightened. It is used only in wood.

The machine bolt has a square or hexagon head which is held with a wrench to prevent the bolt from turning as the nut is tightened.

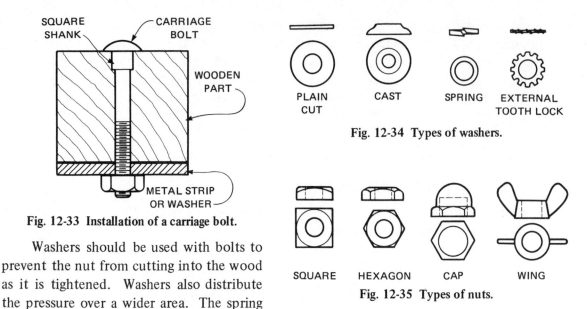

Fig. 12-33 Installation of a carriage bolt.

Fig. 12-34 Types of washers.

Fig. 12-35 Types of nuts.

Washers should be used with bolts to prevent the nut from cutting into the wood as it is tightened. Washers also distribute the pressure over a wider area. The spring lock and external tooth (star) washers are used to prevent the nut from working loose. See figure 12-34.

Several types of nuts used on bolts are shown in figure 12-35. The cap nut is used where appearance is important. It conceals the bolt end, and also reduces the possibility of an accident by catching on the end of a protruding bolt.

The wing nut is used where finger pressure is enough to secure the members in place. Wing nuts also work well where frequent changes or adjustments are necessary.

Whenever possible, apply oil to the threads of a nut before fitting it to a bolt. This helps to prevent corrosion, (which makes it difficult to remove the nut).

FLUSH PLATES

Plates drilled and countersunk to accommodate screws to strengthen joints are made of metal about 1/16 inch thick and 1/2 inch wide. Figure 12-36 shows some of the types most commonly used on screens and small frames.

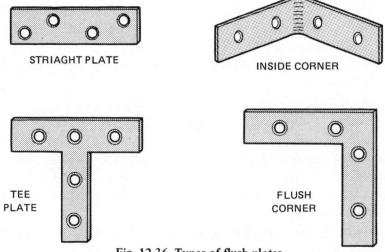

Fig. 12-36 Types of flush plates.

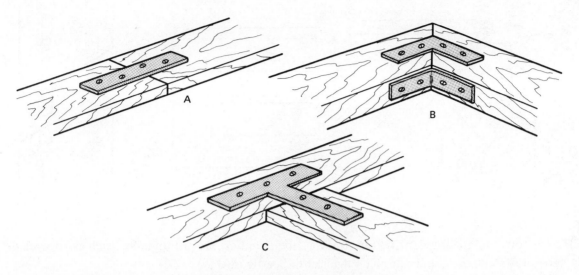

Fig. 12-37 Applications of flush plates.

Applying Flush Plates

1. Place the plates in the desired position on the lumber. Mark the center of the holes on the lumber with a scratch awl and drill the pilot holes.

2. Fasten the plates to the lumber with flathead screws. The screw heads should be driven flush with the plate. Lengths of screws selected depend on the thickness of the lumber.

3. Figure 12-37, A, shows how the straight flush plate is used to fasten and reinforce a butt joint. At B, two types of plates are shown applied to a miter joint. At C, a T-flush plate is shown applied to an angle-butt joint.

WOOD DOWELS

Wood dowels are used for joining various types of wood joints together. They are usually made of hardwood such as birch or maple and come in several forms. See figure 12-38. Diameter sizes range from 3/16 inch to 1 inch, up to 36-inch lengths.

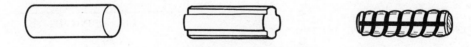

Fig. 12-38 Types of wood dowels.

The longitudinal and helical groove types are better for joinery. The grooves allow air to escape from the dowel hole and distribute the glue evenly.

In many cases a dowel joint is the most practical joint to use. This is true where the members to be fastened are thin, and where cutting away of material to make other types of joints might weaken them. The dowel joint saves material and is as strong as many other types of joints. It is often used in place of a mortise and tenon joint.

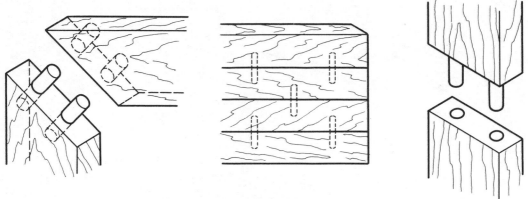

Fig. 12-39 Dowel joints.

Dowel joints are identified by the way the members are put together, such as a doweled-butt, doweled-miter, and doweled-edge joint. See figure 12-39.

Dowels can also be used to pin mortise and tenon joints, to strengthen members, to avoid warpage, and to provide anchorage for screws driven into end grain. See figure 12-40.

The size of the dowel should have a diameter about one-third as thick as the thinnest piece to be doweled. Generally, the 5/16 inch or 3/8 inch sizes are used.

The dowel should be long enough to enter into each member at least one inch. However, circumstances can alter this rule. For example, when running a dowel into end grain, it should be longer. The location of dowels should be as close to the midsection of the wood as possible.

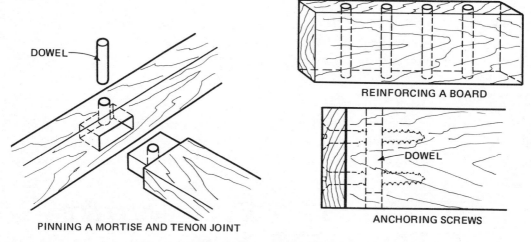

Fig. 12-40 Miscellaneous applications of wood dowels.

Making a Dowel Joint

1. Prepare the surfaces of the joint members so that they are square and straight. When placed together, they should fit perfectly.

2. Lay out the location of the dowels. A few layout methods are shown in figure 12-41.

3. Determine the size of the dowel and, with the aid of a doweling jig (see unit 10, figure 10-47), bore the necessary holes to a uniform depth. Clean the chips from the holes.

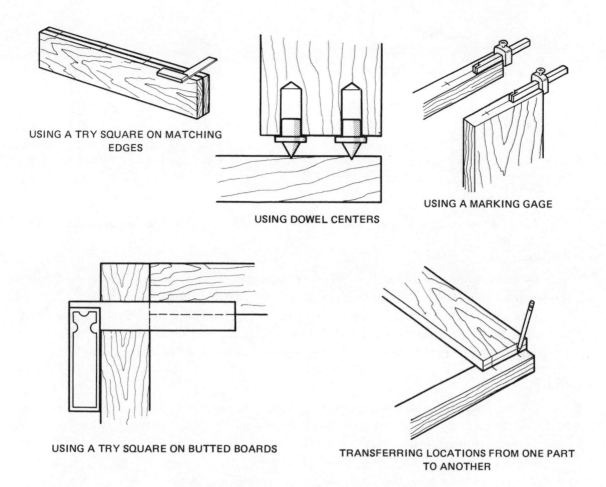

USING A TRY SQUARE ON MATCHING EDGES

USING DOWEL CENTERS

USING A MARKING GAGE

USING A TRY SQUARE ON BUTTED BOARDS

TRANSFERRING LOCATIONS FROM ONE PART TO ANOTHER

Fig. 12-41 Techniques for laying out the dowel holes.

4. Cut the dowels about 1/8 inch shorter than the combined depth of matching holes.

Fig. 12-42 Dowel pointer.

5. Point the dowels at each end with a dowel pointer, figure 12-42. This assures alignment of the dowel with the hole as it is fitted into place.

NOTE: Do not glue the dowels until a trial assembly is made. If any holes are out of alignment, plug and rebore them.

6. When the trial assembly is satisfactory, disassemble it and apply a thin coat of glue to the dowels, holes, and faces of the joint.

7. Assemble the glued parts and clamp them well.

Check for squareness and make any necessary adjustments.

NOTE: To check for squareness of rectangular assemblies, measure the diagonals from corner to corner. They should measure the same.

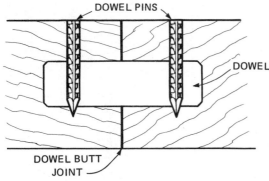

Fig. 12-43 Application of dowel pins.

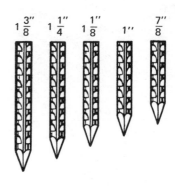

Fig. 12-44 Barbed dowel pins (actual size).

BARBED DOWEL PINS

Barbed dowel pins are used to pin tenons into mortises and to clinch dowels in doweled joints. See figure 12-43. This method produces a very strong joint.

This metal fastener is made in lengths from 5/8 inch to 2 inches and in gauge sizes from 8 through 12. See figure 12-44. They are driven and set in the same manner as a finishing nail. The length should not be more than two-thirds the thickness of the board.

GLUE

Gluing is a process of joining material together with a film of liquid glue. Glue is spread on the surfaces to be joined and clamped together until the glue is dry. The glue penetrates into the wood pores, forming a bond between the two surfaces.

The types of glue commonly available for gluing woodwork are the vegetable, fish, animal, casein, and plastic resin glues. The vegetable and fish glues are cold liquid glues. They are not used as often as the other types because they do not have great holding power. But they work well where slow setting is necessary, and on surfaces which do not easily absorb glue.

Animal glue is stronger than fish or vegetable glue. It flows into joints well, is stainless, and sets quickly. Because it is water soluble, excess glue is easily cleaned.

Animal glue does have some problems. It takes time to prepare. It must be used while it is hot and it breaks down when exposed to moisture.

To prepare animal glue, soak glue chips or pellets overnight before heating in a double boiler. The temperature should not go over 150 degrees Fahrenheit (66° Celsius). The correct mixture for softwoods is one part glue to one and one-half parts water. The correct mixutre for hardwoods is one part glue to two parts water. In general, it should be of a consistency that will run freely from the glue brush.

Casein glue is prepared from a dry casein glue powder and water. It is superior to the liquid and animal glues because it holds up well under heat and moisture. However, it is not completely waterproof and, therefore, is mainly used for inside work. Ordinary casein glue stains certain woods. However, a special nonstaining casein glue can be used.

Casein glue is used cold and begins to set after ten or fifteen minutes. It is usually made one part glue powder to one part water by volume. Detailed instructions for its preparation are given on the container.

Plastic resin glues are waterproof and are used where work is exposed to much moisture and dampness. Like the casein glue, plastic resin glues are in powder form and are prepared by adding water. Two parts of powder to one part cold water by volume produces a satisfactory consistency. The mixture should look like heavy cream. It is applied to the surface in a very thin film. If enough glue is used, a small amount flows from the joint when it is clamped. This excess should be wiped off right away with a damp cloth.

Plastic resin glues set up in four to eight hours and require two to seven days to develop full strength and become waterproof. Weldwood® and Cascamite® are examples of trade names of this type of glue.

Using Glue

1. Prepare the joint so that the surfaces touch at all points. Check the fit by clamping the joints before gluing and inspecting the fit.

2. Determine how many clamps are needed and how they are to be used. If many parts are to be glued to make up a unit, establish a gluing order.

3. Have the necessary tools ready for testing and correcting any alignment problems.

4. Prepare the glue according to the manufacturer's specifications. Apply it in a thin film on the surfaces.

5. Clamp the members together as tightly as possible.

6. Remove any excess glue which flows from the joints with a wood chisel or putty knife and damp cloth.

7. Check the clamped unit for squareness and alignment.

8. Make any necessary adjustments. Loosen the clamps slightly and correct the position of the members with blocks of wood or by tapping members into position.

9. Tighten the clamps, check again, and allow the joint to dry for the time specified by the glue manufacturer. Generally, six hours is allowed for drying softwoods and eight hours or more for hardwoods.

REVIEW QUESTIONS

A. Short Answer or Discussion

1. a. What types of wood screws are most commonly used by the carpenter?

   b. Show by simple sketches how they are sized for length.

2. What portion of the wood screw is measured to determine its gauge size.

3. a. Why is a screw superior to a nail as a fastening device?

    b. What are the limiting factors in its use?

4. How does driving with a Phillips screwdriver differ from driving with the types used for slotted screws?

5. a. What are the advantages of using a screwdriver bit in a brace for driving or removing screws?

    b. When should a brace and a screwdriver bit not be used for driving a screw?

6. Sketch the necessary views to show how a screwdriver should fit in a slotted screw head.

7. a. What is the purpose of dowel centers?

    b. Show by a simple sketch how they are used.

8. What preparation is necessary when fastening two boards together with flathead wood screws? Clarify the answer with a sketch.

9. Describe a technique which can be used when driving soft metal wood screws to reduce the possibility of having them twist off.

10. How can screw holes be concealed?

11. Should a clearance hole be drilled for driving a screw eye? Explain.

12. a. How is the size of a Phillips screwdriver specified?

    b. What size should be used for a 7-gauge Phillips screw? What size should be used for a 20-gauge Phillips screw?

13. What size bit is used to counterbore for sinking the head of a number 12 slotted head wood screw?

14. What is the purpose of flush plates?

15. What is the advantage of a dowel joint over many of the other types of joints?

16. what type of dowel is preferred for dowel joints? Why?

17. For what type of walls are star expansion anchors used?

18. What special precaution should be taken when drilling hard masonry?

19. Why should washers be used under the heads of nuts?

20. Why must the joints of a glued joint fit perfectly?

21. a. What are the types of glues used for gluing woodwork?

    b. What types are commonly used for indoor work?

    c. What type is used for outdoor work?

B. Completion

1. A _____ screw and a _____ screw do ńot have their slots extend to the sides of the head.

2. The surface of an iron roundhead wood screw is usually _____ or _____ to help prevent _____.

3. The pilot hole is drilled to receive the _____ portion of the screw. If a number 5 slotted screw is used in the hole and the wood is soft, the size of the hole in fractions of an inch should be _____.

4. For obtaining the greatest holding power, at least _____ the length of the screw would enter the board.

5. A square-shank screwdriver can be turned with the aid of a _____.

6. The length of a screwdriver is measured from the _____ to the _____.

7. Toggle bolts are generally used as fastening devices on _____ walls.

8. For seating an expansion shield 2 1/2 inches long and using a 3/8-inch lag screw, a hole _____ in diameter must be drilled to a depth of at least _____.

9. The _____ drill and _____ drill are used for drilling in hard masonry.

10. A carriage bolt differs from a machine bolt by the _____ of its _____.

11. When making a dowel joint in the end grain of wood, the joint should be prepared so that the dowel extends at least _____ into each member.

12. A dowel can be used to _____ a mortise and tenon joint.

13. Dowel pins are used for _____ dowels.

14. A disadvantage of ordinary casein glue is that it _____ certain types of wood.

15. A glue which is _____ is required for outdoor work.

C. Identification and Interpretation

1. Identify the types of fastening devices shown in figure 12-45.

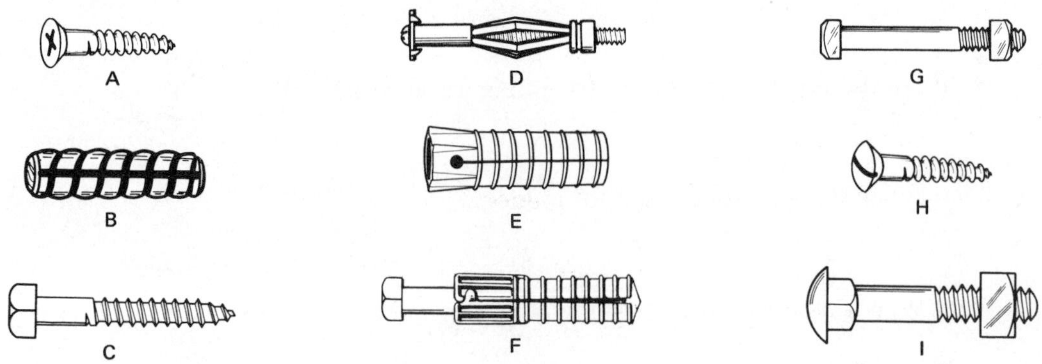

Fig. 12-45

2. Identify the fastening devices in the assembly shown in figure 12-46.

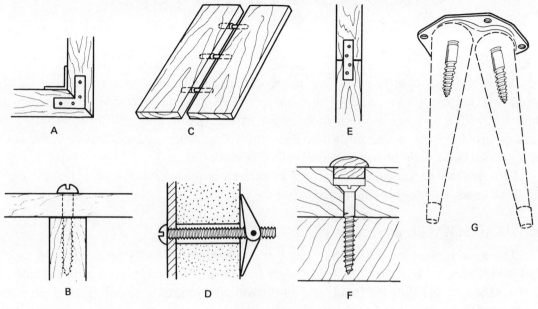

Fig. 12-46

3. Interpret the meaning of the numbers 1 1/4 and 11 found on the label of the box of wood screws shown in figure 12-47.

Fig. 12-47

Unit 13 SMOOTHING TOOLS

SCRAPERS

A finely finished surface must be made smooth before the finishing coats of shellac, varnish, or lacquer are applied. Cross-grained, curly- or wavy-grained wood should be smoothed with a scraper. A sharpened scraper used correctly smooths surfaces that a hand plane might chip. For a fine rubbed varnish finish that brings out the beauty of the grain, the wood surface should be hand scraped rather than sanded.

Scrapers can be classified into three general categories — hand scraper blades, single-handle scrapers, and double-handle scrapers.

THE HAND SCRAPER

The hand scraper blade is a rectangular or curved piece of tool steel about 1/16 inch in thickness (figure 13-1, A and B). It is slightly harder than a saw blade. A scraper blade can be sharpened by grinding or filing, and burnished to produce a square, turned edge or a bevel turned edge (figure 13-1, C and D). The burr on the bevel-edge type can be formed more easily than the burr on the square-edge type. To produce the burr on the sharpened edge of a scraper, a burnisher is used to rub and roll the edge.

A rectangular shaped blade is used for flat surface work. It is especially useful for scraping areas (corners, etc.) which are difficult to finish with any other type of tool.

The swan-neck shape is used to scrape surfaces of molding and curves that cannot be scraped with straight blades. That portion of the blade is used which conforms to the curvature to be scraped.

A scraper removes shavings by the action of a scraping burr rather than by a cutting edge as in a plane. It takes thin shavings and curls them up at very short intervals due to the shape of the hook or burnished edge. See figure 13-2. Blades which are square edged can be pushed and/or pulled to get the cutting action.

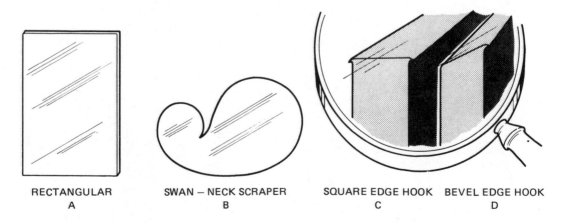

RECTANGULAR   SWAN — NECK SCRAPER   SQUARE EDGE HOOK   BEVEL EDGE HOOK
A   B   C   D

Fig. 13-1 Types of hand scrapers.

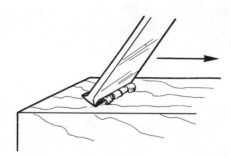

Fig. 13-2 Scraping action of scraper blade.

Using a Hand Scraper Blade

1. The blade can be held with one hand (figure 13-3) or both hands. When both hands are used, place them on the blade as though holding a book to read.

2. When using a rectangular blade with a pull stroke, set the blade as shown in figure 13-4. Pull the scraper with an even easy pressure and keep the blade at the same angle throughout the stroke.

3. If a push stroke is used, reverse the angle of tilt so that the opposite edge does the cutting.

    NOTE: Cutting can be done by a push and pull stroke, if both edges are burnished.

4. When using a swan-neck scraper, fit the blade into the curvature to be scraped and use it in the way described for the hand scraper.

PULL SCRAPERS

Pull scrapers can be classified as fixed handle, figure 13-5, or adjustable handle, figure 13-6. The adjustable-handle pull scraper has a socket on the end of the handle. This allows the scraper blade to be adjusted to various angles. This type of scraper works like a hand scraper except that the blade is held in position in a

Fig. 13-3 Using the hand scraper blade with one hand.

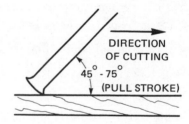

Fig. 13-4 Hand scraping with a pull stroke.

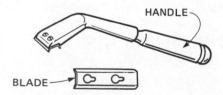

Fig. 13-5 Fixed-handle pull scraper.

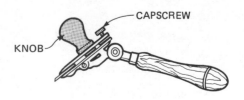

Fig. 13-6 Adjustable-handle pull scraper.

frame while the handle is being pulled. It is convenient for scraping floor surfaces close to a wall that cannot be reached with a floor sander.

The fixed-handle pull scraper comes with a single- or double-edge preformed blade. Single-edge blades are usually fixed in the handle. Double-edge blades are locked in place by screws so that they can be reversed or replaced as the edges become worn. It is not necessary to burnish these preformed blades.

Using a Pull Scraper

1. When using the fixed-handle type, proceed as follows:

    a. If a double-edge blade is used, screw the blade onto the head.

    b. Hold the handle with one hand and use the palm of the other hand to apply pressure on the head.

    NOTE: The amount of material scraped away is determined by the pressure applied to the head.

    c. Pull the scraper toward the body with a steady stroke. Keep the handle parallel to the surface being scraped. Uneven gouging can occur if the angle of the blade is changed during the stroke. The pressure on the head should be the same from the start to the end of the stroke.

    NOTE: When scraping finished surfaces (paint, etc.), try to get under the finish. Gliding the edge over finished surfaces dulls the blade rapidly.

2. When using an adjustable-handle scraper, proceed as follows:

    a. Select and examine the cutter for sharpness.

    b. Lock the cutter in place with the cap and screw on the head of the scraper. The hooked (turned) portion of the blade should face the operator.

    c. Adjust the blade angle by rotating the head at the joint provided for this purpose. By trial and error adjust this angle until the scraper edge cuts effectively.

    d. Pull the scraper toward the body as described for the fixed-handle type.

THE CABINET SCRAPER

The cabinet scraper, figure 13-7, is a double-handle type of scraper. It looks like a spokeshave. It is worked and held like a spokeshave, but it has a flat bottom and is limited to flat surfaces.

The thickness of the shaving can be adjusted by turning the adjustable thumbscrew, shown in figure 13-7. The blade is held in the

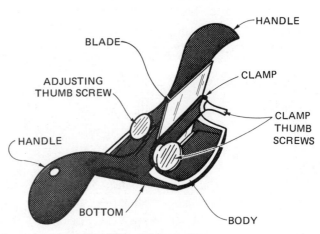

Fig. 13-7 Cabinet scraper.

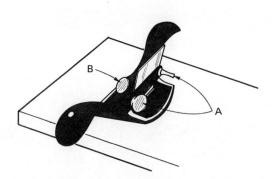

Fig. 13-8 Position of the scraper for adjustments.

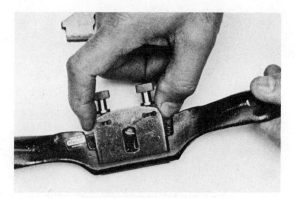

Fig. 13-9 Inserting the blade.

frame a fixed distance from the bottom of the scraper so that shavings of the same thickness are removed. The bottom of the scraper is short and does not have the leveling action of a longer plane.

A great deal of downward pressure can be applied to the handles of this scraper. Thicker shavings can be taken with a cabinet scraper than with a hand scraper blade.

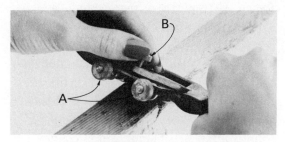

Fig. 13-10 Using the cabinet scraper.

This type of scraper is used mainly for final smoothing before sandpapering. It removes the slight ridges left by other planing tools. It is also used to smooth surfaces that are difficult to plane because of curly or uneven grain.

Adjusting and Using the Cabinet Scraper

1. Place the scraper in a convenient position for making adjustments. See figure 13-8.

2. Loosen the adjusting thumbscrew, B, and the clamp thumbscrews, A, so the blade can be easily inserted.

3. Insert the blade from the bottom with the bevel side toward the adjusting screw, figure 13-9.

4. Bring the edge of the blade even with the bottom of the scraper body. This is done by placing the bottom on a flat surface and pressing the blade lightly against the wood. Tighten the clamping screws.

5. Bow the blade by tightening the adjusting thumbscrew, B, to make it project enough to take a thin shaving.

   NOTE: If one corner of the blade projects too far, it can be drawn in by tapping the side of the blade near the top.

6. Try the scraper and change the adjustment until it takes a thin, even shaving. Hold it turned a little to the side (at a slight diagonal) to start a cut.

   NOTE: The cabinet scraper is usually pushed, as in figure 13-10, but it can be pulled. Dust instead of a shaving indicates a dull scraper.

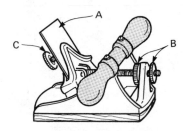

Fig. 13-11 Scraper plane

Fig. 13-12 Burnisher

THE SCRAPER PLANE

The scraper plane has a wider and longer bottom than the cabinet scraper. The bottom can have a wooden block screwed to the surface as shown in figure 13-11. The blade is heavier and wider than that of the cabinet scraper. The thickness of the shaving can be varied by changing the angle of the blade by adjusting the thumb nuts, B. Thumb nut C clamps the blade, A, in place. It is used in much the same manner as a cabinet scraper.

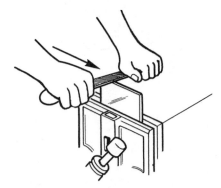

Fig. 13-13 Draw filing a square edge.

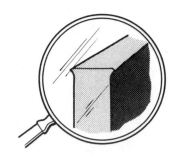

Fig. 13-14 Showing wire edge turned from face.

THE BURNISHER

The scraper blade burnisher, figure 13-12, has an oval shaped blade about four inches long. The blade is made from tool steel, hardened and ground to a smooth surface. It is used for turning the edge of a scraper blade to form a hook edge.

Sharpening the Square-Edged Scraper Blade

1. When sharpening a rectangular blade, proceed as follows:

   a. Place the blade in a bench vise. With a mill file remove and joint the worn cutting edge. The file should be held flat on the cutting edge and 90 degrees to the face of the blade when draw filing the edge (figure 13-13). The filed edge should look like the enlarged view in figure 13-14.

   b. The wire edge shown in figure 13-14 must be removed. To remove this edge, place the cutting edge flat on a fine grit oilstone (A, figure 13-15). The blade edge must be square on the face of the stone. If the face of the stone is not true use the edge.

   c. The face of the blade should be whetted smooth. Place the face on the oilstone as shown in B, figure 13-15. The edge of the blade should then look like the enlarged view, figure 13-16. This view shows that the wire edge still remains, and more whetting is necessary.

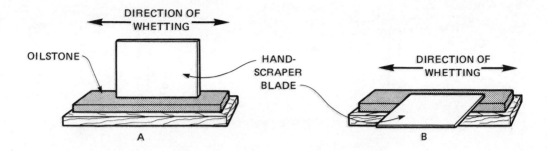

Fig. 13-15 Whetting the hand scraper blade.

Fig. 13-16 Enlarged view of the blade.

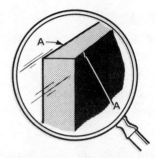

Fig. 13-17 Showing refined edges.

d. Wipe off the stone and repeat steps b and c until the wire edge is removed. The enlarged view of the edge should now look like figure 13-17. When the edges, A-A, are sharp, they are ready to be burnished.

2. When sharpening the swan-neck shaped scraper, proceed as follows:

a. Draw file the curved edge holding the file at right angles to the face of the blade. Rotate the cutter in the vise so that its entire edge can be sharpened.

NOTE: The portion of the blade which forms a V shape should be sharpened with a small knife-edge type file.

b. Whet the edge with a slipstone and smooth the sides on a flat oilstone.

Burnishing a Square-Edged Scraper Blade

1. Hold the blade flat on a clean wood surface. Lay the burnisher flat on the surface of the blade near the sharpened edge as in figure 13-18. Take several firm strokes with the burnisher across each face of the blade.

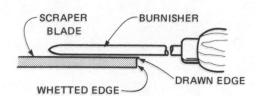

Fig. 13-18 Drawing an edge.

2. Clamp the blade firmly in a vise. Pass the burnisher over one edge of the blade, holding the burnisher at 90 degrees to the face for the first stroke.

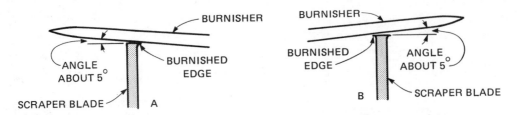

Fig. 13-19 Burnishing the edges.

3. With each stroke, gradually tip the burnisher so that the handle end is tilted about 5 degrees down from the horizontal (A, figure 13-19). Take each stroke the full length of the blade.

4. Burnish the other edge in the same manner (B, figure 13-19). The burnished edge should look like the enlarged view, figure 13-20. In that figure, A-A shows the scraping edges.

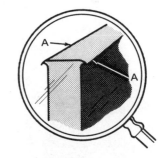

Fig. 13-20 Showing finished edges.

Sharpening the Bevel-Edged Scraper Blade

NOTE: Scraper blades with bevel edges are used in the pull scraper, cabinet scraper, and scraper plane.

1. Test the edge for straightness with a try square and note the high spots.

2. Clamp the blade in a vise and joint the edge with a flat mill file as shown in figure 13-21.

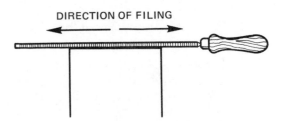

Fig. 13-21 Jointing the blade.

3. With the file held flat on the straight side of the blade, remove the old scraping edge as in figure 13-22.

4. File a bevel edge on the scraper at an angle of about 45 degrees. A draw filing technique (moving the file along the edge so that cutting is done on both the forward and return stroke) produces a straight beveled

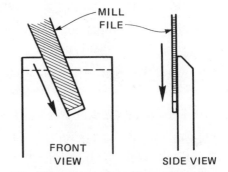

Fig. 13-22 Removing old scraping edge.

edge. See figure 13-23. File until a wire edge appears on the side opposite to the bevel.

5. Whet the bevel and straight side of the edge on an oilstone. Use the same technique described for whetting a bench plane iron. In this case the angle of the bevel should be slightly greater than 45 degrees.

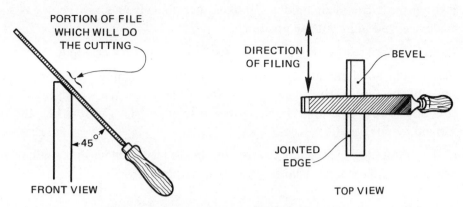

Fig. 13-23 Draw filing a beveled edge.

6. Round the corners slightly by tilting the blade and whetting the extreme ends of the bevel.

7. Clamp the blade in a vise with the blade above the vise jaws and burnish the edge.

8. With a burnisher, take a full stroke across the width of the blade, figure 13-24. Hold it with both hands at the angle shown in A, figure 13-25. Apply only enough pressure to start the edge to turn.

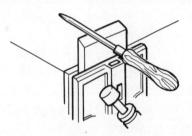

Fig. 13-24 Burnishing beveled edge.

9. Take several more strokes with the burnisher, decreasing the angle of the burnisher with each stroke, as in B and C, figure 13-25. Increase the pressure on the last strokes so enough steel will be turned over to support the scraping edge.

10. If the edge is turned too far or if there are any small nicks in the turned edge, use the tip of the burnisher under the cutting edge to turn it back. See D, figure 13-25.

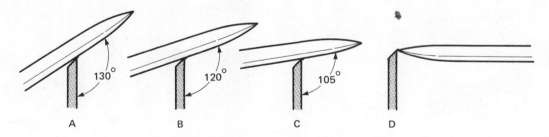

Fig. 13-25 Steps in burnishing a beveled edge.

Sharpening Fixed-Handle Pull Scraper Blades

NOTE: Both the single- and double-edged blades are ground because their edges are usually too hard to be filed. To grind these blades, proceed as follows:

1. Tighten the blade in its holder. Unlike other plane blades, sharpening is done with the blade clamped in its cutting position.

2. Adjust the tool rest so that it can be used as a support for grinding.

3. Use the old bevel already on the edge as a guide for applying the blade at the correct angle to the face of the wheel. Move the blade across the wheel, taking light grinding cuts until a fine burr appears along its entire edge. This burr is like the hooked edge formed by burnishing.

4. If it is a double-edged blade, reverse the blade in its holder and sharpen the opposite edge in a similar manner. No burnishing is necessary.

FILES

The types of files commonly used by the carpenter are wood files and rasps. Wood files are used for smoothing edges and small curves that are difficult to smooth with other tools. They come in a variety of shapes, such as flat, square, half-round, and triangular (figure 13-26). These files are available with teeth of varying degrees of fineness. They range in length from four to fourteen inches. The parts of a file are shown in figure 13-27.

The spacing of the teeth and the angle at which the teeth cross the surface of the file are known as the *cut* of the file. A single-cut file has teeth that run in parallel

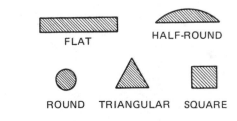

Fig. 13-26 File shapes.

Fig. 13-27 Parts of a file.

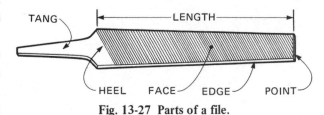

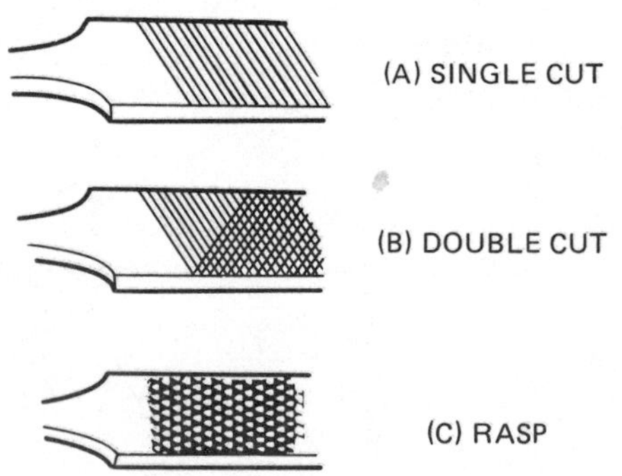

Fig. 13-28 Types of file teeth.

Fig. 13-29 Degrees of tooth coarseness.

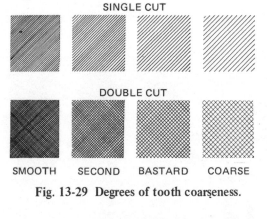

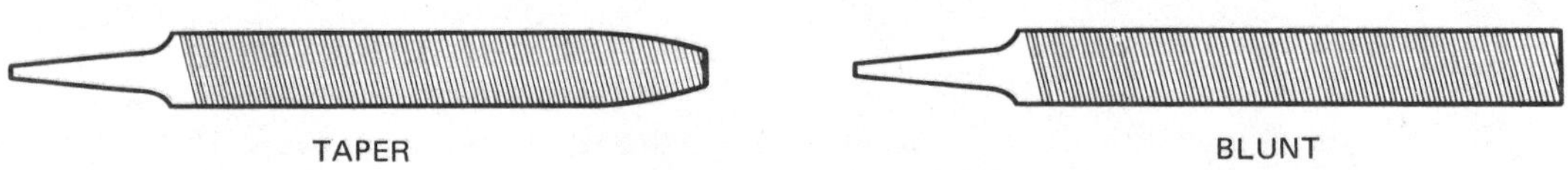

Fig. 13-30 File contours.

lines diagonally across the surface (A, figure 13-28). Single-cut files are classified as rough, bastard, second cut, and smooth. See figure 13-29. A double-cut file (B, figure 13-28) has a double series of teeth crossing each other at an angle. Double-cut files are also classified as rough, bastard, second cut, and smooth. See figure 13-29. The rasp (C, figure 13-28) has a surface covered with triangular-shaped teeth instead of serrations. Rasps are used where much stock is to be removed before using a wood file.

As files increase in length, they become large in cross section. The general contour of the file can be taper or blunt shape, figure 13-30.

The point of a taper shape can be inserted into small openings and the opening gradually worked larger. The taper also makes surface filing easier because the span of cutting increases gradually.

The blunt shape increases the rate of filing. Because its edges are straight, they can be used to file inside corners effectively. Certain blunt-shaped files have one edge that is plain so that when filing a surface to a corner, the plain edge does not cut into the side of the work.

FILE HANDLES

Files should not be used without handles (figure 13-31) except in special cases such as when jointing a handsaw. If a file used without a handle meets an obstruction, the pressure of the hand against the tang can result in injury.

Two types of handle are made for files — wood handles of various sizes with metal ferrules into which the tang is driven, and metal handles which have a clamping device for inserting and holding the tang. Metal handles, although more expensive, are often preferred because they are easily and quickly transferred from one file to another. Also, if they should work loose, they can be tightened, which is sometimes difficult with wood handles.

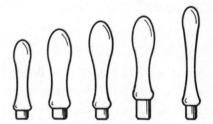

Fig. 13-31 File handles

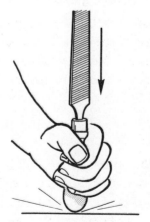

Fig. 13-32 Inserting a file.

Inserting a File in a Wood Handle

1. Choose a proper size handle. This can be determined by the length of the file and the size of the tang. Long and heavy type files require large handles.

2. Insert the tang into the hole at the ferrule end of the handle.

3. Grasp the handle as shown in figure 13-32. While holding it in this position, strike the end of the handle against a solid, flat surface. (Placing a scrap board on a workbench provides an adequate surface.)

4. Continue striking the surface until the tang has entered the hole short of its full length.

NOTE: The ferrule prevents splitting of the handle. However, if the tang is driven too far into the handle, splitting can occur.

Removing a File Handle

1. Hold the file in the right hand with the handle up. See figure 13-33.

2. Place the ferrule against an edge and tap sharply against the edge until the file is worked loose.

NOTE: Use a scrap of wood to avoid damaging the edge of the workbench.

Using a File for Straight Filing

1. Clamp the work securely. Both hands must be used to control the file.

2. For rough filing, hold the file as shown in figure 13-34. For accurate filing, hold the file as shown in figure 13-35. The hand or fingers on the toe of the file are used to apply pressure to produce the cutting action.

3. Hold the file firmly and parallel to the surface of the work and push it across the work. Use a uniform pressure to produce a good cutting action. Use the full length of the file to do the cutting.

NOTE: Do not rock the file.

4. On the return stroke, lift it clear of .the work. Cutting is done only on the forward stroke. Lifting the file on the return stroke allows the worker to see the results of his filing and prolongs the life of the file.

5. Constantly check to see that the surface is being filed flat. Use a straight-edge for this purpose.

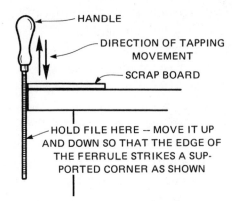

HANDLE

DIRECTION OF TAPPING MOVEMENT

SCRAP BOARD

HOLD FILE HERE — MOVE IT UP AND DOWN SO THAT THE EDGE OF THE FERRULE STRIKES A SUPPORTED CORNER AS SHOWN

Fig. 13-33 Removing a handle.

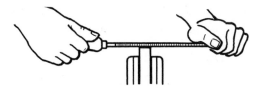

Fig. 13-34 Rough filing.

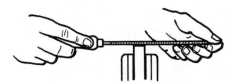

Fig. 13-35 Finish filing.

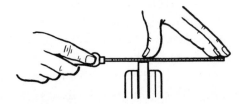

Fig. 13-36 Position for file if rounding has occurred.

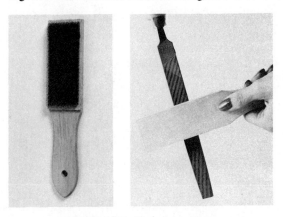

Fig. 13-37 Cleaning a file.

6. If rounding has occurred, hold the file as shown in figure 13-36. The thumb and fingers provide downward pressure over the full length of the file. This assures a more perfect horizontal stroke.

7. Clean the file as it becomes clogged by brushing with a file card as shown in figure 13-37.

8. Continue to file, checking for flatness from time to time, until the required filing is completed.

Caring for Files

1. Keep files stored so that they are not in contact with one another.

2. Keep the teeth clean by the use of a file card. If the teeth become clogged with resinous materials, clean them by soaking the file in turpentine or other suitable solvent. Teeth that are clogged with soft metal, such as aluminum, must be cleaned individually with a sharp point.

3. Do not allow oil to collect on files. Although this prevents rusting, it also acts as an adhesive and causes clogging of the teeth. Oil can be removed by rubbing the teeth with chalk. The chalk absorbs the oil and is then brushed out with a file card.

4. Keep files stored in a dry place to avoid rust.

5. Do not strike files against surfaces or use them for prying or wedging. They are brittle and can break.

REVIEW QUESTIONS

A. Short Answer or Discussion

1. Why is scraping rather than planing done when an especially fine finish is required?

2. Describe the special uses of each type of hand scraper blade?

3. What advantage is there in preparing a hand scraper blade with a square edge rather than with a bevel edge?

4. Why should the corners of the hand scraper blade be rounded?

5. At about what angle should the hand scraper blade be held? How does changing this angle affect the scraping?

6. How do the two types of pull scrapers differ?

7. How does the use of the pull scraper differ from that of the hand scraper?

8. What is the main use of a cabinet scraper?

9. Which of the scrapers have a square-edged blade and which have a bevel-edged blade?

10. How are the worn edges of scraper blades removed?

11. What is meant by the cut of a file?

12. Classify the file cuts according to their use.

13. How does a rasp differ from a file? What advantage does this give it in removing wood?

14. When does a blunt-shaped file have an advantage over a taper-shaped file?

15. How can oil be removed from a file?

B. Completion

1. A scraper blade is dull when _____ instead of _____ result from its use.

2. The most suitable scraper for removing old varnish from the corners of floors is the _____.

3. For the finest finish, the _____ should be used.

4. After planing, but before sanding, the _____ is most suitable for use.

5. Of the various types of scrapers, only the _____ and the _____ can be mechanically adjusted for thickness of shaving.

6. Before burnishing an edge it must be _____.

7. When turning the edge of a square-edged blade, the burnisher is started at _____ degrees to the edge of the blade and on successive strokes is moved to _____ degrees to the edge.

8. When turning the edge of a bevel-edged blade, the burnisher is started at _____ degrees to the face of the blade and is gradually moved to _____ degrees to the face.

9. The main difficulty in using files for wood smoothing is the tendency of the teeth to _____.

10. The main use of files in woodworking is _____.

Unit 14 COATED ABRASIVES

An *abrasive* is any sharp, hard material that wears away a softer material when the two are rubbed together. The term abrasive includes grinding wheels, oilstones, and coated abrasives. A *coated abrasive* is an abrasive sheet made by gluing small abrasive particles to a backing.

The coated abrasives used by the carpenter are called *sandpapers*. These produce a smooth finish on wood surfaces, remove excess material, and smooth and polish finishes which have been applied to wood surfaces. Each type of sandpaper has special characteristics which affect its performance. A knowledge of these is essential in determining the type of sandpaper to choose for use on the job.

The basic elements which control the operation and performance of sandpaper and other abrasives are as follows:

- *Abrasive Grain.* The abrasive grain does the job of cutting.

- *Backing.* The material to which the abrasive grain is applied. The element carries the abrasive grain into action.

- *Bonding.* The process by which the abrasive grain particles are firmly fixed (by means of an adhesive) to the backing.

- *Flexibility.* The ability of the product to be adapted to required operating conditions.

Coated abrasives can be divided into two general classes, natural and artificial. Natural abrasives are found in nature; artificial abrasives are produced in controlled electrical furnaces. The natural abrasives used on wood are flint and garnet. Emery, also classified as a natural abrasive, is used for polishing metals.

Flint is the abrasive used on ordinary sandpaper. When crushed, flint breaks up into sharp crystals, but these crystals lack the hardness and durability of other abrasives. Therefore, ordinary sandpaper has a short life.

Garnet is harder and tougher than flint. When the garnet crystals finally break down in use, they fracture sharply and thus present new cutting surfaces. While garnet paper is more expensive than flint sandpaper, it is more satisfactory and lasts longer. It has almost totally replaced flint sandpaper.

The artificial abrasives, aluminum oxide and silicon carbide, are not often used by the carpenter. Silicon carbide coated abrasives have uses in sanding leather, plastics, glass, and low tensile metals (aluminum, brass and so forth). Aluminum oxide is the stronger and more durable of the two artificial abrasives. It is effectively used in woodworking and finishing high-tensile metals. For certain woodworking operations (power sanding, etc.), it is preferred to garnet.

CLASSIFICATION OF GRAIN SIZES

Abrasive particles are graded to uniform sizes by sifting through screens to various sizes termed *grains* or *grits*. The standard commercial grain sizes are classified in table 14-1.

The numbers in the table listed under the silicon carbide, aluminum oxide, and garnet columns reflect the number of openings per linear inch which the grain has been sifted through. The figures under the column headed "Equivalent in Symbol Series" are symbols used to show grade or size of grit.

The grain size number is most often used in identifying the grade of sandpaper. Note that for garnet, grain sizes range from 280 (very fine) to 20 (very coarse).

The grades most commonly used by the carpenter are numbers 60, 80, 100, and 120. Grades coarser than 60 or finer than 120 are seldom used on wood. When a surface is rough or wavy, a number 60 grade is used, followed by the finer grades until the desired smoothness is obtained. It is necessary to use a coarser grade of flint paper than garnet to get similar results.

Silicon Carbide	Aluminum Oxide	Garnet	Equivalent in Symbol Series	Flint	Emery
600			12/0		
500	500		11/0		
400	400		10/0		
360					
320	320		9/0		
280	280	280	8/0		
240	240	240	7/0		
220	220	220	6/0	4/0	
				3/0	
180	180	180	5/0		3/0
150	150	150	4/0	2/0	2/0
120	120	120	3/0		1/0
				1/0	
100	100	100	2/0		
				½	½
80	80	80	1/0		1
				1	
60	60	60	½		1 ½
50	50	50	1	1 ½	2
				2	2 ½
40	40	40	1 ½		
				2 ½	
36	36	36	2		3
30	30	30	2 ½	3	
24	24	24	3		
20	20	20	3 ½		
16	16		4		
12			4 ½		

Table 14-1 Sandpaper abrasive grain sizes (natural and artificial) and symbol numbers applied.

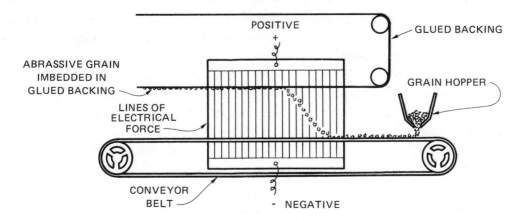

Fig. 14-1 The electrostatic process of applying abrasives to a backing.

BONDING AND DISTRIBUTION ON COATED ABRASIVES

The abrasive grains on coated abrasives are held in place by means of a bond. There are three bonds: animal glue, resins, and varnish, used for coated abrasives. The way the abrasive grains are fixed in the bond bed is known as *coating* which is classified as open or closed.

A coated abrasive is open coated when each abrasive grain is set at predetermined distances from one another, and the surface coverage is about 50 to 70 percent. Open-coated abrasives do not clog quickly and are good for jobs where the sanded material tends to clog the abrasive paper.

Closed or regular coating completely covers the surface of the backing. It is best used on jobs where a great deal of material is to be removed. Close-coated papers are also used where heavy working pressure is applied such as in the case of sanding end grain and hardwoods. This is the type commonly used in hand sanding wood.

Coated abrasives can be obtained that have the abrasives applied by means of a special electrostatic process. See figure 14-1. This process applies the grains or grits to the backing so that each particle takes an upright position. In this process, the grains or grits are passed into an electrostatic field where they become charged, one end of each grain becoming positive, and the other negative.

A negative electrode or pole used in creating the electrostatic field attracts the positive end of the grain particle and repels the negative end. Thus the grain is turned and applied in an upright position on the backing. The result is a sanding or abrading surface that uses a much higher percentage of keen upright points. Furthermore, the pattern of the grain particles is very uniform. All products made by this process are identified by the special electrocoated trademark on the backing of the material and on the package label.

BACKINGS

The materials used for backings on coated abrasives are paper, cloth, combination, and fibre combination. Paper backings are classified by weight and are indexed to the relative strength of the paper. When ordering, the weight must be specified if other than standard weight backing is desired.

Waterproof paper backings are made for use where lubricants are used to improve the abrasive action of the sandpaper. Generally, only the artificial abrasives are applied on this type of paper. In the woodworking trade, it is used for rubbing hard varnish and lacquer finish coats.

Cloth backings have greater strength and flexibility than is usually possible with a paper backing. There are two weights or grades of cloth – jeans and drills. Jeans is a light-weight, strong cloth; and drills is a heavier, stronger, and more stretch-resistant cloth. Cloth-backed abrasives are mainly used on power-driven sanding devices.

Combination backing is a stronger paper stock combined with a lightweight cloth. It is used on severe sanding operations requiring a coated abrasive stronger than the paper-back type.

Fibre combinations, vulcanized fibre combined with drills, test at strengths far greater than any paper or cloth. They are mainly used for disc operations or portable sanders where very high speeds and great stresses and strains are met.

FLEXING

The flexing (finish) of coated abrasive products involves breaking of the bond bed. Its purpose is to make easier application of the product. When applied, it is identified by a number on the backing.

There are two types of flexibility, 90 degree and 45 degree. When the flexing runs crosswise of the sheet, as in figure 14-2, the flex is said to be 90 degrees. This type of flex is commonly used for abrasive products for flat belt sanding operation. When the material is flexed at angles of 45 degrees, the flexing runs toward each of the two edges of the product (figure 14-3). This results in a product that is flexible in all directions and is easy to use on contours.

Fig. 14-2 90-degree flexibility.

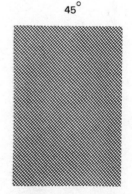

Fig. 14-3 45-degree flexibility.

SIZES AND IDENTIFICATION OF ABRASIVE PAPERS

Sandpaper is made in rolls and in 9-inch x 11-inch sheets. Sheets are packaged in quires (24 sheets) and reams (480 sheets), but any quantity can be purchased in separate sheets.

Information which identifies the type of coated abrasive is found on the package label. It includes the following items:

1. The name and/or trademark of the manufacturer.

2. The product use name.

3. The grit size (by a grit screen number and a grit symbol number).

4. The type of backing.

5. The type of abrasive and electrostating (if applicable).

6. The coating (shown only when open) and filler added to bond.

7. Finish (indication of flexibility).

8. Quantity and dimensions.

When ordering coated abrasives, it is necessary that all of the specifications in figure 14-4 be listed. Similar information, but not as complete, is printed on the back of each sheet of abrasive paper (figure 14-5).

SANDING

Sanding should be done only after all operations with edge tools have been completed. Using edge tools on a surface after it has been sanded dulls the tools rapidly because of the fine abrasive particles embedded in the wood.

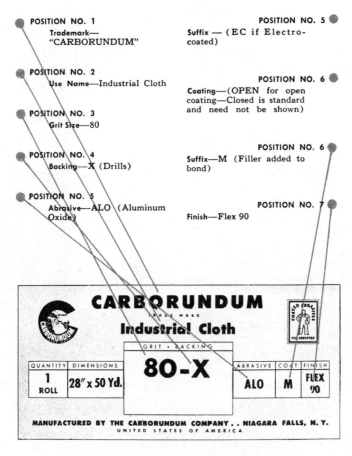

Fig. 14-4 Typical identification marks – labels.

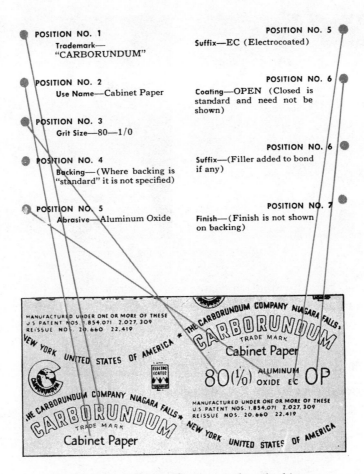

POSITION NO. 1
Trademark—
"CARBORUNDUM"

POSITION NO. 2
Use Name—Cabinet Paper

POSITION NO. 3
Grit Size—80—1/0

POSITION NO. 4
Backing—(Where backing is
"standard" it is not specified)

POSITION NO. 5
Abrasive—Aluminum Oxide

POSITION NO. 5
Suffix—EC (Electrocoated)

POSITION NO. 6
Coating—OPEN (Closed is
standard and need not be
shown)

POSITION NO. 6
Suffix—(Filler added to bond
if any)

POSITION NO. 7
Finish—(Finish is not shown
on backing)

Fig. 14-5 Typical identification marks — backing.

Generally, sandpaper can be used most effectively for hand sanding by tearing it into four equal parts. Several techniques for doing this are described later in this unit.

Mostly, sanding should be done with the grain. For faster and easier cutting, it is sometimes done at a slight angle to the grain. Final sanding is then done by rubbing entirely with the grain to remove any scratch marks which have resulted. Sanding should not be done across the grain as it is very difficult to remove the scratch marks created.

As sandpaper is used, it becomes filled up with fine wood particles which tend to reduce its abrasive action. These particles should be removed by occasionally slapping the sandpaper against a hard surface.

Great care should be used to avoid rounding corners when sanding. Working to the corner rather than over it helps to avoid this. Wrapping the sandpaper around a rectangular block also helps as the block permits better control of the sandpaper and a more even distribution of the pressure.

When sanding concave surfaces, wrap the sandpaper around a half-round file, dowel-shaped stick, or other cylindrical object which fits the curve.

To sand convex surfaces, apply a strip of sandpaper to the curve and use the fingers or palm of the hand to conform the sandpaper to the curve. Proceed to sand, keeping an even pressure on that part of the sandpaper in contact with the surface.

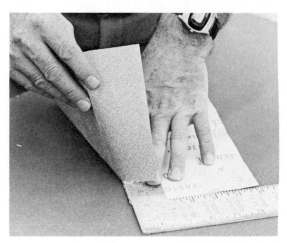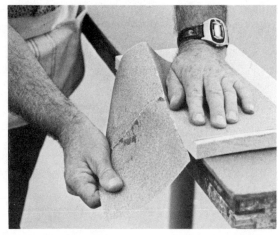

Fig. 14-6 Methods of tearing sandpaper.

When sanding keep in mind that any scar or scratch, no matter how small on the sanded surface, can show up after finishing coats of stain or varnish are applied. Inspect the surface by looking across it from several angles to detect any scratches.

Cutting and Folding Abrasive Papers

1. To cut abrasive papers, proceed as follows:

   a. Place the 9-inch x 11-inch sheet of paper on a bench, coated-side down.

   b. Hold the back edge of a steel square on the center line of the paper and tear the paper against the edge of the square (A, figure 14-6).

   c. Place the two pieces together and tear them crosswise in a similar manner. Each of the four pieces are easy to hold and use.

   NOTE: Abrasive papers can be torn by placing the tooth edge of a discarded hacksaw along the center line to tear against. They can also be torn by placing them over the edge of a bench or board. See B, figure 14-6.

2. If the sandpaper is to be used in the hand without a sanding block, it can be folded as follows:

   a. Mark the two center lines on the smooth side of the paper.

   b. Tear on the line, A-B.

   c. Fold part 1 under part 2.

   d. Fold parts 1 and 2 under 3.

   e. Fold parts 1, 2, and 3 under part 4.

   NOTE: This technique of folding ensures that the coated sides will not be in contact with each other and therefore, will not become dulled from contact with each other.

FOLD UNDER 2	FOLD UNDER 1
A	TEAR
FOLD UNDER 3	4

Fig. 14-7 Folding sandpaper.

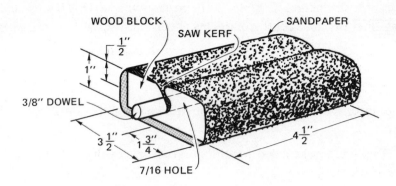

Fig. 14-8 Plan for making a sanding block.

Making a Sanding Block

1. Cut a piece of wood 1 inch x 3 1/2 inches x 4 1/2 inches.
2. Bore a 7/16-inch hole lengthwise through the block, figure 14-8.
3. Cut a saw kerf lengthwise in the face of the block down to the hole.
4. Wrap a half sheet of sandpaper (3 1/2 inches x 11 inches) around the block and insert the ends of the paper in the saw kerf.
5. Force a piece of 3/8-inch dowel through the hole to wedge the paper in place. This type of block provides for four sanding surfaces with little waste of paper.

Some mechanics prefer a soft surface on the sanding block. If this is desired, glue a piece of cork or rubber to the bottom of the block. In this case, the block must be made narrower so that the sandpaper sheet covers all four surfaces of the sanding block and allows for fastening the paper in the saw kerf.

Sandpapering Flat Surfaces

1. Examine the surfaces of the wood to be sanded to see if any additional smoothing with a plane or scraper is necessary. Clean off any chips or dust which are present.
2. Select the proper type sandpaper and wrap it around a sanding block. Use fairly coarse sandpaper until the surface is in a smooth condition.
3. Sand with an even, medium pressure and in the direction of the grain of the wood. Avoid rolling the block over the edges as they will become rounded.

    NOTE: Remove any dust or chips that get between the sanding block and the back of the sandpaper. If the dust builds up, the cutting surface will be uneven.

4. Use finer grades of sandpaper until the desired smoothness is obtained.
5. Inspect the surface for scratches. If any are found, continue to sand until they are removed.

Using Sandpaper on Surfaces to Which Finishes have been Applied

1. Before doing any sanding, be sure that the finish is completely dry. If the finish is completely dry, a slight scratch on the finish will appear white. Make the scratch in a place that does not show.

2. With finishing sandpaper, (220 to 280), go over the surface lightly and evenly to remove any dust or other foreign particles which have settled on the surface as it dried.

   NOTE: This type of sanding is best done with a cushioned block or by hand alone. Do not try to get a perfectly smooth surface by sanding, as this can result in sanding through the finish coat to the bare wood.

3. After the finish is evenly and lightly sanded, remove all the dust with a clean cloth free from lint.

   NOTE: Tack cloths are made for the purpose of cleaning finished surfaces by manufacturers of finishing materials.

   A vacuum device can also be used for the removal of dust.

4. Follow the preceding steps (1 through 3) for all further finish coats.

5. On the last coat use a fine waterproof sandpaper with linseed oil or water as a cutting lubricant. This produces a finer finish than is possible by dry sanding.

6. After the final sanding, the finish can be brought to a higher luster by applying pumice, and then rotten stone used with oil or water.

REVIEW QUESTIONS

A. Short Answer or Discussion

1. List three uses for sandpaper.

2. What general factors determine the makeup of coated abrasives?

3. Identify three types of natural abrasives.

4. Which type of natural abrasive is most suitable for woodworking? Why?

5. Identify two types of artificial abrasives.

6. Which artificial abrasive is preferred for sanding woodwork?

7. What advantage do cloth-backed abrasives have over paper-backed ones?

8. For what type of sanding is waterproof sandpaper most commonly used?

9. What is meant by an electrocoated abrasive?

10. What are the features of electrocoated abrasives?

11. What grades of sandpaper are most commonly used by the carpenter? List them from the coarsest to the smoothest.

12. Explain the terms open coating and closed coating.

13. Under what conditions are open or closed coatings preferred?

B. Completion
1. Sanding is generally done _____ the grain.
2. Of the natural abrasives, _____ is preferred to _____.
3. An 150 garnet paper is _____ than an 80 garnet paper.
4. Flint papers range from the smoothest, _____ to the coarsest, _____.
5. If no indication of the type of coating appears on the label, the coating is _____, which is standard.
6. The designation for electrocoated papers is _____.
7. Regardless of the method used to cut or tear sandpaper, the coated side should be placed _____.
8. _____ has to do with the ability of the sandpaper to be bent easily without breaking.

APPENDIX

DECIMAL EQUIVALENTS OF NUMBER SIZE DRILLS

No.	Size of Drill in Inches	No.	Size of Drill in Inches	No.	Size of Drill in Inches	No.	Size of Drill in Inches
1	.2280	21	.1590	41	.0960	61	.0390
2	.2210	22	.1570	42	.0935	62	.0380
3	.2130	23	.1540	43	.0890	63	.0370
4	.2090	24	.1520	44	.0860	64	.0360
5	.2055	25	.1495	45	.0820	65	.0350
6	.2040	26	.1470	46	.0810	66	.0330
7	.2010	27	.1440	47	.0785	67	.0320
8	.1990	28	.1405	48	.0760	68	.0310
9	.1960	29	.1360	49	.0730	69	.0292
10	.1935	30	.1285	50	.0700	70	.0280
11	.1910	31	.1200	51	.0670	71	.0260
12	.1890	32	.1160	52	.0635	72	.0250
13	.1850	33	.1130	53	.0595	73	.0240
14	.1820	34	.1110	54	.0550	74	.0225
15	.1800	35	.1100	55	.0520	75	.0210
16	.1770	36	.1065	56	.0465	76	.0200
17	.1730	37	.1040	57	.0430	77	.0180
18	.1695	38	.1015	58	.0420	78	.0160
19	.1660	39	.0995	59	.0410	79	.0145
20	.1610	40	.0980	60	.0400	80	.0135

DECIMAL EQUIVALENTS OF LETTER SIZE DRILLS

A	0.234	H	0.266	O	0.316	U	0.368
B	0.238	I	0.272	P	0.323	V	0.377
C	0.242	J	0.277	Q	0.332	W	0.386
D	0.246	K	0.281	R	0.339	X	0.397
E	0.250	L	0.290	S	0.348	Y	0.404
F	0.257	M	0.295	T	0.358	Z	0.413
G	0.261	N	0.302				

DECIMAL AND MILLIMETER EQUIVALENTS OF FRACTIONAL INCHES

Inch	Decimal Inch	Millimeter	Inch	Decimal Inch	Millimeter
1/64	0.0156	0.3969	33/64	0.5156	13.0969
1/32	0.0312	0.7938	17/32	0.5312	13.4938
3/64	0.0469	1.1906	35/64	0.5469	13.8906
1/16	0.0625	1.5875	9/16	0.5625	14.2875
5/64	0.0781	1.9844	37/64	0.5781	14.6844
3/32	0.0938	2.3812	19/32	0.5938	15.0812
7/64	0.1094	2.7781	39/64	0.6094	15.4781
1/8	0.1250	3.1750	5/8	0.6250	15.8750
9/64	0.1406	3.5719	41/64	0.6406	16.2719
5/32	0.1562	3.9688	21/32	0.6562	16.6688
11/64	0.1719	4.3656	43/64	0.6719	17.0656
3/16	0.1875	4.7625	11/16	0.6875	17.4625
13/64	0.2031	5.1594	45/64	0.7031	17.8594
7/32	0.2188	5.5562	23/32	0.7188	18.2562
15/64	0.2344	5.9531	47/64	0.7344	18.6531
1/4	0.2500	6.3500	3/4	0.7500	19.0500
17/64	0.2656	6.7469	49/64	0.7656	19.4469
9/32	0.2812	7.1438	25/32	0.7812	19.8438
19/64	0.2969	7.5406	51/64	0.7969	20.2406
5/16	0.3125	7.9375	13/16	0.8125	20.6375
21/64	0.3281	8.3344	53/64	0.8281	21.0344
11/32	0.3438	8.7312	27/32	0.8438	21.4312
23/64	0.3594	9.1281	55/64	0.8594	21.8281
3/8	0.3750	9.5250	7/8	0.8750	22.2250
25/64	0.3906	9.9219	57/64	0.8906	22.6219
13/32	0.4062	10.3188	29/32	0.9062	23.0188
27/64	0.4219	10.7156	59/64	0.9219	23.4156
7/16	0.4375	11.1125	15/16	0.9375	23.8125
29/64	0.4531	11.5094	61/64	0.9531	24.2094
15/32	0.4688	11.9062	31/32	0.9688	24.6062
31/64	0.4844	12.3031	63/64	0.9844	25.0031
1/2	0.5000	12.7000	1	1.0000	25.4000

ACKNOWLEDGMENTS

Appreciation is expressed to the following companies for their contributions to the publication of this edition.

American Screw Company, Providence, RI
Behr Manning Company, Troy, NY
Bostitch - Northeast, Inc., Medford, MA
Carborundum Company, Niagara Falls, NY
Cleveland Twist Drill Company, Cleveland, OH
Desmond - Stephen Manufacturing Company, Urbana, OH
Diamond Expansion Bolt Company, Garwood, NJ
Disston Division, H.K. Porter Company, Inc., Philadelphia, PA
Greenlee Brothers and Company, Rockford, IL
High Production Machine Company, Inc., New Britain, CT
Hyde Tools, Southbridge, MA
Independent Nail and Packing Company, Bridgewater, MA
Industrial Bolt and Nut Company, Newark, NJ
Ingersoll-Rand Company, Proto Tool Division, Fullerton, CA
Irwin Augur Bit Company, Wilmington, OH
John Wiley and Sons, Inc., New York, NY
Keuffel and Esser Company, Inc., Hoboken, NJ
Lufkin Rule Company, Saginaw, MI
Millers Falls Company, Greenfield, MA
Nicholson File Company, Providence, RI
Omark Industries, Inc., Portland, OR
Powernail Company, Chicago, IL
Red Devil, Inc., Union, NJ
Rockwell International, Pittsburgh, PA
Simonds Saw and Steel Company, Fitchburg, MA
Speedfast Corporation, Long Island City, NY
Stanley Tools, New Britain, CT
L.S. Starrett Company, Inc., Athol, MA
Swingline Industrial Corporation, Long Island City, NY
Warren Tool Corporation, Warren, OH

Appreciation is also expressed to the photographers: Donald D. Pavloski, Ike Lee, and Linda Morrell.

Delmar Publishers Staff:

Publications Director — Alan N. Knofla
Source Editor — Mark W. Huth
Associate Editor — Judith E. Barrow
Copy Editors — Angela LaGatta, Noel Mick

The material for this text has been classroom tested at Marquette Senior High School, Marquette, MI, in the High School Woods Class.

INDEX

A current catalog including prices of all Delmar educational publications is available upon request. Please write to:

Catalog Department
Delmar Publishers
50 Wolf Road
Albany, New York 12205

Or call Toll Free: (800) 354-9815